Pronunciation Fundamentals

Language Learning & Language Teaching (LL&LT)

ISSN 1569-9471

The LL&LT monograph series publishes monographs, edited volumes and text books on applied and methodological issues in the field of language pedagogy. The focus of the series is on subjects such as classroom discourse and interaction; language diversity in educational settings; bilingual education; language testing and language assessment; teaching methods and teaching performance; learning trajectories in second language acquisition; and written language learning in educational settings.

For an overview of all books published in this series, please see
http://benjamins.com/catalog/lllt

Editors

Nina Spada
Ontario Institute for Studies in Education
University of Toronto

Nelleke Van Deusen-Scholl
Center for Language Study
Yale University

Volume 42

Pronunciation Fundamentals. Evidence-based Perspectives for L2 Teaching and Research
by Tracey M. Derwing and Murray J. Munro

Pronunciation Fundamentals

Evidence-based Perspectives for L2 Teaching and Research

Tracey M. Derwing
University of Alberta

Murray J. Munro
Simon Fraser University

John Benjamins Publishing Company

Amsterdam / Philadelphia

TM   The paper used in this publication meets the minimum requirements of the American National Standard for Information Sciences – Permanence of Paper for Printed Library Materials, ANSI z39.48-1984.

DOI 10.1075/lllt.42

Cataloging-in-Publication Data available from Library of Congress:
LCCN 2015005095 (PRINT) / 2015010019 (E-BOOK)

ISBN 978 90 272 1326 6 (HB)
ISBN 978 90 272 1327 3 (PB)
ISBN 978 90 272 6859 4 (E-BOOK)

John Benjamins Publishing Co. · P.O. Box 36224 · 1020 ME Amsterdam · The Netherlands
John Benjamins North America · P.O. Box 27519 · Philadelphia PA 19118-0519 · USA

We dedicate this book to our sisters, who have had such important influences on our lives, and who are so important to us still.

Table of contents

Foreword

We wrote this book to serve as a resource for anyone who is interested in second language pronunciation. Teachers of pronunciation will find a practical presentation of theory and research to inform classroom choices. We have deliberately avoided including material that is readily available elsewhere (e.g. an introduction to basic phonetics; classroom exercises and activities) in favour of building a foundation for understanding how, why, and when to implement pronunciation instruction. Applied language researchers will also find a useful overview of research on pronunciation encompassing its historical roots, its main foci, and its methods. We have elaborated on the major themes and findings that characterize this field while looking critically at the strengths and limitations of specific studies. Although we have focused heavily on English as a second language (ESL), in part because much of the research involves second language (L2) speakers of English, many of the principles outlined here will apply in the instruction of pronunciation of other languages as well.

This book is the product of several years of collaborative research on issues of L2 pronunciation of English. When we first met, we were both teaching ESL to immigrants in the evenings, while attending graduate programs in Linguistics during the day. At that time, many of our students were Vietnamese refugees. Although some of them had a good command of English grammar and vocabulary, nearly all of them struggled to make themselves understood. Because of our Linguistics background, we were asked to teach stand-alone pronunciation classes for the students with the most serious problems. These experiences led us to a lifelong curiosity about the sources of communication difficulty that L2 learners face and the ways their problems can be addressed. When we started teaching ESL, pronunciation had already gone from a primary focus of L2 classrooms under the recently-abandoned audio-lingual method to a largely neglected concern under the communicative approach. In the second language acquisition (SLA) community there was considerable pessimism about the need for pronunciation teaching and its benefits, yet it was exceptionally clear to us that our students needed support. We had few up-to-date materials, and most of those were not helpful. As a result, we resorted to trial and error, developing new practices for our students. The results were mixed. In some instances, we saw clear improvement, both in perception and production; in others, we empathized with our students' frustration at how slowly change seemed to come, and how difficult their interactions were in their everyday lives. We would have loved to have a book like this one, which could have given us insights about the nature of our students' L2 pronunciation challenges, as well as pedagogical suggestions.

Our initial teaching experiences led us to the research that we have been conducting together over the last two decades. It has been most rewarding, and we hope that our work will help other language learners benefit from new knowledge about pronunciation learning and teaching.

How to use this book

The chapters in this book were written as stand-alone units so that they can be read in any order, with one exception. We recommend that readers start with Chapter 1, where the essential terminology used throughout this book is explained. It is possible to revisit the definitions of all expressions in SMALL CAPITAL LETTERS by referring to the Glossary at the end of the book. We have assumed a basic knowledge of linguistics, phonetics, and the International Phonetic Alphabet (IPA). If the book is serving as a text in a course on pronunciation teaching, readers without such basic knowledge will find it helpful to supplement it with other materials that offer ideas for activities and provide information on the IPA. Abundant useful volumes and other resources, both online and in print, are available and are referenced at various places throughout this book. Furthermore, instructors using this book as a course text are invited to access the discussion material and an expanded glossary on the John Benjamins website. Please see http://dx.doi.org/10.1075/lllt.42.additional for this supplementary content.

Acknowledgements

Our deepest gratitude goes out to the students we met in our first years of teaching. We gained far more from them than they did from us. As we write this, we can still picture many of those individuals in our minds; several had a profound impact on us. These were bright, well-educated people who had overcome unthinkable adversities, only to be foiled by English pronunciation. There have been many students since then, and many participants in research studies, whose comments and diligent participation have been a tremendous inspiration.

We owe an immense debt to our co-teachers from that era, including Patti Dunne, Ron Smyth, Judy Cameron, Jeff Bullard, and Leslie Crawford, who were so generous with their ideas and time. Since then, many former students and research assistants (who in some instances became colleagues) have made significant contributions to our work, including Marian Rossiter, Ron Thomson, Susan Morton, Wendy McFeely, Jennifer Foote, Cliff Burgess, Kama Jamieson, Jean Wang, Herman Li, Amy Holtby, Natasha Penner, Gloria Mellesmoen, Enric Llurda, Sarvenaz Hatami, and Debra Elliot. Our co-investigators, Grace Wiebe, Mike Carbonaro, John Levis, Kazuya Saito, Erin Waugh, and others, have influenced our thinking for the better. We also thank two students who made helpful comments on earlier versions of this book, Lynn Sawyer and Patricia Watson. Thanks also to Laurie Scheffer, who worked on the author index.

Jennifer Foote and Sarvenaz Hatami deserve special mention for their work on the Glossary, the References, the general formatting of the book, and their overall meticulous assistance, to say nothing of their good humour assisting with these picky, boring tasks.

We also acknowledge the invaluable role our teachers and mentors played in our research careers: Jim Flege, Terry Nearey, Baha Abu-Laban, and Kathi Bailey. We have drawn tremendously on the input of our colleagues, both within the area of L2 pronunciation and in applied linguistics and phonetics generally, as well as our co-workers in our respective departments.

We thank Robert DeKeyser for encouraging us to write this volume. We are extremely grateful to Beth Zielinski, Bruce Derwing, Ron Smyth, Yue Wang, Ron Thomson, and Alan Borden for reading and commenting on individual chapters. Any remaining errors are clearly our own.

We also thank our friends, who patiently listen to what must seem like extremely esoteric stories filled with excruciating minutiae about our research. Special mention also goes to Chloe and Stewie Derwing, and Teddy and Owen Munro. Finally, and most importantly, we thank our spouses, Alan Borden and Bruce Derwing, who have been supportive in every way.

CHAPTER 1

Key concepts

In a report in <u>Flight Safety Digest</u>, Cushing (1995) described two interactions involving airline pilots, both of which entailed confusion between the words <u>two</u> and <u>to</u>:

> *ATC cleared the aircraft to descend "two four zero zero." The pilot read back the clearance as, "OK. Four zero zero." The aircraft then descended to 400 feet (122 meters) rather than what the controller had meant, which was 2,400 feet (732 meters).*
>
> *In another case a captain, who was the pilot flying, heard his co-pilot say, "Cleared to seven." He began a descent to 7,000 feet (2,135 meters), but at 9,500 feet (2,898 meters) the co-pilot advised the captain that 10,000 feet (3,050 meters) was the correct altitude. The co-pilot's communication, which the captain had heard as <u>cleared to seven</u>, was in fact <u>cleared two seven</u>-meaning the assigned runway for landing was 27L. (p. 3)*

The first confusion caused a major accident leading to four deaths, while in the second case, the error was corrected in time to prevent a tragedy. These examples show how human lives can depend on seemingly tiny details in spoken communication.

Introduction

The examples presented above are stark illustrations of the importance of speech INTELLIGIBILITY, the most fundamental characteristic of successful oral communication. When we say that an utterance is intelligible, we mean that listeners can understand the speaker's intended message. Without this property, there cannot be genuine communication. Rather, the listener may misinterpret the utterance to mean something that was not actually meant, as in the cases above, or may understand nothing at all if the speech is very unclear or masked by noise. The first of these situations may well be the more dangerous – the case in which listeners believe that they have understood when, in fact, they have not.

Although these may strike you as extreme, air traffic incidents are not the only cases of life and death consequences of speech characteristics. Another example concerns the treatment of many refugee claimants or ASYLUM SEEKERS. Immigrant-receiving countries such as Australia and Canada sometimes engage consulting companies to identify the places of origin of refugee claimants on the basis of their language use, including their PRONUNCIATION. This process—LANGUAGE ANALYSIS FOR THE DETERMINATION OF ORIGIN (LADO)–may aim to establish the validity of the asylum seeker's claim. People's lives hang in the balance, sometimes solely because of how they pronounce certain words. A group of Australian linguists have severely criticized some LADO outcomes because of a lack of transparency in the methods used and analyses that are "sometimes of shockingly low quality" (Fraser, 2009, p. 115). (For more information on LADO, see the website of the Language and Asylum Research Group at ⟨http://www.essex.ac.uk/larg/⟩).

In addition to these dramatic examples of the importance of pronunciation, there are countless ways in which speech patterns affect everyday life, particularly for speakers of a second language (L2). One of the most obvious of these is the frustration some L2 speakers incur when they try to express themselves but are not understood. Of course, not all L2 speakers experience such difficulty; many have ACCENTS that are noticeable, but which don't interfere with their ability to communicate. A more subtle aspect of L2 pronunciation, however, is the SHIBBOLETH nature of foreign-accented utterances. By this we mean that interlocutors are extremely sensitive to accents different from their own and can often tell almost immediately when someone is an L2 user (Flege, 1984). This sensitivity evokes a wide variety of responses to the speaker. When interlocutors judge that an L2 speaker has low proficiency because of a strong accent, they may adjust their own language to help foster communication, through a process known as Foreigner Talk (Ferguson, 1975; Varonis & Gass, 1982). In such a situation, having an accent actually affords an advantage to the L2 speaker. Another reaction to accented speech is not at all beneficial: listeners may evaluate the L2 user negatively and respond in a discriminatory fashion (Lippi-Green, 2012). In fact, researchers have documented numerous cases in which both L1 and L2 users have been harassed, denied employment or refused accommodation because of their speech patterns (Munro, 2003; Nguyen, 1993; Purnell, Idsardi & Baugh, 1999). Speakers with a strong L2 accent or low-prestige L1 pronunciation may feel considerable apprehension each time they engage with a new interlocutor because they cannot predict how the communicative exchange will go. In contrast, native speakers of high-status dialects are more likely to assume that new encounters will be successful.

Oral communication is such a fundamental part of everyday life that if pronunciation patterns get in the way, action is essential. This book covers the concepts needed for understanding the *whys* and *hows* of assisting L2 speakers to develop more effective oral production skills. As our starting point, we will define some important terms that appear repeatedly throughout the book. These are foundational notions that serve as the basis for much of the research we will discuss.

Essential terminology

When referring to pronunciation we mean the ways in which speakers use their articulatory apparatus to create speech. This concept encompasses all the individual speech sounds in a particular language as well as the prosodic and VOICE QUALITY features that are shared by speakers of that language. SEGMENTALS are the individual CONSONANTS and VOWELS in a language's phonological inventory. Of course, these vary from one language to another. The synonymous terms PROSODY and SUPRASEG-MENTALS refer to those aspects of speech that are superimposed on the sequences of sounds that comprise words, phrases, and larger units. Prosody includes word and SENTENCE STRESS, rhythm, intonation, juncture, and tone. In popular usage, accent can include vocabulary or grammatical choices that distinguish one speech community from another. However, in this volume, we will restrict our definition of accent to a way of pronouncing that is specific to a given speech community. Within a particular first language (L1), accents can be tied to different regions, social classes, and ethnicities. Different accents also characterize L2 users' speech, typically reflecting some phonological characteristics of the L1. Although accent features vary in salience, it is generally quite easy for most people to recognize a non-native speaker or a speaker of the same language from another country, even on the basis of very short stretches of speech. For instance, Canadians can recognize that an Australian speaker comes from a different dialect region (although they may mistakenly think the speaker is British or from New Zealand). Likewise, an Argentinian speaker of Spanish can recognize that a Mexican is from a different dialect area.

In interactions with certain speakers, you may sometimes feel that you must work especially hard to understand what they are saying. You may grasp everything they utter, but only with considerable effort. Other speakers may seem very easy to interact with – you immediately understand their speech with little or no conscious exertion. The difference between these two kinds of speakers is in their COMPREHENSIBILITY, by which we mean the amount of effort that must be put in to understanding speech. Differences in comprehensibility are not confined to L2 speakers. It's possible to experience both low and high comprehensibility with interlocutors who share the same L1, and even the same accent. You have probably encountered native English speakers who mumble, speak very softly, or have speech disorders. In the end, you might understand everything they say, yet come away feeling that you have had to strain to do so. This is because their comprehensibility has been compromised. In the case of L2 speakers, differences in comprehensibility can arise for exactly the same reasons; however, they can also be due to segments, prosody and voice quality that differ from what listeners are accustomed to hearing. When speech patterns run counter to our expectations, we require more time to cognitively process what we have heard.

When producing an utterance, the speaker always has a particular message in mind. The degree to which that message is received as intended by an attentive listener defines the intelligibility of the utterance, a concept we referred to at the beginning of this chapter. Another basic dimension of speech is FLUENCY. Some people use this term interchangeably with proficiency. For instance, "Alan is fluent in Hebrew," might be intended to mean that Alan has a very good command of Hebrew grammar, vocabulary, and so on. However, this is not the definition of fluency that we will use throughout this book. Instead, we will refer to fluency to describe the rate and the degree of fluidity of speech, as signalled by the presence or absence of hesitation markers, self-repetitions, and filled and unfilled pauses. Of course, fluency varies a great deal across native speakers – it is not an exclusively L2 phenomenon. Fillmore (1979, reprinted in Riggenbach, 2000) identified four levels of L1 fluency such that highly fluent speakers are "creative and imaginative in their language use … able to express their ideas in novel ways, to pun, to make up jokes, to attend to the sound independently of the sense, to vary styles, to create and build on metaphors, and so on" (51). At the low end of the scale, Fillmore saw L1 fluency as "simply the ability to talk at length with few pauses" (51). The latter definition is much closer to the way in which fluency is interpreted in L2 speech research. Nonetheless, beginner-level speakers do tend to have more dysfluencies, such as inappropriate pauses and a slower rate (commonly measured in syllables per second) than speakers who are at intermediate or more advanced levels. This aspect of their speech is partly due to low proficiency (i.e. limited command of vocabulary and grammatical structures); however, it is also believed to be due to cognitive fluency. As Segalowitz and Hulstijn (2005) observed, irrespective of the language a speaker uses (L1 or L2), fluency has the relatively stable characteristics of a trait. Speakers who are slow talkers in their L1 are unlikely to be fast talkers in their L2, regardless of their proficiency level, as a result of cognitive function. In particular, Segalowitz (2007) argues that access fluidity (speed of lexical access) and attention control (ability to focus and refocus attention in real time) underlie the general cognitive fluency exhibited in speakers. In a study comparing ratings of L1 and L2 fluency in spoken narratives, Derwing, Munro, Thomson and Rossiter (2009) found significant correlations in low proficiency learners who had recently arrived in Canada, though the strength of the relationship declined somewhat in later years. Of course, L2 fluency can be influenced by a variety of situational factors, such as fatigue, enthusiasm, or use of alcohol. From a pedagogical standpoint, instructors can address only the L2 proficiency component of fluency, since they have no control over the cognitive capabilities of learners. Fortunately, research has shown that fluency can be enhanced in the classroom (Nation, 1989).

Table 1.1 sums up the major points raised so far by presenting the most pervasive terms in the contemporary research literature on L2 speech. Because we will use this terminology over and over throughout the book, we encourage you to consider the terms carefully and clarify their meanings in your own mind before reading further.

One of the most important messages we hope you will take away from this chapter has to do with the partial independence of the speech dimensions we have described above. Perhaps the most important point of all is that accent and

Table 1.1. Some basic pronunciation terminology

Term	Definition	Synonyms
pronunciation	All aspects of the oral production of language, including segments, prosody, voice quality, and rate	
segments	The individual vowels and consonants in the phonological inventory of a given language	speech sounds, phones
prosody	The aspects of speech that carry across an utterance: stress, intonation, rhythm	suprasegmentals
accent	A particular pattern of pronunciation that is perceived to distinguish members of different speech communities	different speech patterns, salient speech differences
comprehensibility	The ease or difficulty a listener experiences in understanding an utterance	effort, processing difficulty
intelligibility	The degree of match between a speaker's intended message and the listener's comprehension	actual understanding, comprehension
fluency	The degree to which speech flows easily without pauses and other dysfluency markers	fluidity

intelligibility are not the same. Speakers with FOREIGN ACCENTS do not *necessarily* fail to get their messages across effectively. While this lack of congruence has been commented on informally for many years, our first empirical report on the distinction was a study of Mandarin speakers' extemporaneous oral productions (Munro & Derwing, 1995a). From a set of recorded picture narratives, we selected individual sentences and presented them to listeners who transcribed them in standard orthography and rated them for strength of accent on a 9-point scale. When we considered only the perfectly correct transcriptions, which, by definition, indicated full intelligibility, we observed that the corresponding ACCENTEDNESS ratings ranged across the full 9-point scale. In short, a particular utterance could be heavily accented and yet be fully intelligible. This partial independence must be carefully considered in pronunciation teaching, particularly in determining instructional priorities Munro & Derwing (2015b). Comprehensibility and intelligibility are more closely related to each other than they are to accent, but they are not 100 percent correlated either. That is, it is possible to be somewhat difficult to understand and yet be fully intelligible. Empirical data also point to the independence of fluency and accent, which are only weakly correlated (Pinget, Bosker, Quené & de Jong, 2014). Numerous combinations of these speech dimensions are possible, as can be seen in Tables 1.2 and 1.3, where we have compared the extremes of intelligibility and comprehensibility, and intelligibility and accent.

Table 1.2. Results of possible intelligibility and comprehensibility combinations

Intelligibility	Comprehensibility	Result
High	High	Utterance is fully understood; little effort required
High	Low	Utterance is fully understood; great effort is required
Low	Low	Utterance is not (fully) understood; great effort is exerted
Low	High	Probably rare. Utterance is not fully understood; however, the listener has the false impression of having easily determined the speaker's intended meaning

Table 1.3. Results of possible intelligibility and accentedness combinations

Intelligibility	Accentedness	Result
High	High	Utterance is fully understood; accent is very strong
High	Low	Utterance is fully understood; accent is barely noticeable
Low	Low	Not relevant to pronunciation; however, an utterance could be unintelligible because of problems with grammar or word choices, or non-linguistic factors such as noise
Low	High	Utterance is not (fully) understood; accent is very strong

Nativeness and Intelligibility Principles

Levis (2005) described two basic orientations to pronunciation instruction: the NATIVENESS and INTELLIGIBILITY PRINCIPLES. In the former, the goal is to develop L2 speech that is indistinguishable from that of a native speaker. The Intelligibility Principle, on the other hand, holds that the goal is intelligible speech, irrespective of how native-like it sounds. Phoneticians have often emphasized the latter. Sweet (1900), for instance, discussed the importance of intelligibility as something distinct from native-like performance, and Abercrombie (1949) argued that the vast majority of L2 learners (other than secret agents) need only comfortable intelligibility. Gimson (1970) even suggested specific strategies to help learners compensate for individual sounds that they could not produce. However, pedagogical practice has not always conformed to the Intelligibility Principle. During the AUDIOLINGUAL era in the mid-20th century, for example, great emphasis was placed on highly accurate pronunciation. Learners were expected to replicate the segmental and prosodic characteristics of native speaker models, which were often presented through recordings. In the last twenty years, however, both research and practice have placed a sustained emphasis on intelligibility, perhaps because there is now empirical evidence, first, that few adult learners ever achieve native-like pronunciation in the L2 (Flege, Munro, & MacKay, 1995) and, second, that intelligibility and accentedness are partially independent (Munro & Derwing, 1995a).

An evidence-based approach to pronunciation teaching and teaching materials

Just thirty years ago, very few supports were available to teachers of pronunciation. Despite the existence of some textbooks, most instructors had limited access to sophisticated materials and little or no direction on how they should proceed, apart from drills and MINIMAL PAIR practice. For instructors who had not studied an L2 themselves, where they might have been exposed to PHONETICS and other aspects of pronunciation, there was a dearth of guidance. Although some speech researchers were actively working on L2 pronunciation at that point, most research studies from the time were of limited value to practitioners. The studies that did exist tended to be directed at teachers of academically-oriented language in programs at the secondary and post-secondary levels, but were not intended for communicative ESL classrooms, which were gaining in popularity in the early 1980s. Teachers were thus left, for the most part, to rely on their own intuitions and their observations of their students' linguistic behaviour. In some instances, that was enough to motivate them to devise appropriate activities for their students, but in other cases, instructors felt inadequately prepared to deal with pronunciation and therefore avoided teaching it.

More recently, applied linguistics researchers have turned their attention to L2 pronunciation, using an expanded range of techniques to obtain information that is potentially helpful in contemporary L2 classrooms. If we focus on the Intelligibility Principle, then certain approaches to research become mandatory. The concept of intelligibility involves both speakers and listeners, and any assessment of intelligibility must make reference to listeners' perceptions, as well as L2 speakers' productions. It isn't possible, for instance, to measure intelligibility using acoustic analyses or any other type of instrumentation that does not incorporate the listener's perspective. Research on speech intelligibility in general has been conducted for many decades. It is now widely accepted that measurement of this construct is best achieved by presenting speech to listeners and having them respond to it, perhaps by writing down the words they have heard, or by filling in blanks in a cloze task. Recent work on L2 speech has included a number of other techniques for eliciting listener responses. In some of our studies, we have required L2 speakers to produce sets of true and false sentences (e.g. *Some people drink coffee at breakfast; Grass is usually orange.*). These utterances are played to listeners, who must make a true or false judgment. The listeners' responses, then, serve as a measure of how intelligible the sentence productions are (Munro & Derwing, 1995b). Other researchers have presented listeners with recorded picture narratives or mini-lectures from L2 speakers, followed by questions to evaluate the listeners' comprehension – another type of intelligibility assessment. Studies of intelligibility are ultimately intended to help teachers to distinguish aspects of accent that are detrimental to intelligibility from those that, although salient, do not cause communication problems for listeners.

Another facet of the intuition-based approach to language teaching has to do with the assumptions that materials developers incorporate into textbooks. Research evaluating teaching materials can provide instructors with useful guidelines about what is reasonable to teach. For example, Levis (1999) determined that several of the intonation patterns covered in textbooks directed at L2 students are not easily distinguished by native speakers, and therefore are not appropriate for instruction purposes. Another assumption made by some materials developers is the intuition that all minimal contrasts carry equal weight and thus deserve equal attention in instruction. However, as Catford (1987) pointed out, some contrasts are considerably more important than others. In a corpus-based analysis of minimal pairs in English, Levis and Cortes (2008) noted that the members of some pairs occur far less frequently than their counterparts (e.g. should/shoed). In addition, many pair members do not share the same lexical class (e.g. thigh/thy) and are thus not likely to cause communicative problems in context. As the authors point out, "it is difficult to find a context in which both are likely" (p. 199). This type of research is useful for teachers in deciding which contrasts may be worthy of class time (after establishing what learners' difficulties are). It is our hope that L2 pronunciation research, which is currently going through a period of intense interest, reaches a tipping point, such that it remains a popular area of study by applied linguists.

Setting the record straight

When new ideas are presented or old ideas are revisited, it is inevitable that some misinterpretations and conceptual confusions will arise. We have a few pet peeves that we would like to address, and now is as good a time as any! First, many authors refer to "perceived foreign accent" as though it could be distinguished from some other type of foreign accent. We reject this idea because, in our view, accent is by its very nature, a perceptual phenomenon. This relates to our notion of intelligibility and the necessary involvement of both a speaker and a listener. An accent is, by definition, something that is noticed by listeners; therefore, there is no kind of accent other than a perceived accent.

Second, we have concerns about the view that speech evaluation carried out without the participation of listeners-for example, through the use of acoustic measures-is more "objective" than ratings or other listener evaluations that are labeled as "subjective." In our view, the terms "objective" and "subjective" are largely unhelpful in understanding the nature of speech assessments. Rather, we must return to our earlier point that dimensions such as accent and intelligibility simply cannot be measured without recourse to listeners. An ACOUSTIC MEASUREMENT of a vowel, for instance, can be useful for some purposes, but it cannot tell us definitively whether the vowel will be perceived as target-like or not. Because human listeners take into account context at multiple levels, their perceptions may accommodate deviations from an expected target. These deviations might be very apparent in acoustic data, yet have little or no importance from the standpoint of intelligibility. When we compare rating data with acoustic measures, then, the difference has much more to do with the usefulness of the information we can extract from each approach, rather than with the purported objectivity of the assessment.

A third issue we would like to address is a quite specific misinterpretation of some of our research findings. Several years ago we carried out a study in which we compared the effectiveness of segmental instruction versus suprasegmental instruction (Derwing, Munro, & Wiebe, 1998; Derwing & Rossiter, 2003). Our research design called for three conditions: a control group, which received no pronunciation instruction, a segmental group, which received instruction on consonants and vowels, and a suprasegmental group, which received prosodic instruction only. One of the study's outcomes was that only the suprasegmental group showed a significant improvement in comprehensibility in unrehearsed picture descriptions, although both instructed groups improved on sentences that they read aloud. This result provided us with an answer to one of our research questions: Can prosodic instruction benefit L2 speakers' comprehensibility in extemporaneously produced speech? Regrettably, the implications of this study have been misinterpreted: for example, Celce-Murcia, Brinton, Goodwin with Griner (2010) state "We feel that the artificial instructional dichotomy in the Derwing and Rossiter [2003] study (i.e. teach suprasegmentals versus teach segmentals) is unproductive in that for any given group of learners there are going to be features from both domains that are problematic for communication and thus should be taught" (p. 33). We fully agree with their observation about variability in learners, but Celce-Murcia et al. seemed to have missed our point: we never suggested that teachers should restrict themselves to one of the kinds of instruction that we used in the study. In fact, we expressly stated that both segments and suprasegmentals have a place in the L2 pronunciation classroom. In order to isolate the effects of the interventions, the design of the experiment required us to offer classes that were limited to one or the other focus of instruction.

Finally, when we have spoken at conferences, we have often been queried about what should be taught and whether there are some aspects of L2 pronunciation that are off limits. Our response is that intelligibility and comprehensibility should be priorities, but it is important that teachers be flexible in accommodating students' needs and wishes, keeping in mind the time available. The question of whether to teach English interdental FRICATIVES (the PHONEMES at the beginning of the words 'thigh' and 'thy') often comes up, given that they are not very important to either intelligibility or comprehensibility, even though they are a salient feature of accent. We would not advocate spending a lot of time on these sounds, but certainly a few minutes would be a small price to pay to address students' self-perceived needs. On a related point, we want to emphasize that the relative importance of phonemes is language-specific. Findings regarding FUNCTIONAL LOAD that are true for one particular L2 are not necessarily applicable to another (Saalfeld, 2012).

Overview of *Pronunciation Fundamentals: Evidence-based Perspectives for L2 Teaching and Research*

To contextualize the current state of affairs in L2 pronunciation teaching and research, it is helpful to know what has gone before. *Chapter 2: Pronunciation Teaching Historical Overview*, briefly surveys the long history of pronunciation teaching, and describes several early research studies, now long neglected, that offer insights of continuing value.

When conducting research, developing curricula, choosing activities, or providing individual attention, it is helpful to understand some aspects of the L2 phonological acquisition process itself. *Chapter 3: A Pedagogical Perspective on L2 Phonetic Acquisition* covers the major themes in acquisition research. *Chapter 4: Pronunciation Errors and Error Gravity*, focuses specifically on the nature of L2 pronunciation errors, their causes, and their importance to communication.

In *Chapter 5: Pronunciation Instruction Research*, several practical questions are addressed. We examine surveys of teachers, classroom-based intervention studies, and research related to issues surrounding the planning and implementation of L2 pronunciation activities. One aspect of L2 pronunciation that deserves special attention is assessment. In *Chapter 6: Assessment of L2 Pronunciation*, both standardized instruments and informal, classroom-based assessments are considered.

As with other aspects of language learning and teaching, technology plays a growing role in L2 pronunciation, with new software applications being released at an increasing pace. *Chapter 7: The Role of Technology*, examines some of the developments, both good and bad in this field.

The importance of accent extends beyond purely linguistic boundaries. In *Chapter 8*, we explore the *Social Aspects of Accent and Intelligibility*. Issues such as speaker identity, accent discrimination, and a changing global context in which World Englishes are increasingly important are discussed. Another social issue of concern is covered in *Chapter 9: Ethics of Accent Reduction*. The roles of entrepreneurs, speech pathologists, and L2 teachers are surveyed, with a critical eye on motives, claims, and student needs.

We conclude with *Chapter 10: Future Directions*, in which we recommend further avenues for L2 pronunciation research and comment on ideal outcomes for improved communication, such as the enhancement of native speakers' listening skills.

CHAPTER 2

Historical overview of pronunciation

In 1665, Owen Price, Master of arts and professor of the art of pedagogy, published a book with this remarkable title: "The Vocal Organ, or a New Art of Teaching the English Orthographie, by Observing the Instruments of Pronunciation, and the Difference Between Words of Like Sound, Whereby Any Outlander, or Mere English Man, Woman or Childe May Speedily Attend to the Exact Spelling, Reading, Writing or Pronouncing of Any Word in the English Tongue Without the Advantage of its Fountains, the Greek and the Latin." Price was not the first to develop a program for pronunciation study, however. Even earlier, in 1617, Robert Robinson had produced a manual entitled "The Art of Pronunciation," which was intended for both native and nonnative speakers of English. Perhaps for reasons of personal identity, people have a proprietary sense of their first language. So, for centuries people have concerned themselves with English pronunciation and speaking 'correctly.' Everyone seems to have an opinion about how others speak and how they should speak.

Introduction

Phonetics as a field of study goes back perhaps 2.5 millennia to the time of the Sanskrit scholar Panini, and has been described by Ohala (2006) as one of the oldest and most successful of the behavioral sciences. Prior to the 20th century, documentation of the application of phonetics to the teaching of pronunciation is quite sparse, though a few scholars have presented historical accounts. Kelly (1969), for instance, discusses the topic in a detailed survey of language teaching that highlights the relative historical neglect of pronunciation in the classroom. The textbook by Celce-Murcia et al. (2010) focuses specifically on pronunciation teaching, pointing out the fundamental distinction between intuitive and analytical orientations to pronunciation instruction. The authors also describe the pronunciation-specific techniques used in language teaching methods from the late 20th century on.

One of the most carefully focused surveys to date is by Murphy and Baker (2015), who provide a detailed consideration of the last 150 years of ESL pronunciation teaching in terms of four overlapping "waves":

> Wave 1. A *"precursor" period* beginning in the mid 1800s, during which pedagogical specialists began to reject conventional conceptions of language teaching in favour of an intuitively-based emphasis on spoken communication.

Wave 2. The *reform movement* initiated in the late 1800s that saw the development of the INTERNATIONAL PHONETIC ALPHABET (IPA) and the application of principles from phonetics to language pedagogy.

Wave 3. The influence of Communicative Language Teaching (CLT), which, by the mid-1980s, spawned the development of new teaching materials to facilitate the incorporation of pronunciation in CLT classrooms.

Wave 4. The application of *empirical research* to pronunciation instruction, which began in earnest in the 1990s.

In this chapter we will offer our own selective survey of historical developments in English pronunciation instruction. One aspect of the field that we find quite striking is that English pronunciation teaching for L2 speakers did not arise as an entirely independent pursuit. Rather, it developed along with a variety of other pedagogical traditions that were often aimed at native speakers, and the benefits for L2 learners were often an afterthought. Our goal in the sections that follow is not to replace other accounts of the history of pronunciation, but instead to focus briefly on four particular threads that have helped to inform teaching. The first of these is the extensive literature describing the English sound system. Teaching materials and related innovations are our second area of concern, while our third is the vast literature on L2 speech perception and production that has appeared in speech science and applied linguistics publications. Our fourth topic is the least developed line of work, but is growing rapidly – empirical research on classroom pronunciation instruction.

Descriptions of English phonetics for teaching purposes

At a minimum, teaching pronunciation requires a basic knowledge of the sound system of the language being taught. Teachers need to know how vowels and consonants are articulated, and how they vary according to context, as well as the fundamentals of prosody. For contemporary English, there is no shortage of suitable reference materials. In fact, descriptions of English phonetics have existed for centuries, some of the earliest practical materials dating back to the 1600s. It may come as a surprise that these accounts were geared partly to the "mere" native English speakers mentioned above, as well as to "outlanders." The reasons for the diversity of Owen Price's audience are rooted in the complexities of English orthography and in sociolinguistic influences, two factors that continue to affect thinking about pronunciation in the 21st century.

Orthography

Nearly everyone agrees on one fact about English: its spelling is notoriously difficult. Unlike the writing systems of many languages, in which sound can be readily predicted from spelling and vice versa, English lacks a straightforward correspondence between the two. In terms of symbol-sound correspondences, English has countless examples of each of the following:

- *one-to-many* relationships, in which a single letter represents several different sounds, as when ⟨g⟩[1] is pronounced /g/ in *go*, /dʒ/ in *page*, /ʒ/ in *rouge*, and /f/ in *rough*.
- *many-to-one* relationships, in which different spellings can be used for a single sound, as when /ɛ/ is spelled ⟨e⟩ in *bed*, ⟨ea⟩ in *bread*, ⟨ie⟩ in *friend*, ⟨a⟩ in *any*, and ⟨oe⟩ in *foetid*.

Learning to read English orthography and to spell correctly when writing are challenging enough for native English speakers, but can be even more so for L2 learners, especially those who speak L1s like Spanish and Finnish that have nearly phonetic writing systems. To complicate matters, the "sound value" of particular letters in English differs from that of other languages. For instance, ⟨i⟩ is most commonly pronounced as /aɪ/ or as /ɪ/ in English (e.g. bite, bit), but as /i/ in European French, Spanish, Italian, and Portuguese.

English spelling inconsistencies, which go back many centuries, are partially rooted in sound change. For instance, even though the Anglo-Saxon sound system evolved quite dramatically after the Norman invasion of England in 1066, many Old English spellings were retained, so that orthography failed to reflect the new ways in which words were actually produced. As Rogers (2005) notes, Old English had no phonemic distinction between the fricatives /s/ and /z/. Later on, these consonants became separate phonemes, yet writers continued to use ⟨s⟩ for both. During the early Middle English period, when French was the language of government in England, written English was not widely used, and spelling was seen as a "free for all" by many scholars who simply employed their own preferred spellings. As a result of their dialectal differences, many possible spellings co-existed for a number of English words. At the same time, countless lexical borrowings from French led to a mixture of French and English spelling conventions. Still another source of orthographic complexity in English was the Great Vowel Shift. This systemic change in vowel pronunciations affected a very large part of the English vocabulary. The following examples illustrate two changes that took place:

- Words spelled like *boot* were originally pronounced with /o/, just like *boat*. They changed to be produced with /u/, but the ⟨oo⟩ spelling was retained.
- Words spelled with ⟨i⟩ like *bite* were originally pronounced like *beat*. They shifted to contain /aɪ/, but the spelling persisted.

---

1.   Here we use angle brackets (⟨ ⟩) for spelling to distinguish orthographic representations from phonetic symbols.

These illustrations help explain why the sound values of spellings such as ⟨oo⟩ and ⟨i⟩ in English differ from those of other languages, which did not undergo the shift.

Fortunately, with the introduction of the printing press in England in 1476, spellings became more standardized than they had previously been. Also, the appearance of dictionaries, especially Samuel Johnson's in 1755, guided writers to a common orthography. However, this consistency did not make English spelling any more "logical," and during the centuries before radio and television, literate people sought rules on how to pronounce the words they read and on how to correctly spell the words they already knew. Owen Price, a Welsh school teacher, was just one of a number of scholars who catered to consumer demand by writing books on English spelling and pronunciation. While his work was intended to help people make sense of a complex system, other public figures advocated more drastic measures. Throughout the history of English, and right up to the present day, calls for spelling reform have been common. Benjamin Franklin, for instance, proposed adding new letters to the alphabet to represent consonants that have no single-letter correspondences: /ŋ/, /θ/, /ð/, and /ʃ/. George Bernard Shaw wanted to abandon the Roman alphabet altogether and create an entirely new spelling system. Apart from attempts to develop a "universal language," few linguistic enterprises have been so doomed to failure as these, and not much has changed in English spelling for several hundred years. As a result, the spelling conventions of English continue to challenge its users. ESL learners may take some comfort in knowing that native speakers also have plenty of difficulties: they frequently mispronounce words like 'epitome' (/ɪˈpɪrəmi/), 'victuals' (/ˈvɪr̩lz/), and 'Edinburgh' (/ˈɛdn̩bəə/), have trouble distinguishing *it's* from *its* and *their* from *there*, and can't remember the number of m's in *accommodate*. To this day, English language resources include rules for determining sound from spelling (PHONICS) as well as lists of commonly misspelled and mispronounced words. Moreover, conveying the pronunciation of English words on the computer screen or printed page necessitates some sort of transcription system. While the *International Phonetic Alphabet*, which adheres to the principle of *one symbol-one sound*, serves as a standard for linguists, many other representations are still used by textbooks and dictionaries. It must indeed be very frustrating for English learners to discover first that the orthography is inconsistent and then that even the ways of getting around that problem lack standardization!

Sociolinguistic influences

While the complexity of English orthography was one factor that fueled the public's desire for instruction on pronunciation, another is the social stigma associated with sounding "low class," "uneducated" or simply "incorrect." The rigidly class-based nature of British English society has had quite remarkable linguistic repercussions. Some dialects spoken in the UK emerged as high prestige varieties while others came to signal low social status. Of course, there is nothing inherently low class about any way of speaking, but when a pronunciation style comes to be associated with a particular segment of the population, the stereotypes held about that community are evoked by their oral language. In short, we sometimes make judgments about people, both negative and positive, because of the way they pronounce words. In highly class-conscious situations, upward social mobility can depend on speakers' willingness to modify their productions so as to sound like the people with whom they choose to identify. This phenomenon is well illustrated in George Bernard Shaw's 1912 play *Pygmalion*, which was adapted to the popular musical screenplay *My Fair Lady*. Though Shaw actually had little scholarly knowledge of phonetics, one of his aims was to bring the public's attention to this newly popular science as a technique for accent modification. In the story, a linguist named Henry Higgins[2] manages to transform a poor flower girl into an elegant lady largely by changing her speech to a style that fools even the most discerning listener into thinking she is a duchess.

While most aspects of Shaw's play are pure fiction, the story brings home the importance of speech in human social evaluation, a topic we address in more detail in Chapter 8. In many countries, class consciousness is a less significant social force today than in Shaw's time, but prejudicial attitudes about speech are still widespread. Lippi-Green (2012) gives numerous examples of the ways in which people negatively judge others on the basis of the way they talk. For example, residents of the "deep south" of the USA (e.g. from Mississippi, Alabama, and Arkansas) have often been portrayed in television and film as socially backward and unintelligent. Stereotyping occurs when listeners attribute negative characteristics like these to a *particular* speaker of a Southern USA dialect, even when they know nothing about that speaker as an individual. Similarly, deep-rooted racism in the United States explains why AFRICAN AMERICAN VERNACULAR ENGLISH (AAVE) is also often regarded as a low-prestige variety, though its current influence in hip-hop music and among young white Americans indicates an interesting sociolinguistic trend. Of most importance to us, however, is the fact that foreign-accented English is often judged negatively. Immigrants may be subject to harassment, stereotyping or outright discrimination because of their accents. It is critical to understand that foreign accents themselves do not "cause" prejudice. Rather, when listeners hear and recognize non-native patterns of speech, their previously internalized attitudes and feelings about immigrants, "foreigners," or

---

2.   Shaw once commented that the fictional Higgins had some "touches" of the deceased real-life phonetician, Henry Sweet, though it has been argued that Shaw may have been trying to deflect attention from resemblances between his character and Daniel Jones (1881–1967), who was living when Pygmalion was completed (Collins & Mees, 1999).

"outsiders" may be evoked. In this way, foreign accents serve as shibboleths – markers of a speaker's status as an outsider.

Given the long history of accents as a factor in social judgments, it is quite natural that some scholars have invested their time in learning about and in teaching particular articulations and speech styles. Owen Price's book starts with several rather grotesque diagrams depicting the human vocal tract that illustrate how particular speech sounds should be produced. Another speech specialist was Alexander Melville Bell (1819–1905), an "elocutionist" who taught his clients to speak carefully and to move their bodies gracefully when orating. In addition to assisting people with speech disorders such as stuttering, he developed an interest in teaching English pronunciation to the deaf. (He was married to a deaf woman.) For this purpose he invented *visible speech,* a written system that, in some respects, resembled a phonetic alphabet. It not only used symbols to represent discrete speech sounds, but actually went a step further, incorporating information about the use of the vocal tract directly into the symbols. By considering how a visible speech character was written, a speaker could determine how the articulators should be positioned to produce the sound. Figure 2.1, for instance, shows how the actions of the tongue and lips could be represented by iconic symbols.

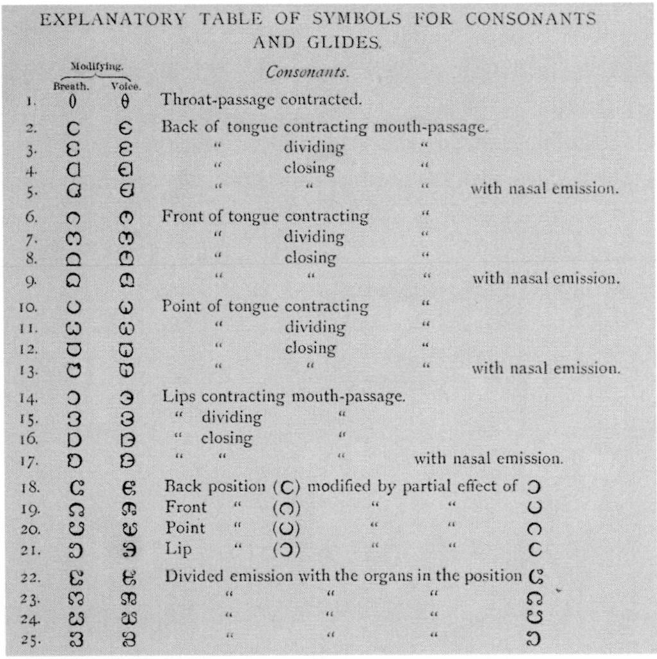

Figure 2.1. An excerpt from A.M. Bell's Visible Speech (1867, p. 39) showing how symbols were used to encode articulatory information

The Bell family, immigrants to Canada and the United States from Scotland, were well known for their technical accomplishments, most notably A. M. Bell's son, Alexander Graham Bell, inventor of the telephone. Like his father, he worked extensively with the deaf, and also married a deaf woman. It is not so well known, however, that the telephone was to some extent a by-product of his attempts at designing a device that would represent speech on the printed page—a new, automatic kind of visible speech. That goal did not become a practical reality until much later, when other inventors commercialized the Kay *Sona-Graph* in 1951, a device which allowed researchers to visually inspect the acoustic components of speech in detail.

In the interim, the connection between academic work and pedagogy was a close one. Most of the earlier figures in the speech and hearing sciences were also teachers. A key representative of this tradition in the UK was Henry Sweet (1845–1912), one of the most famous of all phoneticians and a major thinker on language pedagogy. His 1900 handbook for language learners, *The Practical Study of Languages*, provided a great deal of useful advice. Since he was a phonetician, we would hardly expect him to be an unbiased commentator on the importance of pronunciation, and indeed, he identified phonetics as *the* fundamental aspect of L2 learning. Apart from serving as a handbook on both learning principles and the structure of English, his manual may have been the first to distinguish accent from intelligibility, noting that pronunciation need not be perfectly native-like, but that L2 speakers should have "sufficient accuracy of pronunciation to insure intelligibility" (p. 152).

In North America, Noah Webster (1758–1843), a schoolteacher and education reformer, became concerned that the teaching materials used in American schools, which were published entirely in the UK, were culturally and linguistically biased toward Britain. His response was to publish a best-selling book for children, affectionately known as the blue-backed speller (Webster, 1936), which taught reading, spelling, and pronunciation. His greatest accomplishment, however, was his *American Dictionary of the English Language* (1828), which became the first authoritative source on American pronunciation.

The 20th century saw the appearance of a variety of new publications on English pronunciation that would serve as references for both native speakers and L2 learners. In the UK, Henry Sweet's student Daniel Jones published an authoritative book on RECEIVED PRONUNCIATION, and A. C. Gimson's book *Introduction to the Pronunciation of English*, which first appeared in 1962, is still in print today. Other noted British phoneticians were David Abercrombie, who wrote extensively on pronunciation teaching for second language speakers, and his student Peter Ladefoged, who brought the British tradition to the USA. In addition to many important contributions to the field of phonetics, Ladefoged served as a linguistic consultant on the film *My Fair Lady*.

In the USA, Clifford Prator published his *Manual of American English Pronunciation for Adult Foreign Students* in 1951. A revised 4th edition of this book by Prator and

A CLOSER LOOK: Otto Jesperson, Danish linguist (1860–1943)

Otto Jesperson was a well-known Danish linguist who was concerned with the importance of good pronunciation. His 1904 book, entitled *How to Teach a Foreign Language,* was reprinted for the next 50 years. Jesperson was particularly eager for teachers to make use of IPA, which he thought would transform language teaching practices: "The use of phonetics and phonetical transcription in the teaching of modern languages must be considered as one of the most important advances in modern pedagogy, because it ensures both considerable facilitation and an exceedingly large gain in exactness. But these means must be employed immediately from the very beginning" (p. 170). Jesperson went on to say that "Just as easy as it is to get a good pronunciation in this way, just as difficult is it to root out the bad habits which may become inveterate during a very short period of instruction according to a wrong or antiquated method" (p. 170). In other words, he anticipated some aspects of the AUDIOLINGUAL METHOD more than 60 years before its advent. Jesperson's essay "What is the use of phonetics?" appeared in *The Educational Review* and is available online. It is a striking reminder that scholars now largely forgotten had a lot of interesting ideas well worth considering.

Robinett (1984) is still available, as is Robert Lado's and Charles Fries' *Pronunciation: Exercises in Sound Segments, Intonation and Rhythm,* which originally appeared in 1958. Another noteworthy scholar in the United States was Pierre Delattre, a French immigrant, who published some of the most important early research in acoustic phonetics using the sound spectrograph, an instrument that displays sound visually for analysis. He published comparisons of the sound systems of a variety of languages, particularly English, French and Spanish. Despite his technical accomplishments, Delattre identified himself first and foremost as a language teacher. In his obituary, Eddy (1974) described Delattre's remarkable level of commitment to pedagogy:

> As director of the beginning French course at the University of Colorado, he went much further than training the staff and teaching associates in regular weekly meetings. He visited the classes of each of them, and twice in the first semester personally gave an oral test, recorded by him on tape, to each of the 400-odd beginning students, the results of which went directly into the improvement of teacher training and teacher performance. Even more intense and careful was the individual attention he gave to each student in the classes he conducted personally. For him education was unthinkable without the basic one-to-one, student-to-teacher dialogue. (pp. 513–514)

Delattre's research was motivated in great part by his enthusiasm for teaching, while at the same time it served as a basis for several textbooks geared toward language learners.

Classroom teaching materials and innovations

Handbooks on language learning have existed for a long time, while printed and AV materials developed specifically for classroom pronunciation instruction are a more recent innovation. A major push in materials development came with the Audiolingual Method of teaching, which appeared in the mid-20th century and revolutionized language pedagogy, especially in North America. The method, based on behavioural psychology, emphasized oral/aural skills, requiring learners to listen to native speaker models and imitate them as closely as possible, in accordance with the nativeness principle. A variety of drills were used to teach pronunciation and grammatical structure implicitly, rather than through explanations and rules. Audiolingual teaching took advantage of post World War II advancements in science, technology and manufacturing, which made audio recording devices, projectors and, eventually, the language laboratory widely accessible. Learner textbooks were accompanied by AV materials such as filmstrips, records, and tapes that could be used in teacher-fronted lessons as well as for individual practice in the lab.

Textbooks

With the new emphasis on spoken language in Audiolingual teaching, pronunciation was seen as a central concern, and new pronunciation textbooks began to appear. It is not our intent here to survey the scores of texts that have been published since that period. Instead we will compare some very old, but still used textbooks with some more recently published books as a way of contrasting instructional materials in North America over the past half-century. One difference to note is the contrast between drill-based practice and more contextualized and quasi-communicative activities. Another has to do with the quantity and quality of material covering prosody.

Post-war classroom materials reflected the prevailing belief that difficulties in L2 learning were primarily the result of cross-linguistic INTERFERENCE from the L1. CONTRASTIVE ANALYSIS was used to identify similarities and differences in the sound inventories of the L1 and L2 and, on that basis, to predict areas of ease and difficulty for learners. European French speakers, for instance, would be expected to have difficulty with English lax vowels such as /ɪ/, which does not appear in the French phonological repertoire. The primary technique for teaching pronunciation was to require students to "listen and repeat," and very little time was spent on explanation or on explicit presentation of rules. A detailed program of drills for this purpose was developed in a 3-volume series, *Drills and Exercises in English Pronunciation* (published in 1966 and 1967 and still in print), which was accompanied by audio recordings and a teacher's manual. These drills were entirely mechanical, requiring students to mimic a model, while following along on the printed page. On the surface at least, the series appeared to place considerable emphasis on suprasegmentals, with the second and third volumes devoted to stress, intonation and rhythm. However, it is not clear that the latter volumes were used as much as the one covering vowels and consonants. Apart from focusing on minimal pairs and adhering to the Audiolingual principles of repetition and practice, the program was intuitively designed rather than research-based, though it must be recognized that the available research on pronunciation at that time was minimal. Topics were not ordered in any particular way, and no distinction was made between high and low-priority problems. The same is true of one of the most enduring publications in the field: Nilsen and Nilsen's *Pronunciation Contrasts in English*, first published in 1971 and still in print in a later edition (2010). This short volume consists primarily of lists of minimal pairs of English words to be used for "practicing" vowel and consonant distinctions, presumably through repetition after a model. The lists are accompanied by simple articulatory diagrams and lists of languages lacking the English distinctions in question, so that the teacher can anticipate the problems of particular learners. Though Contrastive Analysis can predict *general* tendencies for learner errors, we have little faith in accurately predicting a *particular* learner's errors using this or any other a priori method, and we seriously question the value of attempting to cover "everything" in a pronunciation class when instruction is based on the Intelligibility Principle. As a result, we do not see these early materials as having much to offer to contemporary language classrooms. In addition, the exercises in Audiolingual publications were often devoid of contextualization. Words, phrases, and entire sentences might be repeated in isolation, and the activities were structured so that learners had no need to even know *what* they were actually saying, let alone *when* a particular intonation pattern might be appropriate.

The emphasis on generative PHONOLOGY in the theoretical linguistics of the latter part of the 20th century had virtually no lasting impact on pronunciation teaching methods or materials. However, a number of post-Audiolingual pronunciation textbooks were published, covering approaches consistent with COMMUNICATIVE LANGUAGE TEACHING (CLT) and with more recent thinking and research on pronunciation. It should be noted, however, that the beginnings of CLT marked a general de-emphasis on pronunciation on the grounds that it was unteachable and that learners would acquire whatever skills they needed through simple exposure to the L2. In spite of this negative view of pronunciation, an important influence for several decades has been Judy Gilbert's *Clear Speech*, which, along with a teacher's manual, first appeared in 1984. Gilbert's work marked a reconsideration of the role of prosody in L2 learning. Although aspects of stress, intonation, and rhythm had long been considered important, many early texts ordered topics with segmentals first, with an expected progression from small (segmental) units to larger ones (words, phrases, and sentences). Prosody in connected speech was scheduled for a "later time" in a course of instruction, which, in practical terms, may never have actually arrived in the classroom. The *Clear Speech* series starts, rather than ends, with connected speech and gives it a prominent role in the exercises. Another feature of Gilbert's (and others') textbooks has been the development of a much wider range of exercises and activities than mechanical "listen and repeat" drills. The newer techniques not only engage learners by keeping them interested, but also embed the material in a meaningful context that is impossible to obtain with rote drills.

Technological developments

Perhaps the single most important 20th century technological innovation for pronunciation teaching was the analog tape recorder. Devices for recording and playing back speech were not readily available to the public, let alone schools, until after World War II. Until that time, aural/oral instruction was greatly restricted in two ways. First, the only pronunciation model normally available to a class of learners was the teacher. The appearance of professional recordings provided access to a wider range of speakers, both male and female, as well as different speaking styles and rates. Some pedagogical specialists saw these materials as obviating the need for native-speaking teachers, while technological enthusiasts even proposed that language teachers would no longer need to speak the language they taught [see Richards & Rodgers, 2014]. A second restriction of early 20th century teaching was that learners had no opportunity to hear and critique their own oral productions. Although the language laboratory could be used for teaching many different aspects of speaking and listening, its invention was motivated in great part by an interest in pronunciation. Early labs used multi-track tape systems so that learners could hear model speakers and then record, play back, and re-record their own voices. The instructor could monitor learners' performance and provide intervention. An innovative variation on this theme was the Bell and Howell *Language Master*, a portable recorder/player for use by small groups or individuals. Small magnetic-striped cards showing pictures, printed words, or full sentences, could be inserted into the machine for playing a model production. Students could then produce and record their own speech for comparison with the model.

The advent of advanced digital technologies has greatly expanded the possibilities for pronunciation instruction. Apart from the more convenient and higher quality recording and playback available with current devices, potential future developments include automated pronunciation assessment and feedback with individually tailored instruction, and perhaps aural/oral interactions in virtual worlds that promote improved speaking skills. However, dramatic benefits of new technology have yet to be realized.

Research on adult phonetic learning

Within the phonetics community, a major research stream developed in the late part of the 20th century that reflected a growing interest in cross-linguistic perception and production. Findings from perceptual studies showed that adults tended to have considerable difficulty DISCRIMINATING and IDENTIFYING certain speech sounds from other languages, including languages learned in adulthood. A series of investigations by Winifred Strange and her colleagues (Miyawaki et al., 1975; Sheldon & Strange, 1982; Strange & Dittmann, 1984) focused on a phenomenon that is particularly well-known to the general public: difficulties with English /l/ and /ɹ/ experienced by Japanese speakers. Early evidence showed that perceiving this distinction, which is not phonemic in Japanese, was often very difficult for adult Japanese listeners without English experience. Moreover, even with feedback-based training or many years of residence in an English-speaking area, perception tended not to improve much. Subsequent studies of infants by Janet Werker and her colleagues (Werker & Tees, 2002) pinpointed a fundamental change in speech perception that occurs by about 10 to 12 months of age. By that time, children lose the ability to perceptually distinguish certain sound contrasts that do not occur in the language spoken around them. Catherine Best (Best, McRoberts & Sithole, 1988; Best & Tyler, 2007) proposed her *Perceptual Assimilation Model* (PAM) to account for these "perceptual blind spots," that appear in childhood and seem to remain with us for the rest of our lives. PAM aims at explaining how listeners tend to perceive foreign segments in terms of what they already unconsciously know about the phonetic properties of their L1. Still another piece in the phonetic learning puzzle was added by James Flege, whose *Speech Learning Model* (SLM) focuses on the role of language experience in phonetic learning (Flege, 1995). His model ties pronunciation difficulties to perceptual processes with the goal of explaining why some L2 segments are learned more readily than others.

Because the research tradition described above has been closely associated with laboratory-based investigations published in phonetics and technically-oriented speech journals rather than with classroom studies or teaching interventions, it has sometimes been regarded as only peripherally relevant to applied linguistics. However, if pronunciation specialists ignore this rich literature, they run the risk of missing out on valuable information about the cognitive-developmental aspects of pronunciation learning. In particular, these studies suggest that the importance of phonetic perception has been seriously underestimated in L2 classrooms. Promising experimental research indicates that, through strategic manipulation of perceptual input, improvement in production can be effected. For instance, segmental identification training can lead to automatic improvement in segmental production (Bradlow et al., 1997). Intriguingly, a parallel benefit for intonation had been reported many years earlier by de Bot and Mailfert (1982). Also, modifying phonetic input to draw listeners' attention to fine-grained details can improve their perception (Guion & Pederson, 2007; Wang & Munro, 2004). Finally, exposing listeners to variable input using many different voices appears to assist them in the development of accurate cognitive representations of sounds (Iverson, Hazan, & Bannister, 2005). It is only very recently that researchers have attempted to apply these types of knowledge from the laboratory to pedagogically-oriented materials. Thomson's *English Accent Coach* (2011), for instance, is specifically designed to implement what is known about feedback training with high-variability input.

Research on pronunciation teaching

Jeris Strain was a scholar ahead of his time when, in a paper in *Language Learning* in 1963, he commented that "controlled experimentation is perhaps the largest remaining frontier" (p. 217) in English teaching. Like many more recent specialists, he placed value on *evidence-based teaching* practices. Of course experienced teachers have well-developed intuitions about learners' successes and failures in the classroom, but nearly all teachers would like guidance based on solid evidence about the effectiveness of particular teaching approaches. It simply isn't beneficial to students, or fair to teachers, if every instructor tries to "re-invent the wheel" for pronunciation teaching by finding effective techniques through trial and error. Many issues that interest teachers have the potential to be resolved, at least partially, through empirical research. Here are a few examples:

a. Can classroom pronunciation instruction really lead to improvement?
b. How effective is individual practice using technology?
c. Can we make useful predictions of learners' pronunciation errors on the basis of L1?
d. Can prosody be taught?
e. Does instruction on perception improve production?
f. What are the most important aspects of instruction to focus on?
g. Can learners with long-term(fossilized) pronunciation difficulties learn to speak more intelligibly?

No amount of discussion or debate about the above questions is likely to give us useful insights into the issues they raise. Rather, controlled, systematic studies are needed to provide us with data that may allow us to draw conclusions. Yet, in spite of Strain's call for empirical research more than half a century ago, the number of controlled experimental studies on pronunciation learning is still remarkably small. We feel compelled to comment here on a tendency among researchers to forget about valuable early work, much to the detriment of the field. In Munro and Derwing (2015a) we reference an empirical pronunciation study by Sisson (1970, in *Language Learning*) that provided evidence of pronunciation improvement as a result of two different instructional methods. Strangely, however, the Sisson study has almost never been cited. Its outcomes seem to have been forgotten as a result of a prevailing, and evidently incorrect, orthodoxy of that era, which saw pronunciation teaching as a waste of time. First, Krashen's input-based perspective on second language acquisition (Krashen, 1981), influential in the 1980s, accorded little value to explicit pronunciation teaching. Second, CORRELATIONAL RESEARCH by Purcell and Suter (1980) was interpreted as showing that acquisition of pronunciation was largely outside of the teacher's control (e.g. Pica, 1994). The study, cited numerous times in the research literature, examined the correlations between a number of predictor variables (including motivation, L1, amount of instruction) and the pronunciation scores of adult English learners. One of its findings was that the learners' amount of pronunciation instruction did not significantly correlate with their production scores. This was an interesting finding, but from a methodological standpoint, it is nearly impossible to justify using such data to draw conclusions about teaching. Correlational studies simply do not establish cause and effect; they indicate only the presence or absence of a relationship between two measured variables. The fact that pronunciation performance was not predicted by the learners' length of instruction does not show that their instruction was ineffective. In fact, we know nothing about the kind or quality of instruction received, or whether the research participants were even able to accurately report their instructional experience long after they had received it. Moreover, since the researchers used a sample of convenience, it is very likely that the speakers' instructional experience was confounded with other variables such that it would not be possible to make useful inferences about instruction effects.

When reading the literature in preparation for a research project, beginning scholars may miss important findings that appeared decades earlier, sometimes because older research has not received much attention in literature reviews. In fact, the Sisson (1970) paper offers some useful insights on questions (a) and (b) above. On a different topic, a study by Brière (1966), also infrequently referenced, sheds light on question (c). In his investigation of the predictive value of Contrastive Analysis, Brière found that phonetic characterizations in terms of phonemes or distinctive features are quite inadequate for predicting certain short-term learning difficulties. Yet textbooks claiming to make such predictions have been in print for many decades.

It is commonly noted that prosodic issues have tended to receive less attention in pronunciation research than they merit. However, it is not true that prosody has been neglected altogether. Among the papers addressing question (d) was de Bot's (1983) comparison of the benefits of audio-visual and auditory-only feedback on English intonation. His finding that an audio-visual approach was superior also speaks to question (b).

Although no one could accurately assert that all the issues arising from the list of questions above have been covered in the literature, substantial progress has been made on several of them. Moreover, the relevant research findings go back many decades.

A pedagogical perspective on L2 phonetic acquisition

A young Englishman named Nigel lived in Seville with his Spanish girlfriend. He taught English during the day, but never spoke it outside of class. When his British co-workers wanted to communicate with him, he expected them to speak in Spanish. Nigel even wrote to his parents in Spanish, though neither of them knew the language. Tracey Derwing met Nigel's mother, who had come to visit her son for a few days. She confided that she had to buy a bilingual dictionary to interpret his letters home. Nigel had essentially rejected his British background in favour of a new Spanish identity. Yet despite his keen motivation, his superb knowledge of Spanish grammar and vocabulary, and optimal input conditions, Nigel had a distinctly English accent when speaking his L2 that even a novice Spanish speaker could detect. Many factors affect L2 speech acquisition, some of which are beyond the speaker's immediate control.

Introduction

L2 phonetic acquisition is a diverse area of study arising from the work of applied and theoretical linguists, experimental phoneticians, psychologists, pedagogical specialists, and speech-language pathologists. With such broad scholarly interest in the field, it is not surprising that many different motivations underlie the L2 speech research of the past several decades. It is also quite striking how researchers with different backgrounds and purposes sometimes look at the same set of data and interpret it in very different ways. In this chapter, we cannot cover the full range of concerns addressed by L2 phonetics specialists. Instead, we will examine a selection of key issues that have helped define the field. We begin by focusing on the L2 phonetic learning process and then turn to theoretical questions about factors influencing learners' success and the prediction of problem areas. Next we consider the relevance of research addressing these questions to pronunciation teaching. In some cases, useful applications for the classroom emerge; in others, however, we risk being led in quite the wrong direction. That is because much theoretically-driven research aims at characterizing the nature of L2 knowledge-often in abstract ways-rather than at developing concrete intervention techniques for the classroom. In most cases, abstract approaches to linguistic description have little direct relevance to instruction; rather, they tend to be of interest only to linguists with specialized knowledge of terminology and notational conventions.

Furthermore, theory-driven L2 work may focus on the acquisition of phonological structures that are of little or no importance for speech intelligibility. To determine the usefulness of L2 speech research for teachers, then, we have to take a critical view of goals and underlying assumptions, and evaluate results in terms of their relevance to the goals of language pedagogy.

The phonetic learning process

No one disputes that adult L2 learners are capable of acquiring at least some aspects of the sound system of their new language, though most would agree that uninstructed pronunciation learning does not typically yield optimal outcomes. In other words, some L2 speakers genuinely need guidance to learn to produce comfortably intelligible speech. By paying attention to some of the details of the L2 phonetic learning process, we may be able to develop effective teaching strategies that promote speech intelligibility. In doing so, teaching specialists may benefit from an understanding of the ways in which L2 speech skills develop over time, both through naturalistic experience and as a result of pedagogical intervention. The more we know about the acquisition process, the clearer will be our sense of what to expect from learners and of how to help them achieve their goals. Here are some questions that we might pose:

- What level of achievement in pronunciation can we expect from adult L2 learners?
- What personal, social, and experience factors contribute to successful pronunciation in adults?
- How long does it take for an adult to learn the sound system of the L2? Do aspects of a particular L2 phonological system vary in learning difficulty? Do some aspects take longer than others to learn? Are some aspects never likely to be learned at all?
- In what ways does knowledge of the L1 facilitate or hamper L2 phonetic learning?
- Is acquisition gradual? Do learners slowly approximate the sounds of the L2 over time-or is the process more abrupt?
- Is acquisition linear? Do learners have a learning trajectory indicating continual improvement or are there ups and downs in the learning process?
- What is the relationship between *perceiving* L2 segments and prosody and *producing* them? Do learners sometimes perceive speech distinctions correctly despite inaccurate production? Do they ever produce them correctly without accurate perception?

Although researchers are still far from arriving at definitive answers to most of the above issues, empirical studies over the past few decades have provided us with useful insights on some of them. In the sections that follow we focus mainly on research findings relating to the first three questions and then discuss their applicability to the classroom. Although we touch on some of the remaining questions, we will address them in more depth in later chapters.

Factors influencing phonetic learning

Age

L2 speech research into the phonetic learning process, and particularly the role of age of learning, has been driven to a great extent by a long-standing observation: adult learners do not typically acquire native-like pronunciation, even after many years of experience with their second language and an otherwise high level of proficiency in speaking, listening, reading, and writing. Tom Scovel (1988) refers to this phenomenon as the "Joseph Conrad Effect," pointing out how Conrad's extraordinary mastery of English prose contrasted sharply with his heavy accent in English – actually his third language. The disparity in Conrad's skills is taken not only as an indication of the difficulties involved in acquiring L2 pronunciation, but also as evidence of how adult pronunciation learning seems to be compromised as learners get older, perhaps even to a greater degree than other aspects of language.

The view that "younger is better" when it comes to learning pronunciation has a number of practical implications: age is a factor that many parents consider when deciding whether to place their children in immersion programs at school. Awareness of age also helps us adjust our expectations when we interact with speakers who learned their L2 late in life. Interlocutors often speak more clearly or listen more attentively when engaged with older L2 learners. While age effects have been observed anecdotally for a very long time, a series of landmark studies of L2 English speakers beginning in the late 1960s have led us to empirically-based conclusions about the relationship between age of learning (AOL) and L2 accent. This line of research uses judgments of strength of foreign accent as a measure of pronunciation accuracy. The studies are correlational, with age serving as a predictor or INDEPENDENT VARIABLE, and pronunciation ratings as the DEPENDENT VARIABLE – the phenomenon we want to explain. The central question is, "how close is the relationship between AOL and accent?" Some of the more influential of these studies are listed, along with a few methodological details, in Table 3.1. In each investigation, the researchers followed a well-established procedure. First they collected speech samples from ESL users who had been living in an English-speaking country for several years, but who varied in terms of their AOL. They then presented the recordings to raters-either phonetically trained, untrained, or both-who made judgments of the speakers' strength of accent. The studies differ with respect to the L1s of the speakers, the methods of eliciting the speech samples, the nature of the raters, and the types of rating scales employed. Yet every one of the listed papers yielded a negative relationship between AOL and pronunciation scores: older learners typically had stronger accents (even after many years of L2 experience), and the likelihood of speaking without a detectable foreign accent diminished with increased AOL. In the light of this evidence, we must accept the fact that increased age of learning is indeed associated with less native-like speech.

Table 3.1. Foreign accent rating studies focusing on AOL

Study	L1	N	Native English comparison group	Raters
Asher & García (1969)	Spanish	71	30	19 untrained
Oyama (1976)	Italian	60	10	2 trained
Patkowski (1990)	Various	67	N/A	2 trained
Thompson (1991)	Russian	36	10	8 trained; 8 untrained
Flege, Munro, & MacKay (1995)	Italian	240	24	10 untrained
Flege, Yeni-Komshian, & Liu (1999)	Korean	240	24	10 untrained
Munro & Mann (2005)	Mandarin	32	14	14 moderately trained

How to interpret the AOL facts, however, is a different matter altogether. While nearly all scholars accept the evidence that greater AOL predicts less native-like speech perception and production, the question of *why* that relationship exists is controversial and provokes a great deal of argument, some of it quite acrimonious. Merely observing a relationship between two variables does not tell us about causes. For instance, North American data on annual earnings show that between the ages of 20 and 50, incomes increase significantly with age. However, it would make no sense to conclude that getting older *causes* people to make more money. Rather, the situation is more complicated. For example, the fact that people in their 50s usually have more highly developed work skills and greater work experience than those in their 20s may partly account for the relationship. The complexity that arises in interpreting correlations between variables explains why SLA specialists can accept the available data on age and L2 learning but disagree on what it means. In our discussion below, we present some of the research findings that have been used to argue both for and against the concept of a CRITICAL PERIOD for the acquisition of pronunciation skills. Our goal is not to convince you that one or the other is the correct view, but rather to encourage you to think critically about these perspectives and to understand the reasons why the issue remains unresolved.

Conflicting perspectives on the "Critical Period." The Canadian brain researcher, Wilder Penfield, was one of the first to propose that language learning is affected by a biologically-based change in the brain prior to adulthood (Penfield & Roberts, 1959). Drawing on Penfield's ideas, Eric Lenneberg presented a viewpoint on language learning in which he argued that innate acquisition mechanisms facilitate L1 learning, but cease to operate at about the time of puberty (Lenneberg, 1967), thereby making L2 learning less successful. Such a phenomenon is comparable to one that occurs in various types of birds that are unable to learn their species-specific song unless they are exposed to it before a critical age. The prevalence of foreign accents in adult L2 learners, but anecdotally not in child learners, has often been taken as evidence for the existence of a parallel maturational constraint on human language learning. The theoretical underpinnings of this view are based on a *nativist* orientation to language, which assumes that language acquisition is strongly influenced by universal innate learning mechanisms specific to language. DeKeyser (2000) gives a detailed account of the critical period perspective. Its adherents often point to empirical data indicating the inevitability of foreign accents in adult learners and the strong evidence of changes in accent acquisition by the end of childhood. By way of contrast, virtually everyone learns to pronounce an L1 perfectly, assuming an upbringing in a normal environment (cf. Rymer, 1993). It may be, then, that adult L2 learning develops as a result of somewhat different mechanisms than those that apply in L1 learning. DeKeyser (2000) proposes, for instance, that older learners cannot learn implicitly, but must instead have their conscious attention drawn to L2 phenomena. In fact, as we explain in the next chapter, research evidence does indeed show that the redirection of L2 learners' attention is useful in helping them perceive and produce L2 speech. However, as far as we know, no study has ever shown that instruction or other systematic training can help

A CLOSER LOOK: Oyama (1976)

An influential study of global foreign accent in Italian speakers of English by Oyama (1976) illustrates a methodological approach used with slight variations many times over in L2 speech research. Oyama framed her work as a test of the "sensitive period" proposal. Her objective was to examine the effects of two independent variables – age of L2 learning (AOL) and length of US residence (LOR) – on the strength of foreign accents. She began by recording oral language samples from 60 native Italian speakers and a group of 10 native English controls. The Italian speakers had moved to the US at ages ranging from 6 to 20 years, and their length of residence was from 5 to 18 years. Each speaker produced a reading passage, followed by an extemporaneous narrative of a "danger of death" experience. Two graduate linguistics students then listened to a randomized presentation of the recordings and judged each on a 5-point scale, ranging from "no foreign accent" to "heavy foreign accent." The mean ratings thus served as Oyama's dependent measure. She found that later AOLs significantly predicted stronger accent scores: for the reading passages, the simple Pearson *r* correlation was .83, and for the narratives it was .69. However, LOR bore no relationship to either type of production, with correlations of .02 and –.07, respectively. In short, age of learning was a good predictor of accent strength; length of US residence was not.

adult L2 learners to speak with a perfectly nativelike accent at all times under all conditions. That observation seems consistent with the view that certain language learning abilities are "lost" as we age.

An alternative perspective does not consider the notion of a critical period to be well-motivated. Instead, the AOL effect is understood as the result of a combination of cognitive and experiential factors that affect learning processes as we age. Researchers such as Flege and MacKay (2011) point to the influences of L1 knowledge on speech perception and production, to social factors such as motivation, and to the relatively impoverished language experience of many L2 learners. Singleton (2001) notes that both Penfield's and Lenneberg's ideas about L2 learning and puberty were based mainly on personal experience and anecdotal claims rather than on systematic evidence. He cites empirical studies showing that even child L2 learners often retain foreign accents. Research findings, in fact, do not support the claim that puberty marks an *abrupt* change in language learning abilities. Rather, it seems that the likelihood of "foreign accent-free" speech decreases *gradually* with AOL. Adult L2 learning might therefore be compromised by a combination of factors that happen to be related to age, including developmental changes in general perception mechanisms, L2 experience, motivational effects, and the fact that adults (but not younger children) already have cognitive structures in place that may "get in the way" of some aspects of new language learning. From this perspective, the difficulties adult L2 learners have in learning pronunciation are comparable to the problems they experience in learning other complex behaviours late in life. If so, then L2 learning is not a fundamentally different process from other kinds of learning, including L1 acquisition.

To sum up our discussion so far, applied linguists do not agree on the question of whether a critical period underlies the AOL effect: data are still being discussed that support both sides of this debate. One aspect of the debate concerns the nature of the AOL effect: At what age do changes in learning capabilities occur? Do adult L2 learners *ever* partially or completely overcome the negative effects of age on accent production? And do young learners *always* produce "accent-free" speech? A second important issue is the question of whether AOL effects are mediated by other factors: Can motivation, aptitude, experience and instruction enhance phonetic learning? Most researchers agree that addressing these questions can give us useful insights into the phonetic acquisition process.

The nature of the age effect. Anecdotal evidence suggests that people vary considerably in their ultimate success in L2 phonetic accuracy. You have probably heard stories of remarkably talented adult speakers who seem to pronounce an L2 perfectly. However, as with other common claims, drawing conclusions on the basis of unsystematic information is not a satisfactory way to understand human behaviour. We need data that have been collected and analyzed as systematically and rigorously as possible. In that regard, Theo Bongaerts and colleagues found evidence that *some* adult learners of Dutch can produce native-sounding speech under at least *some* circumstances. Their study was part of a series of investigations of highly-proficient instructed and naturalistic learners whose speech was recorded and then presented to listeners for evaluation in blind listening tasks (Bongaerts, Mennen, & van der Slik, 2000; Bongaerts, van Summeren, Planken, & Schils, 1997). "Blind" assessment means that the listeners had no idea whether they were actually listening to native or non-native speakers of Dutch. In the end, the researchers concluded that the native-like performance of some speakers was the result of a combination of motivation and language experience factors, as well as TYPOLOGICAL PROXIMITY. By this they meant that speakers of languages that are phonologically similar to Dutch, such as English and German, were sometimes able to produce native-sounding Dutch speech, while speakers of more distant non-Indo-European languages like Turkish and Berber were not. Of course, even if adult learners can sometimes produce native-sounding speech, the studies in Table 3.1 suggest that high-achieving L2 speakers like those described in Bongaerts et al. (2000) are the exception rather than the rule. Hyltenstam and Abrahamsson (2001) and Abrahamsson and Hyltenstam (2009) have also emphasized that even the most successful of L2 users are likely to betray their non-nativeness in some circumstances. Nonetheless, an intriguing perspective on exceptional L2 pronunciation in adults was discussed by Ingrid Piller in her analysis of interviews of couples in which one partner's L1 was English and the other's was German (Piller, 2002). Her respondents described their experiences of passing for a native speaker of their L2 on first encounters with interlocutors such as service people in stores. She focused on the length of time it was possible to be perceived as a native speaker, the context, and the satisfaction of having succeeded. These instances appeared to reflect a self-imposed challenge designed to test their own abilities. In fact, the ability to "pass," even if only briefly, was reported to be common, rather than rare.

At the opposite end of the age continuum, research has yielded some dramatic surprises. One of the most important research findings in the study of language acquisition had to do with the age at which speech perception becomes tuned to the native language. In the 1980s, several studies by Janet Werker and colleagues (see Werker & Tees, 2002) demonstrated that, before they reach one year of age, infants cease to discriminate certain phonetic categories that do not contrast in the language spoken around them. For instance, right after birth, babies who are being raised in an exclusively English environment can distinguish consonant pairs such as the Hindi dental and retroflex STOPS, even though these do not occur in the English sound inventory. Dental stops are produced by positioning the tongue tip at the back of the teeth, while retroflex stops require a curling back of the tip of tongue toward the palate. Of course, English infants have no need to produce or perceive such articulations, and over the first several months of life, their ability to discern the difference between them declines to chance levels. Infants exposed to Hindi, however, continue to perceive the difference without difficulty. Training English adults and older children to distinguish these two types of consonants at a perceptual level has proved to be extremely difficult; to adult English ears they sound very much the same. Werker and colleagues' findings, which have been replicated numerous times, point to a change in speech acquisition processes much earlier in human development than anyone had previously expected – and well before Lenneberg's (1967) conception of a critical period defined by puberty. Rather than attributing these findings to a critical period, Werker and Tees (2002) characterized the changes as a PERCEPTUAL REORGANIZATION that results from early L1 experience. A likely benefit of this change is that it actually facilitates L1 learning because it helps infants focus on the phonetic details of the L1 that actually matter and to ignore irrelevant variation. The "cost," however, is that they lose sensitivity to speech phenomena that exist in other languages. Werker's research may help account for findings from another research thread indicating that early L2 learners-including those whose families moved to a new country before they were six years of age-sometimes speak with detectible nonnative accents (e.g. Asher & Garcia, 1969; Flege, Munro, & MacKay, 1995; Flege, Yeni-Komshian, & Liu, 1999). It seems, then, that changes in language learning mechanisms happen very early in life, not nearly as late as theorists

A CLOSER LOOK: Perception and production

Even prior to Janet Werker's research on infant speech perception, the relationship between adult speakers' perception of L2 sounds and their production abilities had attracted the attention of speech researchers. Nearly everyone is aware of the stereotypical difficulty that Japanese speakers often have when attempting to produce the English /ɹ/-/l/ difference. In the 1970s, research by Winifred Strange and her colleagues demonstrated that Japanese speakers actually have trouble *perceiving* the distinction. This influential work helped make /ɹ/-/l/ one of the most studied phenomena in L2 speech. Some studies have focused on poor *discrimination*: an inability to hear the difference between the two sounds. Others indicate problems with *identification*: determining which of the two sounds has been presented. Still other work has examined the effects of perceptual training on these two phenomena. In identification training, for example, learners hear an utterance containing one of the sounds and must indicate which one they have heard. Feedback (right/wrong) is then provided, perhaps on a computer screen or through an audio signal. Such research indicates not only that perception improves with training, but that production sometimes spontaneously improves as well. However, subsequent research has shown that the relationship between perception and production is quite complex. It certainly seems logical that someone who does not perceive a consonant distinction would have trouble producing it. However, poor production is not always tied to poor perception, and the reverse is also true. A few studies have even shown that people can produce certain sound distinctions quite well without being able to reliably hear the difference between them (Sheldon & Strange, 1982).

once proposed. Werker and colleagues' findings are highly relevant to any account of L2 acquisition, though they do not appear to fit well with attempts to explain foreign accents in older learners in terms of a well-delimited critical or "sensitive" period that is complete by puberty, age 12, or age 6, all of which have been proposed. Perhaps it is for this reason that some proponents of critical periods simply ignore the evidence of a perceptual reorganization altogether (e.g. Granena & Long, 2013).

Research comparing older and younger learners provides us with useful information about the AOL-accent relationship. For one thing, the Bongaerts et al. (2000) findings point us in the direction of mitigating factors such as motivation and L2 experience that must be explored if we are to gain a full understanding of the L2 phonetic acquisition process. For another, if a critical period exists, it is *not* sharply delineated. To understand why, consider the hypothetical "critical period" function illustrated in Figure 3.1, which is based on work by Miles Munro and Virginia Mann (2005). The three functions illustrate potential degrees of L2 accent for the onset of language acquisition between birth and early adulthood. We might interpret the figure as showing the "average" amount of accent we would find if we collected data from many speakers at every AOL between birth and adulthood. Each function indicates that foreign accent tends to increase with AOL. We know that to be a fact; however, as we have pointed out, young learners are not *guaranteed* to have "accent-free" speech, and older learners can vary considerably in the levels of nativeness they achieve, with some showing very high levels of performance. In particular, studies by Flege and colleagues indicate a *gradual* change in accent as a function of age, more similar to the sigmoid (the stretched 's' shape) and linear patterns shown in Figure 3.1, and not like the sharp "critical period" function (Flege, Munro, & MacKay, 1995; Flege, Yeni-Komshian, & Liu, 1999).

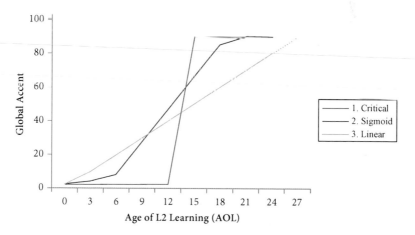

Figure 3.1. Hypothetical relationships between age of L2 learning and degree of foreign accent (see Munro & Mann, 2005)

To gain a clearer understanding of the age-accent relationship, Munro and Mann (2005) used statistical techniques to evaluate the actual shape of the age-accent function. Their primary data consisted of accent ratings on several types of speech produced by native Mandarin immigrants with AOLs between 3 and 16 years. They found that the sigmoid model provided the best fit to the ratings, concluding that "No model of an age-accent connection should ever hope to claim 'before age X, a person is guaranteed to develop a native accent and, after age Y, a foreign accent is unavoidable" (p. 337). They also observed a great deal of variability in the degree of accentedness between different L2 speakers at any particular age and also when the same L2 speaker produced different utterances. The *inter-speaker* differences indicated that the function is only a model of general tendencies and cannot be used to predict the performance of any particular speaker on the basis of age. *Intra-speaker* variability was due to different accent ratings, related to the kind of task performed. Productions of individual words and picture story descriptions tended to be judged more native-like than did sentence and paragraph readings. Finally, the Munro and Mann data showed that although men tended to be rated as more accented than women, no difference between the two genders was found in the general *shape* of the function. This casts still further doubt on the idea that accent and puberty are related, since women normally experience the onset and offset of puberty earlier than men, and would therefore be expected to show earlier changes if puberty were actually relevant.

One final matter of focus in the AOL-accent relationship has to do with the age of learning at which the strength of foreign accents levels off – the offset of the critical period. We have already noted that a decline in phonetic learning begins to occur even before the age of one year. If a critical period actually exists, then it should be possible to pinpoint an AOL in late childhood or early adulthood after which no further declines are observed. On the other hand, as Hakuta, Bialystok, and Wiley (2003) point out, evidence of a persistent decline in language learning success after early adulthood would pose a problem for a critical period account. They presented an analysis of data from the US Census covering Chinese and Spanish immigrants' self-reported English proficiency. A continuous decline in achievement between the ages of 20 and 60 was observed. Some other recent studies have also suggested that aspects of pronunciation may become less native-like as a function of AOL among adults in their 20s and 30s (Baker, 2010; Derwing & Munro, 2013; Derwing, Munro, Mulder, & Abbott, 2010).

Language experience, personal and instructional factors

We have already noted that even among adults sharing an AOL, large variability often exists in L2 pronunciation performance. In Flege et al.'s (1999) study, for example, some Korean learners of English had only moderate foreign accents, scoring as high as 5 or 6 on a 9-point accentedness scale on which '9' meant 'no foreign accent,' while others with the same AOL scored only 1 or 2, indicating that they had very strong accents. So what factors might account for such differences? In other words, what characteristics of speakers might *mediate* the age effect so as to help them do better than expected for people of their age? To answer this question, researchers have carried out studies in which several independent variables have been considered at the same time, with AOL held relatively constant. In one of the best-known studies of this type, Purcell and Suter (1980) performed a multiple regression analysis to determine how well a set of 11 speaker variables would predict L2 pronunciation accuracy. As in other studies we have considered, accent judgments on L2 learners' speech were collected and used as the dependent variable. Of the 11 predictor variables, only 4 showed statistically significant relationships to the judgments: first language, APTITUDE for oral mimicry, length of residence (LOR), and strength of concern for pronunciation accuracy. Note that AOL was absent from this list of predictors because all speakers were adults at their time of arrival in the USA. For that reason, this research is not comparable to the AOL studies in Table 3.1 and does not represent a contradiction in outcomes. Other non-significant predictors included gender and years of instruction. The findings led the authors to develop the following profile:

> If we may be permitted to indulge our imaginations, we might even create a theoretically superior pronouncer. We might call her Nazila (or him Muhammed, since sex is not a meaningful predictor). She is a Persian. She arrived in the United States nine years ago and has remained here ever since. Two years after her arrival, she married Fred, an American, and continues to share a home with him. Although she is a good mimic, Nazila continues to worry about what remains of her "foreign accent." This is all we need to know in order to be fairly certain that Nazila pronounces English very well. Whether or not she has had much or little formal instruction in English or English pronunciation is of no importance. (p. 285)

Purcell and Suter's (1980) final point seems very troubling for advocates of pronunciation teaching. We will evaluate the appropriateness and reliability of their conclusion later in the chapter. First, however, we will turn our attention to other predictors of success in pronunciation learning.

L2 experience. An influential study by Oyama (1976) gave no indication that greater length of residence (LOR) in the US predicted better accent scores among adult L2 learners, while the Purcell and Suter (1980) study showed the opposite. Though both studies aimed at quantifying the effect of exposure to the L2, this contradiction in findings was an early indication that evaluating the benefits of language experience on pronunciation would turn out to be a more complex problem than could be addressed simply by looking at LOR. In fact if we consider a number of research studies focusing on the relationship between pronunciation (including perceptual aspects) and LOR, we find a rather frustrating array of contradictions, some of which are presented in Table 3.2. In reading the table, notice how some investigations of identical

A CLOSER LOOK: Suter (1976)

One of the first comprehensive studies of the influences on accent attainment was Suter (1976) who, like Oyama (1976), recorded speech samples from L2 English speakers, collected accent judgments from listeners, and carried out a correlational analysis to determine which of a set of 20 independent variables were significant predictors of the listeners' ratings. His speaker sample of 61 was quite small, considering the large number of independent variables he aimed to consider. Suter's approach was simply to compute a Pearson r value for the relationship between each variable and the accent ratings. However, Suter's findings were difficult to interpret because some of the variables were intercorrelated. For example, several of them were related to motivational factors, while several others had to do with exposure to the L2. With 20 predictor variables to consider, a table of intercorrelations contains 190 correlation coefficients – far too many to interpret in a straightforward way! As it turned out, only 12 of the original 20 predictors were significantly correlated with the accent scores, but even then, interpretation was difficult. To develop a less overwhelming picture of the results, Purcell and Suter (1980) re-examined the original data using factor analysis, a statistical approach that helps researchers group related predictors together to create composite variables that may provide a clearer understanding of the categories of influences on a dependent variable.

Table 3.2. Studies of the effects of LOR on L2 pronunciation and speech perception phenomena

Study	Focus	Significant effect of LOR?
Oyama, 1982	Global accent	No
Purcell & Suter, 1980	Global accent	Yes
Thompson, 1991	Global accent	Yes
Flege & Fletcher, 1992	Global accent	Yes
Flege, Takagi, & Mann, 1995	r/l	Yes
Larson-Hall, 2006	r/l	No
Flege, Munro, & Skelton, 1992	Final consonants	No
Flege & Liu, 2001	Final consonants	Mixed
Trofimovich & Baker, 2006	Prosody	Mixed
Flege, Bohn, & Jang, 1997	Vowels	Yes
Tsukada et al., 2005	Vowels	No
Baptista, 2006	Vowels	Yes
Munro & Derwing, 2008	Vowels	Yes

speech phenomena actually yielded opposite results. Flege, Takagi, and Mann's (1995) cross-sectional study of Japanese speakers' acquisition of English /ɹ/, for instance, showed better performance by longer-term USA residents, while very similar research by Larson-Hall (2006) did not.

How do we account for the discrepancies in the outcomes of these studies? Several issues that need to be considered were discussed in a comprehensive review by Piske, MacKay, and Flege (2001). We will examine two of these below.

1) Quantifying L2 experience. When discussing L2 experience, we usually mean the extent to which someone hears the L2 spoken and produces utterances in the L2. While it is sometimes assumed that living longer in a country entails hearing and speaking the L2 more, Piske et al. (2001) point out that LOR is not necessarily a good index of listening and speaking behaviour. Some immigrants, for instance, move to a new country and soon begin using their L2 extensively. They work with, make friends with, and sometimes marry people who do not speak their L1. Their L2 experience is therefore much richer than that of other immigrants who choose to keep close ties with their own L1 community and avoid using the L2 when not required to.

Flege and Liu (2001) also observed that LOR does not always correspond to learners' amount of L2 experience. They found that Chinese-speaking US residents with postsecondary instruction at American universities showed an LOR effect, while those without such instruction did not. The difference may have been due to the greater exposure to English in the postsecondary group. But even if we were able to accurately measure a learner's amount of L2 experience – in hours, weeks, or months – we would still have to consider the *quality* of that experience in order to understand its impact. Clearly, a learner who engages in extended conversations in the L2 has a different *kind* of experience than another who interacts only in very short, formulaic exchanges in the L2, even if both have the same amount of exposure over a particular period of time. In a series of longitudinal investigations, Tracey Derwing and her colleagues (Derwing & Munro, 2013; Derwing, Munro, & Thomson, 2008) collected pronunciation data from Mandarin- and Slavic-speaking (Russian, Ukrainian, and Croatian) immigrants to Canada over several years. Recordings of each speaker describing a picture story were made soon after arrival and presented to listeners who rated the speech for accentedness, comprehensibility, and fluency. The speakers had all arrived with a low level of oral English proficiency and had come from similar socio-economic backgrounds. All were well-educated in their home countries. However, after a year in Canada, a significant between-group difference emerged in their productions of extemporaneous speech: the Slavic language speakers outperformed the Mandarin speakers in comprehensibility and fluency (Derwing, Thomson, & Munro, 2006). And after 7 years, the gap increased even further: the Slavic speakers had improved a great deal on both dimensions since the outset of the study, while the Mandarin speakers still showed the same levels of performance as they did at the beginning. One factor contributing to the difference might be the greater structural similarities between Slavic languages and English than between Mandarin and English. These may have facilitated English learning for the Slavic group. However, interviews with the participants revealed another important difference: the Slavic speakers reported many more extended interactions with English speakers-both native and non-native-than did the Mandarin group, as well as greater integration into the new culture. Also striking was the fact that *within* the two groups, speakers who were more integrated into the English-speaking community tended to produce the most comprehensible speech. These findings provide further evidence that simply counting years of residence in a country is far less useful than considering the *quality* of L2 learners' interactions when assessing how experience affects learning.

One way to avoid the simplistic approach of measuring L2 experience in terms of LOR is to have research participants complete detailed questionnaires about their actual L2 (and L1) use in various situations. Flege et al. (1995), for example, had participants retrospectively estimate their typical time spent using English with family, with friends, and at work. A problem with this approach, however, is that participants may be unable to recall their past experiences well enough to provide accurate responses. Recently, Ranta and Meckelborg (2013) developed a more sophisticated technique in which L2 speakers tracked their actual interactions using electronic language logs. In a further development, Surtees (2013) reported a study in which learners used mobile phones to record interactions in their L2, thus affording an unmediated account of their L2 oral experiences. Still another intriguing development is digital language processing hardware that tracks and analyzes language to which the user is exposed. LENA, for instance, is a small, portable device that can count the number of words children hear from their caregivers (see ⟨www.lenafoundation.org⟩). In the near future, applied linguists may use similar innovations to evaluate the speech input and output of L2 learners. Technology-based approaches such as these offer considerable promise for more accurate evaluations of actual language experience over a defined time interval. Nevertheless, one problem that remains is that learners' use of the L2 is not necessarily comparable over different time periods during their lives. Thus language use data collected during the course of a research study may be accurate at the time of the study, without necessarily providing a correct reflection of the use of the L2 over the months or years prior to that point. At present there seems to be no solution to this problem.

2) Identifying the best time for adult phonetic learning. Another issue raised by Piske et al. (2001) is the possibility that adult L2 phonetic learning happens mostly during a short initial period after arrival in the L2 community. In fact, Flege and Fletcher (1992) found that learners with LORs of about 14 years had weaker foreign accents than learners with only a few months of US residence. In contrast, Flege (1988) found no difference in accent scores between residents with 1 year and 5 years of residence. He suggested that the 1-year residents may already have plateaued in their accent learning, such that they did not differ from longer-term residents. On the basis of such findings, we might hypothesize a WINDOW OF MAXIMAL OPPORTUNITY (WMO) for adult phonetic learning that occurs during the early period of residence in the L2-speaking area. Piske et al. (2001), however, noted that accurately pinpointing this "early phase" would require suitable longitudinal data, but that longitudinal investigations of L2 speech learning are very rare.

For researchers, the existence of a WMO would mean that comparing the pronunciation of *very recent* arrivals in a new country with longer-term residents is more likely to yield significant differences than other kinds of comparisons. Recall that Oyama (1976) found no difference in accentedness between 5–11 year residents and 12–18 year residents. But this absence of an LOR effect may be due to not including the WMO within the interval under observation. In contrast, when Riney and Flege (1998) examined pronunciation changes in Japanese college students during their first year of studies and again three years later, they found improvement in some cases-most notably among those who had spent time abroad in an English-speaking country.

In the most extensive longitudinal research on L2 speech development to date, Derwing and colleagues provide a useful perspective on the proposed WMO. Their findings from two studies of accent and other speech dimensions (Derwing & Munro, 2013; Derwing, Thomson, & Munro, 2006) are summarized in Table 3.3. The learners were adult speakers of Mandarin and Slavic languages who had arrived in Canada with limited oral proficiency in English. Over the next several years, speech samples were collected at the comparison intervals shown in the table and were evaluated by listeners on the speech dimensions indicated.

Notice that the Mandarin group as a whole showed no statistically significant improvement on any of the global dimensions at any of the times, whereas the Slavic group did show meaningful changes. Thus, there seems to be no guarantee of improvement on these aspects of speech as a result of simply *residing* in an L2 area. For the Slavic group, no statistical change in global accentedness was detected after 2 years, which suggests that accent acquisition may indeed be susceptible to a WMO. However, the Slavic group *did* continue to improve with respect to both comprehensibility and fluency after the 2-year point, even though they had left ESL classes by that time. From these data it is not possible to determine the exact timing of their improvement – it might have occurred only during the third year or across the entire interval between 2 and 7 years. From Table 3.3, you can also see that both groups showed some improvement in vowel intelligibility during the 1 to 7 year interval. Also, the Slavic group showed improvement in productions of [pʰ] with ASPIRATION, during the first

Table 3.3. Longitudinal improvement on L2 global and specific speech dimensions in two studies based on judgments by native English listeners

Speech dimension	Improvement by comparison intervals					
	2 to 10 months[a]		*2 months to 2 years*[b]		*2 years to 7 years*[b]	
	Mandarin	Slavic	Mandarin	Slavic	Mandarin	Slavic
Accentedness	no	no	no	yes	no	no
Comprehensibility	no	yes	no	yes	no	yes
Fluency	no	yes	no	yes	no	yes
	2 to 10 months				*1 year to 7 years*	
Vowel Intelligibility	yes	yes	–	–	yes	yes
[pʰ] Intelligibility	–	yes	–	–	–	no

Sources: [a]Derwing, Thomson, & Munro (2006); [b]Derwing & Munro (2013). For empty cells, no data are available.

10 months, but not afterward. (Slavic languages, such as Russian, have unaspirated [p] but not [pʰ].) Taken together, the results provide limited evidence of a WMO that may have affected some aspects of their speech, but that comprehensibility, fluency, and vowel accuracy remained more amenable to change (without instruction) after 2 years than did accent or the acquisition of the aspirated bilabial consonant.

Closely related to the WMO is the concept of FOSSILIZATION, according to which L2 learners eventually reach a point at which improvement in their L2 language skills seems to plateau, even when they continue to be massively exposed to the L2 on a regular basis. Although applied linguists have long discussed this phenomenon in connection with pronunciation, evidence suggests that it does not apply to the *instructed* learning of pronunciation. In a teaching study by Derwing, Munro, and Wiebe (1997), for instance, even L2 speakers with a mean of 10 years of Canadian residence showed improved speech intelligibility, at least in the short term, following instruction. More recently, Derwing, Munro, Foote, Waugh and Fleming (2014) provided a pronunciation course to seven adults who had resided in an English-speaking environment for an average of 19 years, but who had never studied English pronunciation before. They showed significant improvement in both perception and production after a total of 17 hours of instruction. In a delayed post-test six months later, they were found to have retained at least some of what they had learned.

Motivation and willingness to communicate. Probably no L2 teacher would doubt that students who are concerned about pronunciation and who try very hard to produce intelligible speech are likely to perform better that those who are less invested in how they sound. In fact, "strength of concern for pronunciation" was one of the factors that predicted pronunciation accuracy in Purcell and Suter's (1980) study. Such a concern is generally understood as an aspect of a learner's motivation to acquire good pronunciation. Research findings offer some support for the view that motivation does indeed contribute to pronunciation learning. For example, Bongaerts et al. (1997) attributed the ability of some of their L2 Dutch speakers to pass for native speakers to their high motivation. Also, Moyer (2007) found significant correlations between accent ratings and a variety of motivational factors, including intention to reside in the US, comfort with assimilation, and a desire to improve pronunciation. While such outcomes appear to confirm our expectations, evaluating motivational influences on language learning in general has posed numerous challenges for empirical research (see Dörnyei & Ushioda, 2011). One concern is finding suitable ways to define and measure motivation. Another has to do with the difficulties in interpreting correlational findings that we mentioned earlier in this chapter. A positive correlation between motivation and good pronunciation does not prove that the motivation actually *caused* the good pronunciation. People who wear bigger shoes tend to be taller, but that isn't because big feet make you tall. Rather, some other underlying variable is responsible for both big feet and tallness. Moreover, other factors that correlate with motivation may influence learning, and may therefore be the "real" causes. For instance, highly motivated learners may also tend to have a special aptitude; in fact, having an aptitude for something may serve as a motivating force. So if such learners do indeed do well at pronunciation, we can't be sure whether the motivation, the aptitude, or both factors are responsible. Still another problem with understanding motivation is that it probably interacts with a variety of behavioural and situational factors as a determinant of particular acquisition outcomes. While a learner might express a strong desire to accomplish something, the actual achievement of that goal may depend on the availability of the appropriate resources, as well as the learner's talents, willingness and opportunities to take the necessary steps to achieve it. Recent work has suggested that a fruitful approach to probing some of the complexities of motivation is the WILLINGNESS TO COMMUNICATE (WTC) framework originated by McCroskey and Richmond (1991) and adapted for L2 learners by MacIntyre, Clément, Dörnyei, and Noels (1998). WTC treats motivational influences as part of a complex array of interacting contributors that predict whether a particular speaker will choose to communicate with someone else in a particular situation. Factors intrinsic to the speaker including personality, communicative competence, and self-confidence are taken into account, along with social influences, like the intergroup climate, and aspects of the immediate situation, such as a desire to interact with a particular individual. We will return to this concept in Chapter 8.

Aptitude for pronunciation. As we have noted, adults vary quite widely in their success in L2 acquisition. Some researchers and theorists have attributed this individual variability to differences in ability that are largely independent of age and experience.

In fact, pronunciation has been singled out as one aspect of adult L2 learning that may be especially influenced by aptitude. Anecdotally, we are all aware of actors who seem very successful at imitating regional or foreign accents, and we have all heard the claim that people with musical talent are "good at accents." It is also a widespread view that some L2 speakers are simply better pronouncers than others because of an underlying talent for pronunciation itself. Research findings provide some support for the latter belief. First, case studies of extraordinary talent have been documented for learners like *Julie*, an English speaker who acquired native-like Arabic pronunciation as an adult (Ioup, Boustagui, El Tigi, & Moselle, 1994). Second, testing specialists have identified individual differences in cognitive abilities that relate to success in phonological learning. When Carroll and Sapon (1959) created the Modern Language Aptitude Test (MLAT), phonological aspects of language figured importantly in their conception of aptitude. The test includes a component focusing on phonetic coding ability, the ability to make and recall links between speech sounds and symbols. The MLAT also assesses rote learning ability with respect to remembering relationships between sounds and meanings. In the more than 50 years since the appearance of the MLAT, research on pronunciation aptitude has been quite limited; however, the evidence that has emerged has generally supported anecdotal observations. Purcell and Suter (1980), for instance, reported a moderate correlation between the ability to mimic speech sounds accurately and L2 pronunciation achievement. More recently, Abrahamsson and Hyltenstam (2008) found that native-like adult L2 users scored high on aptitude evaluations that tapped pronunciation learning abilities. In a study by Milovanov, Pietilä, Tervaniemi, and Esquef (2010), Finnish adults with greater musical aptitude scored higher on English pronunciation than did those with lesser aptitude. Finally, recent work by Hu et al. (2013) indicated a correlation between adults' phonetic coding ability and their L2 pronunciation performance, as well as differences in brain activity between good and poor pronouncers. Despite these intriguing findings, research on pronunciation aptitude is still a field in its infancy. Much more work will be needed to establish the effects and the underpinnings of aptitude differences among learners.

Instruction. Recall Purcell and Suter's (1980) conclusion that the most important influences on L2 pronunciation were beyond the control of L2 teachers. That interpretation was very influential for many years and, in fact, hastened a movement away from the teaching of pronunciation that had already begun by the 1970s. As we noted in Chapter 2, the Audiolingual Method of language instruction had, up till that time, held sway in language classrooms. As Morley (1991) noted, pronunciation had been a central aspect of pedagogy; students were expected to develop native-like accents through listen-and-repeat drills focusing on segments and prosodic patterns. Audiolingual instruction began to disappear with the decline of the behaviorist psychology on which it was based. While the new interest in generative linguistics did not directly engender any successful L2 teaching methods, Stephen Krashen's *Input*

A CLOSER LOOK: Aptitude for pronunciation

Hu et al. (2013) examined in detail the factors contributing to pronunciation aptitude among 109 university students in Germany. The students had all begun learning English at about 10 years of age and had advanced proficiency in English at the time of the investigation. The study consisted of two parts, one a behavioural evaluation and the other an examination of brain activity using functional magnetic resonance imaging (fMRI). For the behavioural component, each speaker recorded an oral reading of a passage often used in speech research called "The North Wind and the Sun." The recordings were then rated by 10 listeners on an 11-point nativeness scale. The authors treated the resulting mean score for each speaker as an assessment of pronunciation "aptitude." They then used the set of mean scores as the dependent variable in a regression analysis to pinpoint the best predictors of aptitude. The independent (predictor) variables, which were selected on the basis of previous studies, consisted of scores on tests of phonetic coding ability, phonological working memory, musical aptitude, verbal and non-verbal IQ, and personality traits such as extraversion, agreeableness, and empathy. Their analysis revealed that phonetic coding ability (which is assessed in the MLAT), together with empathy, predicted the pronunciation ratings moderately well, with no other significant predictors.

For the fMRI portion of the study, eight speakers with high nativeness scores and eight with low scores participated in a brain imaging procedure, during which they imitated, as accurately as possible, sentences in English and German. They also performed a discrimination task in which they had to decide whether pairs of sentences (again in both languages) had the same or different prosodic patterns. A key finding was that brain activity in the better pronouncers differed from that of the poorer pronouncers, suggesting a fundamental difference in the two groups' speech processing.

Hypothesis (formerly called the Monitor Model) (Krashen, 1985), had a major influence on post-Audiolingual instruction. Acceptance of his view-that adults best learn languages through comprehensible input with only very limited explicit instruction-resulted in widespread abandonment of the earlier emphasis on the formal teaching of grammatical structure, as well as pronunciation. The timing of Krashen's research was significant; his theory emerged at the time when the Communicative Language Teaching (CLT) movement was gaining currency. CLT derives from a theory originated by Dell Hymes (1966) and later developed by Canale and Swain (1980) as the Communicative Competence framework. Its components were grammatical competence (linguistic form), sociolinguistic competence (social appropriateness), and strategic competence (conversation repair or enhancement). (Canale later added 'discourse' competence to the model in 1983). Although pronunciation was regarded as an aspect of grammatical competence, CLT classroom activities were guided by the notion that learners would acquire the necessary aspects of language, including pronunciation, through opportunities to communicate. Purcell and Suter's work influenced a move away from pronunciation teaching at roughly the same time as Krashen's theory and Canale and Swain's Communicative Competence model were becoming popular in the early 1980s. This was a perfect storm for major changes in L2 classrooms everywhere, especially in North America.

Despite the decline in pronunciation instruction in the late 20th century, a variety of classroom and laboratory studies have now demonstrated that Purcell and Suter were wrong in concluding that instruction is irrelevant to L2 learners' speech patterns. We will discuss this research in detail in Chapter 5. For now, we will identify two serious problems with the Purcell and Suter (1980) study. First, the researchers were mistaken in their conception of the nature of "pronunciation." The only dependent variable they considered was strength of foreign accent. They did not consider speech intelligibility, comprehensibility, fluency, or any fine-grained details of their subjects' oral productions. Yet, in terms of communicative competence, these aspects of speech are far more important than accentedness. Furthermore, as we have pointed out, they are partially independent of accentedness such that some heavy accents can still be highly intelligible and comprehensible. Had the study been carried out with the same speakers focusing on the latter variables, the results might have been very different.

A second problem with Purcell and Suter's (1980) work is summed up in the adage, "absence of evidence is not evidence of absence." The Purcell and Suter study is a correlational investigation, rather than a systematically designed experimental study. As we noted earlier, correlational studies permit only relatively weak conclusions and disallow causal interpretations. The fact that speakers who reported having had pronunciation instruction did not also have weaker accents does not allow us to conclude that instruction is ineffective. Rather, Purcell and Suter's negative result may simply be due to a research design that is inadequate for assessing instructional benefits. We don't know, for instance, how the speakers in the study interpreted "pronunciation instruction" when they were asked to report on it, and, as Pennington (1998) pointed out in a critical commentary on the Purcell & Suter study, we have little or no idea of the actual nature and quality of instruction given to learners when they report having received it. Perhaps it was poorly or sporadically delivered in some cases, or perhaps the good pronouncers in the study had been provided with pronunciation instruction without realizing or recalling it. Nor do we know what other variables in the study may have been confounded with instruction. It is possible, for instance, that the speakers who received the instruction happened to be mainly students with severe pronunciation difficulties or students who came from one particular L1 background. Since Purcell and Suter did not control these potential influences, their impact on the results of the study is unknown.

For the above reasons alone, we should view the Purcell and Suter findings with considerable skepticism. More importantly, we must take into account findings from more recent studies pointing us toward opposite conclusions. The most compelling evaluation of the benefits of instruction on pronunciation would be an experimental investigation in which subjects are randomly assigned to control (no instruction) and instructed conditions and tested prior to and after the instruction period. Such a study would allow us to compare the instructed group directly with the control group. Of course, we need to keep in mind that the control group might improve simply as a result of doing a spoken test for a second time, but if the instructed group shows statistically more improvement than the control group, we can reasonably conclude that the instruction has been effective. Note that a truly experimental research design requires both random assignment, to reduce the likelihood of confounding factors, and a control group, to ensure that any effects are actually due to instruction. Although the speakers in the Purcell and Suter study were described as "randomly selected" from the student population at an American university, the authors did not use the term "randomly" in its scientific sense. Even if some randomness was involved, the subject group was actually a sample of convenience (i.e. a group of research participants selected on the basis of ready availability and willingness to cooperate). In fact, the overwhelming majority of studies of L2 pronunciation (and of other aspects of SLA) have resorted to that approach. Researchers commonly recruit university or college students who are within a short distance of the research site and who are willing to participate for small monetary rewards. One can't be sure that the performance observed in these students accurately represents how the general population of L2 learners would perform. In other cases, intact classes of language students from cooperating schools serve as participants, typically one class as a control and the other as a test group. However, the members of two such classes may differ in all sorts of ways that threaten the validity of the conclusions. These choices by researchers tend to be viewed as a necessary compromise in the collection of data. However, they also limit the extent to which we can generalize from research outcomes.

At present, we do not know of any true experimental studies of pronunciation instruction. However, several researchers have now published instances of the next-best type: quasi-experimental investigations. These have used controlled intervention *without* true random group assignment. In such cases, researchers must do their best to ensure that the control and instructed groups are as comparable as possible in terms of background, age, and proficiency level, as well as other factors that might affect their performance. The best available evidence coming from such work is that classroom instruction in pronunciation can indeed be effective in improving communicative skills. We will cover some of the relevant studies in Chapter 5, though for the moment you may wish to take an advance look at Table 5.1 for a list.

Other influences

In addition to the factors we have covered in the previous sections, several other influences on pronunciation learning have been proposed by theorists and researchers, but few useful conclusions can be drawn. Research on gender effects, for instance, has not yielded consistently different results between men and women (Piske et al., 2001). Learning styles, personality, and affect have also been considered, but with limited results. One line of work began with a study of university students by Alexander Guiora and colleagues indicating that those who drank a small amount of alcohol pronounced words from an unfamiliar language better than did a control group (Guiora et al., 1972). It was concluded that the alcohol increased "ego permeability," thus facilitating performance. In a similar subsequent study of the effects of hypnosis by Schumann, Holroyd, Campbell, and Ward (1978), students who reported being deeply hypnotized scored better than those who did not. Finally, Guiora, Acton, Erard, and Strickland (1980) attempted to replicate the alcohol study by giving students various doses of valium or a placebo. The valium did not improve pronunciation; instead, the higher the dose, the more the students were influenced by the particular tester that they interacted with. While these studies are thought-provoking and interesting to read, they are much too limited to tell us much, if anything about the process of second language learning.

Applying research findings in the pronunciation classroom

For well over a century, language scholars have articulated their perspectives on the teaching of pronunciation. Not surprisingly, their opinions have varied, especially given the few clear research findings that have been available for them to rely on. However, as mounting evidence converges in favour of the view that adult L2 pronunciation is both learnable and teachable, we might look forward to a future in which pedagogical opinions and practices have a firm basis in sound empirical findings. In the sections that follow, we briefly take stock of what the existing research can offer us at this point.

Age

In Chapter 1, we discussed our reasons for favouring the Intelligibility Principle over the Nativeness Principle as described by Levis (2005). As we pointed out, a focus on producing speech intelligibly is far more relevant to L2 communication than is a preoccupation with sounding native-like. If we accept that position, then we must agree that a considerable body of the research literature on L2 speech has, at most, limited value for the classroom because it focuses on accent rather than on intelligibility or comprehensibility. All the studies listed in Table 3.1 (and many others) feature global foreign accent as the dependent variable. The evidence they provide that AOL exerts a powerful influence on accent gives us a theoretically interesting insight into the L2 acquisition processes. But that finding has little importance in language teaching based on the Intelligibility Principle. Rather, we simply do not know what correlation exists between AOL and intelligibility because large-scale studies of that relationship have not been published. What we do know, however, is that intelligible, comprehensible speech is not only possible in adult L2 learners, but that it is the norm rather than the exception.

Language experience

Though recent research findings should make us skeptical of the importance of AOL in the acquisition of intelligible L2 speech, findings regarding language experience appear to be more useful. Early work indicated that LOR was a poor predictor of accent, but researchers now recognize that LOR is not a satisfactory measure of language experience and that actual experience with the L2 is indeed beneficial under the right circumstances. In the first place, immigrants who integrate well into the target culture such that they use the L2 extensively have better long-term prospects with respect to oral communication skills than do learners who carry out their daily activities mainly within their L1 community or whose interactions in the L2 are mostly limited to specific routines (Derwing & Munro, 2013; Derwing, Munro, & Thomson, 2006). Second, the evidence we summarized earlier points to a Window of Maximal Opportunity shortly after arrival in an L2 speaking area when adult learners seem most likely to improve in certain (though not all) pronunciation skills in the absence of pronunciation-specific instruction (Derwing & Munro, 2013; Munro, Derwing, & Thomson, 2008). The reasons for this constraint have yet to be identified. Perhaps the limits on production improvement after a certain initial interval result from having repeatedly practiced non-nativelike articulatory patterns. When learners mispronounce sounds, words, and prosodic patterns over and over, they establish rehearsed production routines that may be difficult to change. In addition, they may develop perceptual representations based on speech input that they themselves have generated, given that they hear themselves more than they hear anyone else. Two implications that can be derived from these considerations are as follows:

1. Instruction focusing not just on language structures, but also on the knowledge and skills needed for initiating and sustaining effective interaction with others may be helpful to L2 learners, especially beginners. PRAGMATICS instruction, including conversational strategies, may assist speakers to engage in interactions with others in the L2 community to a greater extent, which in turn may lead to enhanced pronunciation learning (see discussion of the Willingness to Communicate framework below).

2. Instruction in pronunciation soon after arrival in the L2 environment is likely to be optimally effective. This is not a new idea; in fact, it was a fundamental principle of the Audiolingual teaching method, which treated language learning as the acquisition of a set of habits. Current work does not treat language as a habit, but it does point to early instruction as potentially beneficial.

Motivational influences

Closely tied to point 1 above are the likely benefits of Willingness to Communicate in the L2 phonetic learning process. Evidence suggests that learners who seek out and exploit opportunities to use the L2 tend to advance in terms of intelligibility and comprehensibility. The WTC framework goes beyond traditional conceptions of motivation by examining the interplay between variables within and outside of learners that influence their communicative choices. This new perspective is valuable to teachers: while we might scoff at the idea of directly teaching "motivation" in the classroom, some of these variables within the WTC model, such as the competence to initiate and sustain interactions, may be enhanced through instruction.

Aptitude

Because studies of aptitude have been based on achievement in terms of accent rather than intelligibility or comprehensibility, we must also avoid attributing much importance to that variable for classroom teaching. Perhaps future research will help us understand how aptitude relates to the ability to acquire intelligible speech. Until we have such information, perhaps the best strategy for teachers is simply to expect variability in learners' success in pronunciation and encourage their efforts to improve.

Instruction

Purcell and Suter (1980) offered a dismal assertion about the irrelevance of pronunciation teaching, basing it on the absence of a correlation between the strength of speakers' accents and the amount of pronunciation instruction received. In a subsequent survey paper on the applications of research in language teaching, Pica (1994) was able to provide almost no advice on what teachers could do to help learners with pronunciation problems. Basing her comments heavily on Purcell and Suter's findings, she concluded: "For the time being, precise pronunciation may be an unrealistic goal for teachers to set for their students and in their teaching" (p. 73). While Pica's interpretation reflected ideas about empirical research on pronunciation at some time in the past, we now know that her conclusion was built on faulty evidence (see Chapter 5).

Summary

Much research on adult phonetic acquisition has emphasized the powerful influence of the learner's age on accent. That well-known finding has proved misleading because it emphasizes what learners *cannot* usually achieve (perfect pronunciation) rather than what they are capable of achieving (intelligible speech). Teachers must remember that accent in itself is not the focus of communicative pronunciation instruction. In fact we have only limited data on the ways in which AOL influences intelligibility and comprehensibility.

Whether or not a critical period account is a useful way of understanding the age-accent connection remains controversial; however, it is clear that learners vary considerably in their speech-learning success. This variability appears to be due to a variety of influences that mediate age effects. Although early research revealed that LOR is minimally relevant to phonetic learning, this does not mean that L2 experience itself is unimportant. Rather, findings now show that learners who gain language experience by interacting regularly in their L2 tend to improve more on dimensions such as comprehensibility, intelligibility, and fluency than those who do not.

In the 1970s, pedagogical theorizing, together with a few correlational research findings, led some SLA specialists to believe that classroom pronunciation instruction was ineffective. That view has now been refuted by evidence from systematic studies showing that communicatively relevant changes in L2 learners' speech can be taught in the classroom. There is no reason to believe that adult L2 learners are "doomed" to unintelligibility. Useful instructional strategies include encouraging students to use the L2 outside the classroom by initiating and sustaining interactions, along with providing in-class instruction on aspects of pronunciation that influence intelligibility.

CHAPTER 4

Pronunciation errors and error gravity

Minh, a Vietnamese speaker, worked as a supervisor at a Canadian window factory. He had recorded a one-minute description of a typical day on the job, which Tracey Derwing subsequently transcribed in standard orthography. Despite listening to the recording several times, she could not understand one particular word. Later in the week, she played the recording for Minh, while they both looked at the transcription. When they got to the unintelligible word, Tracey stopped the recorder and asked Minh what the word was. He said what sounded like 'stockitts', i.e. /stɑkɪts/. Tracey asked him to repeat the word several times, and each time she heard the same thing. She asked if 'stockitts' was a word especially associated with windows. Minh became a bit frustrated and repeated the word a few more times. Tracey finally asked him to write the word, and this was his response: TARGET. *Tracey indicated that she would never have understood Minh's pronunciation of 'target' in a million years-and Minh, somewhat shocked, said, "But I use that word every day!" They worked on the word until Minh could perceive and pronounce it perfectly. He was elated afterwards, and could be heard telling his co-workers next door that he could finally say 'target.' Some errors are more important than others; certainly for Minh, this lesson was a revelation.*

Introduction

Applied linguists have long been interested in the wide variety of errors that occur in L2 production. Both theorists and teaching specialists have tried to explain why errors occur, whether or not they can be predicted in advance, how they should be ranked in terms of their gravity, and what they tell us about the phonetic acquisition process. Addressing these issues is a complex matter for pronunciation specialists, as well as for researchers focusing on other aspects of L2 learning, such as syntax and morphology.

What counts as an error?

The study of L2 learner errors and their remediation is fraught with controversy. In fact, some sources even object to the term 'error' or argue vehemently against error correction, asserting that it is not only useless, but harmful to learners (Truscott, 1996). While heated debates on such matters seem to carry on eternally in some academic circles, they have little to do with the practical reality that language teachers face: L2 production typically includes structures and patterns that differ from those used by proficient members of the larger speech community. And in some cases—though certainly not all—these differences lead to communication breakdowns. Teachers who see their role as one of guiding learners toward the achievement of L2 communicative competence naturally feel a responsibility to address such sources of difficulty. They also realize that they cannot escape this situation by taking the view that 'errors' don't really exist or that the term cannot be used and acted upon in the classroom.

At the phonetic level, nonnative structures and patterns of production form the basis of what is commonly called a foreign accent. As we stress throughout this book, the fact that many L2 users sound different from other members of the community is not, in itself, a problem. However, certain aspects of L2 speech, including Minh's pronunciation of 'target' in our anecdote above, are likely to impede the speaker's success in communication, irrespective of whether the listener is a native speaker or another L2 user. In such cases, not understanding the speaker's intent can be a shared experience of all or most members of that speaker's audience. We take great pains to emphasize the shared aspect of this experience because we want to be clear that we are *not* referring to instances of idiosyncratic loss of intelligibility in which one listener fails to understand something, while 10 others have no trouble at all with the same utterance. That situation might simply reflect the one listener's perceptual (mis-) functioning or may even result from a negative attitude toward the speaker. Nor are we focusing on listeners' expectations of being able to understand (positive bias) or on an unwillingness on the listener's part to even attempt to understand what has been said (negative bias). In reality, situations of these types most certainly do arise in human interactions, and they obviously cannot be addressed by requiring the speaker to make changes. (See Chapter 8 for more discussion.) Rather, they are the result of limited listening skills or prejudicial attitudes, and it is the listener who must try to make the adjustment if communication is to carry on.

Although comprehension of L2 speech can be affected by listener idiosyncrasies and listener bias (negative or positive), a great deal of empirical evidence shows that speech material itself can be a source of unintelligibility. In fact, it is quite absurd to suggest otherwise. All of us have probably experienced situations in which we failed to understand someone-either a native speaker or an L2 user-despite trying our hardest to do so. To untangle some of the issues, we will consider a perceptual study of L2 listeners from different L1 backgrounds (Munro, Derwing, & Morton, 2006). In that investigation, listeners rated a set of intermediate-level ESL speech samples for accent and comprehensibility, and also transcribed them orthographically. The speakers were from Cantonese, Japanese, Polish, and Spanish backgrounds, while the listeners were native speakers of English, Cantonese, Japanese, and Mandarin. Thus, some of the listeners' L1s matched some of the speakers' L1s, and some did not.

Just as expected, the listeners did not always assign exactly the same ratings to particular samples, nor did they all experience identical comprehension difficulties. The fact that some listeners were "out of line" with the others-even those from the same L1 background-on certain judgments probably reflects the idiosyncrasies we mentioned earlier. On another matter, although one might have predicted that the Cantonese listeners would have an advantage when hearing Cantonese-accented English, they actually understood the Cantonese speakers no better than any other speakers. However, their comprehensibility ratings of the Cantonese speakers were better than those of the other speakers. We noted at least two interpretations of this outcome. On the one hand, perhaps the Cantonese listeners really did find the Cantonese-accented speech easier to process, even though it was no more intelligible than other kinds of L2 speech. On the other, their better comprehensibility ratings may have reflected a bias in favour of Cantonese-accented speech: they may have recognized the accent and therefore expected to understand it more easily than the other speech, even though there was no evidence that they performed any better than the other listeners.

Despite the existence of biases and idiosyncrasies in judgments of L2 speech, these aspects of the Munro et al. (2006) study accounted for only a small amount of the variability in the results and are much less important than another very striking outcome. In particular, irrespective of L1 background, the listeners tended to agree quite strongly with one another on their relative judgments of the speakers: INTER-RATER RELIABILITY was high. Moreover, intelligibility was very much a "shared experience" within and across listener groups. The data, in fact, showed that all groups agreed on 6 of the 10 most intelligible speakers and on 5 of the 10 least intelligible ones. Since it seems impossible that the listeners in all groups were 'biased' in precisely the same way, this outcome suggests that the results were mainly due to properties of the speech itself rather than to subjective dislike of particular speakers or speech patterns. 'Errors,' then, were responsible for varying degrees of intelligibility.

In our opinion, it makes little difference how we label the communicatively problematic differences between L1 and L2 speech. Whether we call them 'errors' or something else, they have real consequences that we need to identify and understand. For the purposes of this book, we offer a working definition of pronunciation errors as follows: we mean cases in which a speaker aims to produce an utterance, but as a result of a lack of full control over its segmental or suprasegmental structure, produces something else instead, just as when Minh produced 'stockitts' instead of 'target.' This definition is far from perfect, but it will serve our purposes. Note that we don't include occasional speech blunders, slips of the tongue, or false starts-sometimes called PERFORMANCE MISTAKES-in the error category. Teachers must remember that L2 speakers produce many errors, but that not all errors are equal in terms of their impact on communication. In fact, many errors seem not to pose any serious problems at all, while certain others can cause severe communication breakdowns.

Classifying learners' errors

As we will explain in more detail in Chapters 5 and 6, pronunciation teachers need to be able to identify learners' problems, prioritize them according to how serious they are, and provide effective help. Of course, our guiding principle is that the most serious errors are the ones most likely to impede effective communication. But how do teachers identify those particular issues? In order to carry out beneficial assessments, a general understanding of error classification is essential. The first step in gaining the needed skill is to establish a suitable vocabulary to describe the aspects of L2 speech that make it differ from target-like utterances.

Segmental errors

To classify segmental errors, researchers have traditionally focused on the nature of the difference between an L2 production and the expected target pattern. Some commonly-used terms are summarized with examples in Table 4.1. Keep in mind that the names of these categories are merely metaphors for comparing L2 productions with targets; they should not be interpreted as operations that a speaker actually carries out. It is convenient to think of /sɪk/ (for 'six') as having a "deleted" final /s/, but we do not actually mean that the speaker "started" with a final /s/ and somehow got rid of it. Rather, the processes by which the speaker ended up with /sɪk/ are complex and not fully understood. Later in this chapter, we discuss aspects of the interplay between L2 perception and production that may partly account for such errors.

Table 4.1. Classification of L2 segmental errors

Type	Description	Examples
Insertion	including a segment not present in the target form	/lɪvəd/ for 'lived' (/lɪvd/)
Deletion	not including a segment that is present in the target form	/sɪk/ for 'six' (/sɪks/)
Substitution	replacing a segment in the target form with a segment from a different phonemic category	/kʌt/ for 'cat' (/kæt/)
Distortion	producing a segment in the target form in a way that may be noticeably non-target, but which does not change the phonemic category of the segment	/k/ in 'caught' ([kʰɑt]) produced with audible but short aspiration instead of target-like (longer) aspiration

Note that segmental errors sometimes have effects that extend beyond the segment itself. The insertion error (also called EPENTHESIS) in Table 4.1, for example, actually increases the number of syllables in the word from one to two, and the deletion error changes the word structure from CVCC to CVC.

Prosodic errors

STRESS refers to the prominence that a particular element receives within a word or longer utterance and which causes it to stand out from other unstressed elements. In English, stressed syllables tend to be longer, louder and higher PITCHED than unstressed or weak syllables, though not every stressed syllable has all three characteristics. In other languages, the correlates of stress may be different. Note that in IPA transcription, primary word stress is indicated by a superscript mark in front of the stressed syllable, as in /'æksɛnt/. For teachers, describing cases of misplaced stress in English is usually straightforward. LEXICAL STRESS (word stress) errors occur when a speaker does not stress the correct syllable in the target word. Our database of recordings includes an instance in which a French-speaking politician in Canada pronounced 'develop' (target: /dɪ'vɛləp/) as /dɪvəl'ap/. On the many occasions when we have played this recording, in context, to listeners (both native English and non-native), they have nearly always found it unintelligible and have expressed surprise on learning the speaker's intent. Notice how the speaker's placement of stress on an unstressed syllable in the target form (in this case, the final syllable) also affected the vowel quality such that /ə/ became a full vowel, while the vowel in the second syllable was reduced. Such a pattern is quite common with stress errors of this type.

Errors in sentence-level stress are also fairly easy to pinpoint. Typically, the greatest PROMINENCE in English sentences is placed near the end – on the last content syllable. However, stress may also be used to emphasize a particular word according to the context. Suppose someone asks the following: "Which house is JOAN'S?" (capital letters indicate the prominent word). An appropriate response is sentence A of the two possibilities below, because the position of the stress emphasizes the characteristic (colour) that distinguishes Joan's house from the other possible houses. Answer B does not fit the context because the word receiving emphasis (house) is not the information that the questioner is seeking.

A.   Hers is the BLUE house.
B.   Hers is the blue HOUSE.

Producing and understanding utterances with these types of distinctions often pose problems for ESL learners because many languages do not use contrastive stress in the same way as English. For them, the concept of highlighting a particular word with stress is something completely new.

INTONATION is realized as variations in the pitch of a speaker's voice in an utterance. Though intonation is closely tied to stress in English, it is much harder to identify discrete errors on this prosodic dimension. In some instances it serves a linguistic function, as it does in intonation questions in which pitch rises toward the end to signal an interrogative intention (e.g. You're leaving now?). However, intonation can also convey paralinguistic information about the speaker's attitude toward the listener or toward what is being said. Because of differences in the meaning of particular intonation patterns across languages, L2 speakers' intentions can sometimes be seriously misinterpreted when they transfer patterns from their L1 to their L2 (for example, they may be mistakenly perceived as arrogant, bored or hostile), and they themselves may misconstrue the intentions of native speaker interlocutors if they have not learned how to interpret English intonation contours. In a perceptual study, Gibson (1997) found that Russian listeners were poorer than native English listeners at identifying the attitudes of native English speakers on the basis of intonation. Her native English listeners also did less well than Russian listeners at identifying Russian speakers' attitudes in L2 English productions.

RHYTHM relates to the perception of patterns of stress within phrases, clauses, and longer utterances. It has long been noticed that different languages have a different "rhythmic feel" (Lloyd James, 1940). Pike (1945) is commonly credited with noting that English appears to have a STRESS-TIMED rhythm because of its alternation between stressed and weak syllables. Many other languages, such as Cantonese and French, are classified as SYLLABLE-TIMED because they do not show as much variability between syllables. At one time, it was thought that these timing differences were the result of isochrony-a hypothetical tendency for certain speech units to have approximately equal durations. In English, for instance, it was thought that the time between successive stresses would be about the same, while French syllables were believed to all have about equal duration. However, research in which these intervals were systematically measured did not support expectations (Dauer, 1983), and the notion of isochrony was largely abandoned. The evidence against isochrony, however, certainly does not mean that rhythm classes like "stress-timing" do not exist. Rather, teachers and students have recognized for a very long time that languages like English and Mandarin *sound* rhythmically distinct. It was not until fairly recently, however, that empirical studies confirmed the existence of reliable, measurable timing differences between languages that fit the stress-timed and syllable-timed categories, as well as a third category-MORA-TIMED-which applies to the rhythm of Japanese, as well as a few other languages (Ramus, Nespor, & Mehler, 1999).

At the moment it is not possible to translate these recent research findings directly into specific pedagogical recommendations on how to teach rhythm. However, they do indicate that teaching students L2 rhythm is a well-motivated practice. In particular, evidence suggests that speakers of one type of language may transfer their L1 rhythmic patterns to an L2 with different timing. The transfer of syllable-timing to English speech cannot be considered a discrete error; rather it is the result of a long-term pattern of timing that is not English-like and that is likely to be noticeable to listeners. From a psycholinguistic standpoint, rhythmic patterns can play an important role in helping listeners determine the syntactic structure of an utterance to facilitate their comprehension. The stress that English speakers place on content words (nouns, verbs, adjectives and adverbs) makes those lexical items stand out in English utterances, while the function words (auxiliaries, determiners, and pronouns) are typically relegated to the background. Someone listening to English, then, can process what is said by taking advantage of the information that the stress-timed rhythm conveys. In other languages, processing is facilitated by other linguistic devices. On that basis, we might hypothesize that producing non-native rhythm should sometimes result in a loss of intelligibility for the listener. Tajima, Port, and Dalby (1997) found evidence in favor of that prediction in a study of Mandarin-accented utterances in English. They used digital speech resynthesis to create corrected productions of the utterances such that the revised timing matched that of native English speakers. They also manipulated a set of native English utterances to match the timing patterns of the foreign-accented productions. They then presented the original and revised speech to English listeners, who were required to identify what they heard. As predicted, the artificially-corrected L2 speech was more intelligible than the original and the distorted native productions were less intelligible than their unchanged counterparts.

Other problems

Apart from segments and prosody, a number of other aspects of L2 speech can make it differ from target-like production. Although these properties of speech aren't typically labeled as errors, they need to be taken into account in pronunciation assessments because of their potential to reduce the intelligibility of L2 speech.

Fluency has to do with the fluidity of speech. All speakers of a language-native or non-native-vary in fluency from time to time; however, L2 speech is commonly produced less fluently than L1 speech. By this we mean that it tends to contain more hesitations and false starts, as well as more frequent and longer PAUSES. However, the relationship between pausing and fluency is complex. Wennerstrom (2000) found, for example, that one particular speaker might produce more pauses than another, yet be perceived as more fluent if the pauses occur at appropriate places such as phrase boundaries within an utterance.

Speaking rate, the pace at which a person speaks, usually measured in syllables per second, is an aspect of fluency. A number of studies have shown that L2 speech is typically uttered more slowly than L1 speech (Derwing & Munro, 2001; MacKay & Flege, 2004; Munro & Derwing, 1998, 2001). This difference probably results from the greater time required for lexical retrieval and speech-planning when speaking in an L2. In some situations a slow rate of production may help the listener to adjust to and understand speech that is produced with an accent, so we might view the reduced rate as a built-in enhancement feature of non-native utterances. However, we should not try to extrapolate from that observation. Telling L2 users to slow down their speech to make it more intelligible is probably a poor strategy; evidence shows that when L2 speakers do so, they may actually introduce new errors into their productions such that they are judged as less comprehensible than when speaking at their natural, self-determined rates (Munro & Derwing, 1998). It is quite common to hear listeners complain that they can't understand a nonnative speaker because of a fast speech rate; however, this may be the result of misunderstanding the real sources of comprehension difficulties. L2 speakers make a variety of errors in pronunciation, grammar, and lexical choice. The processing demands that listeners experience can slow down their comprehension, making it seem that the speech is too fast, even when it is actually much slower than what is typical for L1. Thus rate can be a scapegoat for other language difficulties (Derwing & Munro, 1997). Of course, some L2 speakers are actually fast talkers who may indeed benefit from slowing down to facilitate their interlocutors' comprehension.

Voice quality is a result of long-term use of the vocal tract in distinctive configurations (Laver, 1980). As Esling (1994, 2000) observes, some speakers habitually employ laryngeal settings that affect speech in very salient ways, such as high pitch, breathy voice, and creaky voice. He also notes that supralaryngeal settings of the articulators affect voice quality, giving, for instance, dentalized, PALATALIZED, and hypernasalized speech. In addition to these, he comments on the effects of raising and lowering the larynx to change the resonance of the vocal tract, making the speaker sound bigger or smaller. Another setting mentioned by Esling is faucalized speech, which entails expanding the pharynx as occurs during yawning. This setting was once described by Alexander Graham Bell as the 'cry of the peacock' in reference to its commonness in hearing-impaired speech. The effects of habitually using particular vocal postures may help us distinguish one speaker from another, but they may also reflect differences in speech production that arise from L1 influences. When L2 speakers transfer voice quality from their L1 to the L2 the result may sound foreign (Esling & Wong, 1983). However, we do not have much research evidence to help us determine how voice quality affects speech intelligibility.

Other non-linguistic and paralinguistic aspects of L2 speech that influence listening can be important because they sometimes affect comprehension. In this category we include certain speaking habits that are the result of cultural expectations. Speaking very quietly, habitually covering the mouth with a hand, or using foreign-sounding hesitation noises can adversely affect communication, especially when such behaviors are combined with pronunciation errors. Although we don't usually think of these concerns as part of pronunciation, they are often an important issue in the classroom. Teachers need to take note of them and address them if they perceive the behaviours to interfere with intelligibility.

Explaining why pronunciation errors occur

Many theoretical proposals have been offered to explain aspects of L2 pronunciation-so many, that we can't possibly cover them all here. Instead we will focus our attention on a selection of accounts that help us understand the processes that take place when an L2 user perceives and produces speech. It also means that we will avoid more abstract accounts from such fields as generative phonology, which do not readily translate into pedagogically useful information.

It is obvious that many aspects of L2 speech can be attributed to the influence of the L1. The most compelling piece of evidence favouring this view is that foreign accent features often allow us to identify a speaker's L1 background. For instance, French, Mandarin, and Japanese accents in English each have distinctive properties that are reflected in the segmental and prosodic characteristics of those languages. An excellent resource for listening to and analyzing the nature of different accents is the *Speech Accent Archive* (Weinberger, 2015) available at ⟨accent.gmu.edu⟩. This website offers scores of recordings of different accents, along with detailed phonetic transcriptions and analyses. For anyone interested in pronunciation teaching, these are a valuable source of information.

Describing the ways in which L2 speakers produce foreign-accented utterances is an important step; however, speech researchers are particularly interested in *why* non-native speech is subject to L1 effects. While a number of accounts have been proposed, all have limitations. In the sections that follow, we discuss some of the ways in which L1 influences on pronunciation have been characterized by theorists.

Contrastive analysis

One of the best known – and still influential – approaches to errors is the CONTRASTIVE ANALYSIS HYPOTHESIS (CAH). The CAH had close ties to the behaviourist view of language learning that motivated the Audiolingual teaching method. Some underlying assumptions were that language is a system of habits and that learning the habits of the L1, such as particular syntactic structures and the articulation of vowels and consonants, greatly influences the acquisition of the L2. While the CAH was formulated to cover all types of errors, we will discuss only its phonological aspects here. The "strong" version of the CAH (Lado, 1957) assumes that errors in L2 pronunciation can be predicted a priori through a comparison of the phonological inventories of the L1 and L2. In instances in which segments in the L1 and the L2 are the same, POSITIVE TRANSFER is anticipated. However, when the L1 and L2 have different segments or differently organized phonemic categories, knowledge of the L1 is expected to interfere with L2 learning. In short, points of difference between the L1 and the L2 are seen as the source of problems for learners. In the 1950s and 1960s, various comparisons of phonological inventories were used to establish error hierarchies specifying the predicted degree of difficulty posed by different types of sound relationships. For example, Table 4.2 illustrates four of the six error types identified by Clifford Prator (in Archibald, 1998), who offered one of the best-known hierarchies of errors based on the CAH perspective. The examples are for learners of English, though the hierarchy is the same for any L2. For a more detailed account, see Moulton (1962).

Table 4.2. Examples of error types in contrastive analysis

Type	Description	Example	Level of difficulty (1–6)
Positive transfer	L1 and L2 have an identical (or nearly identical) phoneme.	Both Greek and English have the phoneme /m/.	1
Under-differentiation	L1 treats two sounds as allophones of one phoneme. L2 treats the two sounds as separate phonemes.	In Spanish, /d/ and /ð/ are allophones of /d/. In English /d/ and /ð/ are separate phonemes.	4
New item	L1 lacks a sound that occurs in L2.	Cantonese has no /θ/ phoneme.	5
Split	A single item in L1 is realized as two different items in L2.	The Japanese FLAP category /ɾ/ corresponds to the two phonemes /ɹ/ and /l/ in English.	6

Error analysis

Although hierarchies such as the one in Table 4.2 did sometimes appear to give accurate *a priori* predictions of L2 learning difficulties, the success of the CAH was limited. Empirical data contradicting the predicted levels of difficulty were reported in major studies. Brière (1966) found, for instance, that the high front ROUNDED vowel /y/ and the high back unrounded vowel /ɯ/ posed very different degrees of difficulty for English speakers who tried to learn to produce them (/ɯ/ was found to be far more difficult). Yet both these vowels fall in the same level (Level 5) on Prator's hierarchy. At the theoretical level, Wardhaugh (1970) presented a detailed critique in which he evaluated the strong version of the CAH as unrealistic, noting that a weaker version was more promising, though still flawed. The weaker approach entailed post hoc analyses of errors that were not restricted to comparisons of L1 and L2, thus allowing other types of information to be taken into account. Its emphasis was therefore not so much on prediction as on finding ways to account for errors after they occurred. This shift in emphasis toward post hoc interpretations of errors is referred to as ERROR ANALYSIS. One issue that received attention using this approach concerns developmental errors. Flege and Davidian (1984), for instance, observed that the DEVOICING of English word-final stops by Spanish and Mandarin speakers resembles a developmental pattern seen in English-speaking children as they acquire their L1. Moreover, in Spanish and Mandarin L2 learners, devoicing cannot be attributed to interference, because neither language uses final VOICELESS stops. Despite the advantages it affords, error analysis also has limitations. While it was initially assumed that error analysis would provide a new kind of window into the L2 competence of learners, Schachter (1974) observed that a problem of the new approach was its focus on only those errors that actually occurred. It therefore had the potential to give a misleading picture of learners' abilities when they simply chose to avoid particular language structures. In short, learners who make few errors are not necessarily more competent that those who make many. The seemingly more accurate speakers might be those who are sensitive to their own problem areas and do not attempt to use sounds that they cannot articulate well.

Weaknesses of CAH and error analysis as theoretical accounts of L2 speech

The strengths of both CAH and error analysis lie in their ability to draw connections between learner errors and linguistic phenomena such as L1 influences and developmental processes. However, their scope as theoretical models is actually quite limited. Apart from the problems we have pointed out above, the following drawbacks apply:

1. Perception and production are not considered separately in these approaches. Yet it is well established that L2 learners can sometimes perceive differences between L2 sounds without being able to produce them accurately. It is nearly always easy for English speakers to *hear* the difference between the Spanish TRILL /r/ and the flap /ɾ/. However, it is often not so easy to *produce* the distinction. Moreover, cases of the reverse situation – good production despite limited perception – have also been identified (Sheldon & Strange, 1982). A model that does not allow these two aspects of speech to be considered separately is clearly incomplete.
2. CAH and error analysis are not acquisition models in that they offer no obvious way of accounting for changes in learner performance over time. Yet we know that L2 learners do indeed acquire sounds as a result of experience with their new language.
3. A very serious limitation of both approaches is that they offer no obvious way to account for individual learner differences. Because foreign accents can be identified in terms of speakers' L1s, it is sometimes mistakenly assumed that accents are uniform and consistent. However, this is far from the truth. Rather, individual learners, even from the same L1 background, vary a great deal in the types of errors they make during acquisition, the rate at which they learn, and the level of ULTIMATE ATTAINMENT they achieve.

4.   Neither approach gives us meaningful insights into the underlying cognitive pro-
     cesses that lead to pronunciation errors. If we claim, for instance, that knowledge
     of an L1 sound "interferes" with acquisition of a certain L2 sound, we are speaking
     quite abstractly. Someone might well ask what we mean by "interfere." What hap-
     pens in the mind of the learner that accounts for such a phenomenon?

In the next sections, we turn our attention to two more recent approaches to errors
that address some of the problems we have identified above.

Best's perceptual assimilation model

Psychologists have known for several decades that adults' difficulties in phonetic
acquisition are frequently rooted in perception. Surprisingly, however, the extensive
research in this area is often little-known to applied linguists and is frequently ignored
altogether in introductory SLA textbooks. We feel the need to remedy this situation by
emphasizing that perceptual studies are among the most important areas of research
bearing on language acquisition processes-both L1 and L2–and that we can't possibly
discuss L2 pronunciation without giving this area at least some attention.

As we noted in Chapter 3, Werker and colleagues (e.g. Werker & Tees, 2002) found
that infants cease to discriminate many non-native sound contrasts even before they
reach one year of age. For instance, babies raised in an English environment no longer
DISCRIMINATE Hindi dental stops from retroflex stops, while newborns have no difficulty in doing so. Furthermore, older English children and adults have remarkable difficulty in learning to hear the distinction even when they are given extensive training.
In the 1980s, Catherine Best began to probe adults' perceptions to gain more insight
into this phenomenon. The result of her work was the *Perceptual Assimilation Model-*
PAM-which describes the ways in which adults perceive non-native phones. An early
study (Best, McRoberts, & Sithole, 1988) yielded the intriguing finding that native
English adults had relatively little difficulty perceiving the difference between pairs
of click sounds that contrast phonemically in Zulu. This raised a new problem: why
should they be successful at discriminating clicks, but not the other speech sounds
considered by Werker?

Best et al.'s (1988) description of PAM begins with the assumption that native
language acquisition entails the development of perceptual categories corresponding
to particular sounds in the L1. Native English infants, for instance, eventually acquire
categories for such segments as /i/, /ɪ/, and /tʃ/, but not for retroflex stops like /ɖ/,
front rounded vowels like /y/, or UVULAR stops like /q/; of course, they do not have
categories for clicks, either. Later on, perhaps in adulthood, when we hear unfamiliar
sounds from another language, our perceptual systems try to match, or ASSIMILATE,
the sounds to categories that we already know in our L1. In other words, we tend to

hear new sounds through a sort of "perceptual sieve" determined by our L1 knowledge. Best and colleagues were the first to develop a systematic model to describe the nature of the assimilations. They proposed that foreign sounds match L1 categories to varying degrees, and that the nature of the match determines perceptual performance. Here we will present a few key points from the PAM model to help you understand its basics. (For a full account, see Best and Tyler, 2007.)

According to PAM, the reason English adults have such difficulty hearing the difference between the dental (/t̪/) – retroflex (/ʈ/) pair from Hindi is that both foreign sounds assimilate to a single perceptual category in English. In simple terms, as illustrated in Figure 4.1, they both sound like English /t/. Since listeners generally do poorly at discriminating consonants from a single category (we usually don't notice allophonic differences between different instances of /t/ in English), they are generally unable to distinguish the two Hindi sounds. The problem is thus due to what Best and colleagues have termed *Single Category (SC) Assimilation*.

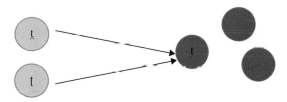

Figure 4.1. Single Category (SC) Assimilation: Two consonant sounds from Hindi (left) assimilate to one category in English (right). The unmarked dots represent other categories in the listener's L1

In certain other cases, however, discrimination of foreign sounds is easy, even if new categories are not created. Note the case of the French dental /d̪/ and uvular /ʁ/ illustrated in Figure 4.2. Neither of these consonants exists phonemically in English, but we typically hear them as ALVEOLAR /d/ and /ɹ/ respectively. Because they assimilate to two different English categories, we have no trouble recognizing that they are different sounds, and the situation is called *Two Category (TC) Assimilation*.

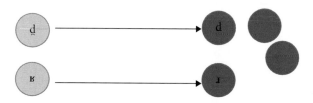

Figure 4.2. Two Category (TC) Assimilation: Two consonant sounds from French (left) assimilate to two different categories in English (right). The unmarked dots represent other categories in the listener's L1

A third pattern is the one associated with English listeners' perception of Zulu clicks (see Figure 4.3). Although Best et al. (1988) considered several different consonants of this type, we will use the dental /ǀ/ and palatal /ǂ/ clicks for illustration. These articulations are often familiar to English ears as, respectively, a 'tsk' sound and an exhortation to a horse to speed up, but English speakers do not use them as components of words, and therefore do not perceive them as speech sounds. Best and colleagues hypothesized that clicks would therefore be *Non-Assimilable* (NA) to any English speech categories. However, because they are acoustically quite different from each other, English listeners can readily distinguish one from the other. So in this case, the sounds are fairly easy to perceive because of the lack of a match to any existing English sounds.

Figure 4.3. Non-Assimilable (NA): Two Zulu click consonants (left) do not match any categories in English (represented by the unmarked dots), but can be readily distinguished from each other

Flege's speech learning model

Best's PAM was not originally developed as a model of L2 learning. Rather, it was intended to account for the ways in which listeners would perceive speech sounds with which they had no prior experience. Flege's *Speech Learning Model* (SLM), on the other hand, was designed to account for L2 phonetic learning over time. Like Best, Flege (1995) took into account perceptual processes, with the view that difficulties in perception are responsible for difficulties in production. He used the term "interlingual identification" to refer to the way in which listeners tend to hear L2 sounds in terms of their own language. His focus, however, was not on hearing the difference between pairs of L2 sounds, but on being able to distinguish L2 from L1 sounds.

Two aspects of Flege's SLM are especially worth noting here. First, it proposes that if an L2 sound is heard to be very similar to an L1 sound, learners are expected to have considerable difficulty perceiving the difference. Conversely, if the sound is heard as very different from any L1 sound, it should be much easier for learners to hear the distinction. Second, the SLM assumes that speech production eventually falls into line with perception: if a distinction is acquired at the perceptual level, production will become more accurate over time. On the basis of these two principles, then, 'new' L2 sounds will tend to be produced more accurately than L2 sounds that are 'similar' to those of the L1. Flege (1987) tested this prediction with respect to two French vowels: /u/, which tends to be heard as very similar to English /u/, but is not identical, and /y/, which is a high front rounded vowel rather unlike any vowel in English. His acoustic measurements of /y/ produced by native French speakers and English learners of French showed no statistical differences, whereas a divergence occurred for the two groups of speakers on /u/. The predictions of the model were thus supported. Additional evidence was uncovered in a more recent study by Thomson, Nearey, and Derwing (2009), which described a statistical approach to estimating the similarity of English and Mandarin vowels. The similarity measures successfully predicted the vowel production accuracy of low proficiency Mandarin learners of English.

Comparing newer and older approaches

When we compare the PAM and SLM with contrastive analysis and error analysis, some especially important differences emerge. Perhaps most importantly, the two older approaches focus on "language product" in the sense that they treat errors and their causes as objects of study. When they "explain" errors, they do so in terms of those objects. In contrast, the PAM and SLM are better understood as process-oriented models that focus not on language as a thing, but on learners and the mechanisms involved in perception and production.

1. PAM and SLM treat perception and production separately. While it is assumed that these two aspects of speech are related, neither model assumes that they are perfectly aligned.
2. The original PAM clearly defines its scope as the perception of unfamiliar speech sounds. SLM and the more recently developed PAM-L2 (Best & Tyler, 2007) both focus on the process of L2 acquisition, and therefore recognize that learners' L2 knowledge and skills can change over time.
3. Although individual learner differences are not a major focus of attention in either PAM or SLM, neither approach assumes uniformity across learners. With respect to the SLM, for example, it is possible that different learners may perceive different degrees of similarity between a particular L1 sound and its L2 counterpart.
4. Though both approaches entail some degree of abstraction, they also specify cognitive mechanisms (assimilation, interlingual identification) by which L2 learners' difficulties arise.
5. Approaches like PAM and SLM that identify acquisition mechanisms have the potential to inform teaching practices. For instance, the link between perception and production posited in SLM strongly implies that perceptual skills should be taught as part of pronunciation instruction.

Other approaches

The CAH is just one of a number of approaches to L2 errors based on the assumption that useful accounts of errors can be developed through analyses of linguistic phenomena. In the case of CAH, the phenomena are the L1 and L2 sound inventories. Phonologists have also proposed approaches that account for learners' errors on the basis of universal language processes and tendencies. Processes such as final consonant devoicing, which we discussed above, as well as deletions and certain substitutions appear to be widespread aspects of both L1 and L2 acquisition. Another matter commonly discussed by phonologists is the concept of *markedness*. Marked phenomena are linguistic features that are less common in the world's languages. All other things being equal, a marked aspect of language should be more difficult for an L2 learner to acquire than an unmarked one. For instance, /θ/ is a marked phoneme because of its crosslinguistic rarity. Coverage of the evidence in favour of such a hierarchy of difficulty is available in Major (1987) and Eckman (2008). None of these hierarchies has been developed for pedagogical purposes, except in the sense that they attempt to predict levels of difficulty. They share with CAH and error analysis the focus on language as a set of objects, rather than a cognitive or social phenomenon. And like the older approaches, they do not account for individual learner differences.

Are theoretical accounts of errors useful in the classroom?

Over the years, ESL teachers have asked us many times to recommend teaching materials that provide lists of pronunciation problems related to a given L1, or that present a direct comparison of the phonology of their learners' L1 and English. The expectation is that teachers should use information about the L1 and L2 to determine in advance the problems that any group of learners will experience.

Compendia that attempt to help ESL teachers predict pronunciation and other errors have been available for many years. In general, these have been based on Contrastive Analysis. Nilsen and Nilsen, for instance, first published such a book in 1971, *Pronunciation Contrasts in English,* which, as a result of its popularity, has been reprinted many times, most recently in 2010. It offers lists of minimal pairs of English words, along with specific languages whose speakers are predicted to have trouble with them. Another textbook, by Swan and Smith (2001), *Learner English: A Teacher's Guide to Interference and Other Problems,* gives basic descriptions of the phonological systems of several languages and makes specific predictions about sounds that will be problematic for each language group. Beginning teachers might be quite excited to discover such resources: how convenient to have a "recipe book" that identifies exactly what you need to teach to any group of learners! But as with other things that seem too good to be true, the value of this type of error prediction for language teachers is at best minimal. In fact, relying on error prediction for guidance in the classroom may actually do more harm than good. Let's consider for example, the acquisition of English stop consonants by speakers of a Slavic language like Russian. Swan and Smith (2001, p. 147) have this to say:

> The sounds /p/, /k/ and /t/ are not aspirated in Russian, which causes learners to mispronounce them at the beginnings of words in English. So for example 'pit' may sound rather like 'bit', 'come' like 'gum', or 'tart' like 'dart'.

As you will recall, aspiration refers to the intense puff of air that follows the release of English voiceless stops in word-initial position, as in 'pit' ([pʰɪt]). To produce English word pairs such as 'pit/bit' intelligibly, Russian speakers need to learn to add this puff of air, since it is not used in their L1. It seems perfectly logical that making such an adjustment might be difficult, especially during the early stages of learning English. But exactly how much of a problem does this articulatory change actually pose? In recent longitudinal research on Slavic speakers of English (Munro, Derwing, & Saito, 2013), we recorded productions of several words beginning with /p/ and /b/ at various time points over a seven-year period after the speakers' arrival in Canada. All of them had low oral proficiency at the outset. Our aim was to determine how well they would acquire aspirated /p/ without focused pronunciation instruction. The speakers' productions were elicited using a repetition task in which they first heard a model in the following form: "The next word is [target word]." They then responded with a different utterance containing the same target: "Now I say [target word]."

After seven years, we randomly presented recordings from different time points to native English listeners who judged whether each production contained a /p/ or a /b/. The results were quite surprising: more than half the speakers (14 of 24) produced the aspirated /p/s with nearly perfect intelligibility, either right from the start or within their first few months of residence in Canada, even though they received no systematic instruction on the aspiration feature. Four of the remaining speakers learned more slowly, but eventually produced intelligible stops most of the time. The remaining six speakers showed long-term problems with aspirated /p/; in fact, two of them actually produced less intelligible stops as time went on. In short, there was dramatic inter-speaker variability in the difficulty posed by this feature, though the majority of learners had only minimal difficulty.

For most of our speakers, then, the Swan and Smith (2001) prediction was wrong. However, we must be cautious in interpreting these findings since they are based on a small number of monosyllabic words produced in a repetition task. It would be inappropriate to conclude that our results are indicative of all aspects of segmental learning for all learners. However, the diverse learning trajectories shown by the speakers are similar to patterns we have seen in other research, such as a study of vowel acquisition by Munro and Derwing (2008). Taken together, our findings point to a serious problem that arises in using linguistic comparisons to predict learners' errors. What matters in this case is not simply that Swan and Smith's global prediction of difficulty with [pʰ] was wrong for most of the Slavic speakers, but, more importantly, that speaker behaviour was far from uniform. It appears to be uncommon for all speakers from a particular L1 background to share identical difficulties, even when they are at similar proficiency levels. Rather, one of the most noticeable aspects of L2 phonetic learning is individual variability. Any speaker's productions can be affected by a wide range of factors, including age of learning, aptitude, previous learning experiences, and the quality and quantity of exposure to the L2. In addition, the speech material to be produced is itself a source of variability; lexical frequency, phonological context, and orthography can all affect the pronunciation of segments. Thus, no two people are likely to speak their L2 in exactly the same way, no matter how much they seem to have in common. And no individual speaker is likely to be consistent across different productions of the same speech sound.

In the light of such complexity, it seems improbable that teachers would be able to make accurate predictions of their students' production difficulties. Even if learners from a single L1 background often do share problems, we must keep in mind that L2 classes commonly comprise learners from multiple L1 backgrounds, so that extensive variability in difficulties is inevitable. For these reasons, it is important that teachers not rely heavily on over-generalized descriptions to determine and prioritize students' pronunciation needs. Instead, they need to set aside time to assess individual learners to identify shared and idiosyncratic problems and provide appropriate assistance. Shared problems can be covered with whole-class activities, while serious difficulties experienced by one learner or only a few learners should be addressed with individual and small group interventions.

Determining error gravity

The study of error gravity is based on the premise that some L2 errors are more serious than others. As we noted in Chapter 1, it is possible to speak with a strong foreign accent, yet be perfectly intelligible. However, some heavily-accented speakers are highly unintelligible. The most likely explanation for this discrepancy in the effects of accent has to do with the nature of the pronunciation problems in such cases: some errors are more likely to compromise intelligibility than others. To gain clarity on this issue, applied linguists went about establishing error gravity studies in a variety of papers in the 1970s and later. Some of these were concerned with the relative importance of different categories of errors, such as grammatical errors vs. pronunciation errors. Others focused on comparing the consequences of different types of pronunciation errors.

However, the results of this body of work were far from uniform. We have summarized some of the often contradictory claims and findings in Table 4.3 below:

Table 4.3. Selected error gravity studies

Order of gravity	Publications
Error Categories	
Phonological > grammatical	Gynan, 1985
Grammatical > phonological (French L2)	Ensz, 1982
Vocabulary > grammatical > phonological (German L2)	Politzer, 1978
No relation between linguistic "correctness" and comprehensibility	Albrechtsen, Henriksen, & Faerch, 1980
Phonological Types	
Prosodic > segmental	Anderson-Hsieh, Johnson, & Koehler, 1992; Johansson, 1978; Palmer, 1976
Segmental > prosodic	Fayer & Krasinksi, 1987; Koster & Koet, 1993
Segment Types	
Consonants > vowels	Gimson, 1970
Vowels > consonants (Spanish L2)	Shairer, 1992
Other	
Nonnative pronunciation > listener distraction and annoyance	Fayer & Krasinski, 1987

Some of the differences in outcomes showing in Table 4.3 may be due to a focus on different L2s. If consonant errors prove to cause more problems than vowel errors in English, there is no reason to assume that the same applies in Spanish. Furthermore, highly contradictory conclusions often result from differences in methodologies, including the tasks and participants, the quality of test materials, and the nature of the analyses. In fact, Albrechtsen, Henriksen, & Faerch (1980) concluded that it was pointless to try to establish firm hierarchies from such studies because of the many differences in methods, L1s, and L2s at issue. While we concur with their critique, debates about relative difficulties continue. One contentious question is whether prosodic problems outweigh segmental errors in the perception of L2 speech. In our view, there is little value in attempting to determine a definitive answer. In the first place, difficulties of each kind depend to some degree on the learner's L1: speakers of languages that are prosodically close to English, such as Dutch, may experience few difficulties with English prosody. Thus, for these learners, prosody may actually be less important than segmentals. In contrast, speakers of syllable-timed languages like Hungarian or French may have numerous problems with English stress and rhythm, such that prosody outweighs segments as a concern. A second issue is that both major and minor errors may occur in both segments and prosody. Perhaps some segmental problems are more detrimental to comprehension than certain prosodic problems and vice versa. Finally, even if we could establish that, on average, more intelligibility problems are due to one type of error, such knowledge will not help us very much in the L2 classroom where we need to assess the seriousness of specific learner errors rather than general tendencies.

Functional load

A potentially useful theoretical perspective on error gravity is the concept of Functional Load (FL), which relates to the importance of linguistic phenomena in distinguishing meanings in a language. A number of pronunciation specialists have discussed the notion of FL as it applies to segments (Brown, 1991; Catford, 1987; Levis & Cortes, 2008). In particular, some phonemic sound pairs are assumed to 'do more work' than others, and the amount of work done should be calculable on the basis of statistical data about the frequency of occurrence of the sounds. One factor in the computation is the number of words distinguished by a given minimal pair. For example, the English /p/–/b/ opposition has a relatively high FL in English, because many minimal pairs are determined by these sounds (pea-bee, pit-bit, pate-bait, pet-bet, pat-bat) in comparison with the /θ/ – /ð/ pair, which distinguishes far fewer words (thigh-thy).

In addition to numbers of actual pairs, computation of FL must take into account the token frequency of the words in the pairs. If both words in a pair are very common, confusion is more likely to arise, and FL is therefore high. When one of the words is uncommon or both are, FL is lower because there are fewer opportunities for miscomprehensions to arise. Another matter to be considered is whether or not the words in any particular pair belong to the same lexical class. Since listeners are far more likely to confuse a noun with another noun than a noun with an adjective, for instance, FL is higher when the lexical class is shared. Table 4.4 summarizes these points. For more elaboration and lists of computed functional loads, good resources are Brown (1991), Catford (1987), and Levis and Cortes (2008).

The FL principle is a theoretical notion based on a well-reasoned argument. However, as we have seen, other theoretical notions such as the CAH have proven to be much less useful in language teaching than their originators anticipated. It is essential that we test the predictions of FL empirically in order to establish its usefulness. Our study of the perception of Cantonese speakers' consonant errors (Munro & Derwing, 2006) was a first step in that direction. From a large recorded database of English

Table 4.4. Some factors to be considered in the computation of functional load

Factor	Outcomes
Type frequency (number of minimal pairs distinguished by the two segments)	more pairs ≡ higher FL*
Token frequency (frequency of occurrence of words in the pairs)	both very common ≡ highest FL one word is uncommon; the other is common ≡ lower FL both very uncommon ≡ lowest FL
Syntactic category of words in the pairs	both words are same part of speech ≡ higher FL

*We use the symbol "≡" to mean "corresponds to."

sentence productions by Cantonese speakers, we identified utterances that contained certain high FL (e.g. /l/ – /n/, /s/ – /ʃ/) and low FL (e.g. /d/ – /ð/, /f/ – /θ/) errors. We then selected utterances that had 0–2 high FL errors and 0–3 low FL errors, as well as sentences with one error of each type. A group of phonetically untrained listeners then heard the sentences in random order and judged them on a scale of comprehensibility. Two key findings emerged. First, low FL errors reduced comprehensibility much less than high FL errors. In fact, sentences with even three low FL errors were judged more comprehensible than sentences with a single high FL error. Second, the effect of high FL errors was cumulative – sentences with two high FL errors were rated worse than sentences with only one. Low FL errors showed no such effect. These findings are preliminary, and as yet represent the only perception-based research on functional load that we know of. However, they indicate that further research along similar lines might prove useful for teachers. In particular, solid information would provide a firm basis for reviewing difficulties encountered by students at the segmental level, and then selecting for attention those that are likely to affect intelligibility because of their functional load.

Summary

L2 learners' pronunciation errors have received a great deal of attention from both theorists and teachers, who have been concerned with their causes, their predictability and their impact on communication. Although research has demonstrated that segmental difficulties, as well as aspects of prosody and voice quality, are the result of a carry-over of production patterns from the L1, it has also shown that individual learner variability is large. L2 speakers from the same background and at the same level of proficiency often have quite different problem areas. As a result, error prediction is of limited value as a pedagogical resource and may actually lead to a misplaced focus in the classroom. Even more important is the finding that different pronunciation errors have different effects on a speaker's comprehensibility and intelligibility. Though many errors are highly salient, only some of them actually matter when communication is the concern. An evidence-based approach to understanding and addressing errors, then, requires that we give considerable weight to individual differences and to variable error gravity.

CHAPTER 5

Pronunciation instruction research

When we were teaching in an ESL program years ago, large numbers of our Vietnamese students struggled with intelligibility. Many had quite sophisticated vocabulary and grammar, but experienced serious communicative problems as a result of their pronunciation. Several of the teachers within the program were frustrated by their own inability to help their students. As one of them put it, "What else can you do, but repeat, repeat, repeat?" As it turns out, many things can be done to facilitate more comprehensible pronunciation, as the research in this chapter shows.

Introduction

As we have noted in earlier chapters, much of the considerable body of research on L2 speech is not directly applicable to language teaching. This should not come as a surprise because researchers often design their studies to evaluate interesting theoretical proposals about the speech acquisition process itself, rather than about pedagogical interventions. It would be unwise to extrapolate from their findings to classroom practices. In a discussion of timing in language teaching, Hyltenstam and Abrahamsson (2001) astutely observed:

> It must ... be considered a misuse of theoretical research when individual results are given an immediate practical interpretation. At the same time, such an approach depreciates applied research. The many complex practical questions addressed in applied research often call for complex answers based on sets of knowledge, at times even sets drawn from different disciplines. The issue of timing in language teaching is no exception. It is simply not possible to handle this complex issue solely on the basis of one isolated area of theoretical knowledge. (p. 162)

Both language learning and language teaching are highly complex enterprises, and require examination from a wide variety of perspectives. In this chapter, we will consider applied approaches to the teaching of L2 pronunciation.

As noted in Chapter 2, in the long history of pronunciation instruction for L2 speakers, good pronunciation was at times considered to be a central objective of effective language teaching. Practitioners of the Audiolingual Method, for example, put a premium on accurate production at both the segmental and prosodic levels, using an approach that required extensive repetition of sentence-length utterances after native speaker models. However, it has been only in the last few decades that researchers have taken an interest in pronunciation instruction: identifying what is happening in language classrooms, the degree to which language teachers have the necessary training to teach pronunciation, and, most importantly, the efficacy of pronunciation teaching in enhancing learners' intelligibility and comprehensibility.

Is pronunciation taught in L2 classrooms?

Researchers have asked this question of language teachers in Australia (Burns, 2006; MacDonald, 2002), Britain (Burgess & Spencer, 2000), Canada (Breitkreutz, Derwing, & Rossiter, 2001; Foote, Holtby, & Derwing, 2011) and the USA (Darcy, Ewert, & Lidster, 2012). An extensive English Pronunciation Teaching in Europe survey was also carried out in 2010 in seven countries: Finland, France, Germany, Macedonia, Poland, Spain, and Switzerland (Henderson et al., 2012). The consensus from each of these studies is that many instructors are hesitant about systematically teaching pronunciation; they report sporadically correcting students' productions in class, and some introduce lessons incorporating aspects of pronunciation, but on the whole, they indicate that their students would prefer a stronger focus on pronunciation than is currently provided. Foote et al. (2011) determined that the 99 instructors who declared that they integrated pronunciation into their language classes spent less than an hour a week, on average, or six percent of their class time on pronunciation. Forty-three percent of instructors indicated that their institutions offered stand-alone pronunciation classes varying in length from ten minutes to three hours. The instructors in these courses placed a heavier emphasis on segmentals than suprasegmentals, but nearly all the instructors included prosodic features to some extent. In a recent classroom observation study of teachers of three grade 6 ESL classes in Quebec (a context which has more in common with EFL), Foote, Trofimovich, Collins, and Urzúa (2013) found that the three teachers, all of whom reported teaching pronunciation in their communicative classrooms, actually devoted very little time or planning to pronunciation in comparison to vocabulary and grammar. Their primary approach to dealing with pronunciation was to correct errors as they occurred on an incidental basis. We can conclude from these studies that pronunciation instruction is somewhat hit and miss; the extent to which it is integrated into general language classes depends on the teacher and the curriculum; a minority of programs offer stand-alone courses. Moreover, there is probably a response bias in several of the surveys cited, because teachers who have no interest in pronunciation instruction are unlikely to have responded at all.

Teaching resources

Another avenue for determining the nature of pronunciation instruction offered in classrooms is an examination of teaching resources. Textbooks are often considered the mainstay of the language classroom (Bragger & Rice, 2000; Chapelle, 2009; Sobkowiak, 2012). Tergujeff (2010) undertook an examination of sixteen general skills English language textbooks commonly used throughout Finland in primary, lower secondary, and secondary classrooms to identify whether they included pronunciation activities, and if so, what the foci of those activities were. She discovered that the texts incorporated several pronunciation activities, the most frequent of which were 'phonetics training,' 'reading aloud' and 'listen and repeat'; however, these activities were almost exclusively focused at the segmental level. Because Tergujeff (2013) also interviewed learners, she was able to ask whether the activities in the books were actually covered in class. The students reported that their teachers seldom skipped any material in the texts, and that they either completed the activities in class or as homework.

Derwing, Diepenbroek, and Foote (2012) carried out a similar survey of integrated skills ESL textbooks designed for adult learners. They analyzed the content of 12 series (48 individual textbooks and six teacher manuals) from several major publishers. The authors found striking disparities across the series, such that some had very little to no pronunciation coverage in any of their texts, while others included a wide range of pronunciation activities at every level within the series. Other series were inconsistent in both the quantity and nature of pronunciation foci across levels. In several textbooks, a pronunciation point would be raised once, never to be seen again; thus there were very few opportunities for review. The authors argued that many of the texts examined did not provide sufficient support to either the learners or the teachers in terms of explanations or range of task types. Unlike Tergujeff (2013), this study did not

A CLOSER LOOK: Conducting research on teaching practices

There are several ways to determine whether pronunciation instruction takes place in language classrooms or not, including surveying teachers, and examining textbooks and other teaching resources, as we have seen. Another approach—in class observation—is perhaps the most effective in that it provides first-hand data about the pronunciation activities and behaviours actually taking place in language classrooms. In an innovative study that entailed observing 32 lessons, surveying teachers, interviewing learners, and analyzing textbook content, Elina Tergujeff (2012) discovered that students in Finnish schools did receive pronunciation instruction, but that it was focused almost exclusively on segmentals. Furthermore, in her classroom observations, she documented significant differences in the range of activities employed by teachers, such that one teacher utilized nine of Tergujeff's ten categories of pronunciation instruction whereas another teacher employed only one. Only four occurrences of any kind of pronunciation instruction were noted in one teacher's lessons, while the other teacher used sixty-two during the same length of time. Thus, overall, Tergujeff found a tremendous difference in both the quality and quantity of pronunciation teaching offered in relatively homogeneous environments.

address the issue of whether teachers actually use the limited pronunciation activities available in these textbooks. In Canada, where the Derwing et al. study was carried out, the ESL adult context offers more flexibility because there is no national curriculum to which teachers must adhere, as is the case in Finnish public schools. Thus, it is quite possible that teachers may choose to avoid the pronunciation activities presented in the textbooks they use in class. A useful line of follow-up research, then, would be a classroom observation study in ESL settings, coordinated across several jurisdictions.

Do teachers have sufficient training to teach pronunciation?

The teacher surveys identified above also probed teacher training. The earlier studies suggested that many language teachers are uncomfortable teaching suprasegmentals because they lack sufficient background; all of the studies demonstrated instructors' perceptions of a need for access to more professional development. MacDonald (2002) carried out in-depth interviews with eight Australian instructors, six of whom declared that they disliked teaching pronunciation and were not good at it. The remaining two said they 'didn't mind' it and that they were 'ok' at teaching it. He categorized the teachers' concerns about pronunciation instruction into the following themes: "formal curricula; learner goals and assessment (including the teacher's role); teaching communicatively and in an integrated way; and teaching and learning materials" (p. 6). The curricula in the various programs in which the teachers worked did not focus on pronunciation; any guidelines that mentioned pronunciation tended to be vague and generally unhelpful. The teachers reported that they rarely or never formally assessed their learners' pronunciation. Instead, they were guided by intuitive notions of intelligibility. Even though they recognized that others might not be able to easily understand their students, they didn't know how to carry out assessments and provide assistance. Some of the instructors also felt that they would embarrass their students by correcting their pronunciation, or hinder their communication by interrupting them, and thus refrained from monitoring their students' speech. MacDonald also noted that not all teachers were able to integrate pronunciation into their teaching; some pointed out that they had not been trained how to do so. Teachers also commented on the paucity of useful pronunciation materials available to them.[1] It was clear from their comments that they were unaccustomed to adapting materials originally intended for emphasizing other skills. MacDonald concluded that English language teachers would benefit

---

1. Since the research cited in MacDonald (2002), several resources have been developed for the Australian market that are freely available through the Australian government, notably Fraser (2001) and Yates and Zielinski (2009).

from explicit training in teaching pronunciation, and that appropriate materials and assessments should be made available for L2 classrooms.

Henderson et al. (2012) asked their 635 European respondents to describe on a scale of 1 – 5 (where 1 = extremely poor and 5 = excellent) the quality of their professional training in the teaching of English pronunciation. The authors interpreted the mean score of 2.91 as indicative of the participants having little or no training. Respondents also had an opportunity to provide open-ended comments, which generally reinforced this conclusion. On the other hand, the teachers were considerably more likely to judge pronunciation as fairly important in relation to other language skills, with average ratings ranging from 3.14 in Macedonia to 4.2 in Spain (1 = least important).

The most recent Canadian ESL survey of language teachers and program directors (Foote et al., 2011) showed an improvement in teacher confidence over the ten years after an earlier survey, but the majority of respondents indicated that most often, their pronunciation-specific training came from sporadic conference presentations, while only 20% had taken a credit course focusing specifically on pronunciation teaching. For those instructors who reported having taught pronunciation courses, the greatest challenges were finding common pronunciation problems in students from different language backgrounds, making activities interesting, and teaching students from a range of proficiency levels in the same class. The authors of this study also scanned Canadian university TESL offerings to determine the availability of for-credit training opportunities geared to teaching pronunciation for ESL teachers. Only six courses were found across the whole country. It is possible that more are offered on an ad hoc basis, but there is no question that teachers have very limited access to professional development in this area.

Should non-native speakers teach L2 pronunciation?

Teachers who have learned the language themselves are generally excellent models. Unless a teacher has an inadequate oral command of the L2 (as sometimes happens in some EFL contexts), our view is that non-native instructors should indeed provide pronunciation training along with other aspects of the language being learned. In some contexts, notably Japan and Korea, native speakers are often hired to teach pronunciation and conversation, while local instructors offer grammar and other skills-based instruction. This practice reinforces the notion that there is something inherently wrong with having an L2 accent, and that only a native speaker has the wherewithal to effectively teach pronunciation. This is a faulty assumption. Consider the Levis, Link, Sonsaat, and Barriuso (2013) study, in which two ESL instructors, one a native speaker of English and the other a high proficiency bilingual speaker, both taught pronunciation classes, following the same curriculum, using the same materials and the same activities. Their students came from similar backgrounds and shared the same pronunciation difficulties. Levis et al. administered pre and post-tests, and determined that the students from both classes made significant improvements as a result of the instruction, regardless of whether their teacher was a native speaker or non-native speaker. On a related point, the issue of who should teach pronunciation in World Englishes contexts has been a matter of serious debate (see Chapter 8), but as Moussu and Llurda (2008) stated in their comprehensive review of non-native English-speaking English language teachers, "many so-called NSs can be far less intelligible in global settings than well-educated proficient speakers of a second language" (p. 318).

Conducting classroom-based research: Is pronunciation instruction effective?

As outlined in Chapter 1, language teachers have taught pronunciation for a very long time, but research focusing on its outcomes did not appear until the latter part of the 20th century. In Chapter 3 we presented a detailed critique of Purcell and Suter (1980), one of the first studies claiming to research whether pronunciation instruction is effective. We argued that their negative conclusion was unwarranted, given the nature of their data. Since that time, the results of several studies have indicated that pronunciation instruction in a laboratory setting may, in fact, be beneficial. For example, de Bot and Mailfert (1982), de Bot (1983), Bradlow, Akahane-Yamada, Pisoni, and Tohkura (1999), and Thomson (2011) showed that perceptual training can have positive effects on L2 oral productions immediately afterward. In fact, the latter study also showed retention of both perceptual and production progress three months after the initial training period. While laboratory research must be viewed as encouraging, pronunciation research in the classroom in the 1980s was practically non-existent. Recognizing an important need, Pennington and Richards (1986) called for studies to determine whether pronunciation instruction, particularly beyond the level of individual sounds, would be effective. They also suggested that it would be important to know whether any positive changes observed as a result of teaching would be maintained over time.

Though classroom-based studies are likely to resonate with directors and teachers within language programs, they are much more difficult to conduct than are laboratory studies. Why are classroom-based studies hard to carry out? A number of logistics complicate matters, starting with ethical approval. Researchers who work with human participants always have to apply to an ethics board at their own university before any study can be implemented, but often with classroom studies, they go through a second ethical review process at the institution where the learners are studying.

Another set of complications concerns locating suitable numbers of participants within institutions. An ideal study requires one or more experimental groups, as well as a control group, and the groups should all be at roughly the same L2 proficiency level. Many language programs may not have two or more classes at the same level, which may require the researcher to carry out the project over more than one semester, in order to satisfy the need for sufficient sample sizes. Even when classes of the same nominal proficiency level are available, it should not automatically be assumed that they are truly equivalent. In fact, schools sometimes group students together for administrative reasons, so that researchers must use pre-defined groups that do not actually match. Classroom studies also require the cooperation of the program director and the collaboration of the classroom teachers involved, some of whom may be asked to alter their lessons throughout the course of the project. Students will have to sign consent forms, which often use daunting and confusing language because of requirements of ethics boards. For refugees who have experienced problems with the government in their countries of origin, having to sign any official papers may seem threatening.

Some of the challenges in conducting classroom research arise because multiple steps are needed. Those L2 students who agree to participate commonly have to complete a pre-test to determine their starting points prior to instruction, perhaps some midpoint testing, a post-test immediately after the end of the intervention and, finally, in some studies, a delayed post-test, to determine whether any changes due to the intervention have been maintained. The next stage in a classroom-based study is to analyse the resulting data. The researchers may choose to do a linguistic analysis, comparing speech samples from each of the assessment points, or they may identify samples from the pre-, post-, and delayed post-test periods, which can be randomized across collection times and played to listeners for their reactions (e.g. fluency, comprehensibility, and accentedness judgements). Together these many steps place great demands on investigators' skills, energy, and time.

A number of difficulties are completely out of the researcher's control. Attrition, for instance, which occurs when a student moves away or leaves the program for some other reason is nearly inevitable in studies carried out over weeks or months. Depending on the design of the study, this may result in unbalanced N's, making classroom comparisons difficult. At the same time, if some of the students in the class under study have not consented to participate, other arrangements have to be made to ensure that they are still provided with the learning opportunities they expect. Any number of other things can go wrong during the course of the data collection period: one of the teachers could fall ill; field trips or fire drills may interfere with the schedule of learning interventions; and so on. Given the long list of problems we have identified above, it is unsurprising that many researchers eschew classroom studies, despite their great appeal from the standpoint of ecological validity. See Figure 5.1 for a graphic of a typical timeline for a classroom-based study.

A. CONCEPTUALIZATION

Idea
Preplanning – literature search and review
Formulation of concrete research questions

B. ADMINISTRATIVE INITIATION

Grant proposal (1 year) (optional)
Home institution ethics
Recruitment of research assistants

C. PROJECT INITIATION

Explanation of research to language school administrators
School approval (may require separate ethics process)
Recruitment and training of teachers at appropriate levels
Recruitment of student participants (informed consent)

D. PROJECT IMPLEMENTATION

1. Training/Testing

Control group	Experimental group(s)
Pre-test	Pre-test
–	Intervention
Post-test	Post-test
Delayed post-test optional, (but optimal, if feasible)	Delayed post-test optional, (but optimal, if feasible)

2. Evaluation of Primary Data

Linguistic analysis	Listener-based analysis
Pre-processing of data: e.g. phonemic or other transcription, preparation of audio files for analysis	Preparation of audio stimuli for random presentation
Actual analysis: e.g. error counts; occurrences of phenomena of interest (e.g. accurate consonant clusters in obligatory contexts); acoustic measurements (mean length of utterance (MLU), pause time, filled and unfilled pauses); vowel or consonant identification	Recruitment and scheduling of listeners (in groups or individually)
Data analysis: Statistical comparisons of speaker groups' performance	Administration of listening task: LBQs and informed consent; Instructions and warm-up; Completion of listening tasks (e.g. standard orthographic transcription for intelligibility; Likert-scale ratings of comprehensibility, fluency, accentedness; T/F assessment; paired comparisons)
	Data analysis: Data entry, input and related processing, statistical analyses comparing speaker groups

3. Interpretation of results
4. Write-up (up to 2 years)
5. Submission for publication and/or conference presentation

Figure 5.1. The steps involved in a classroom-based pronunciation research study

One of the first classroom-based research studies to address pronunciation was that of Perlmutter (1989), who compared the English performance of international teaching assistants (ITAs) in the USA on their arrival and six months later, after a program of training. She found an improvement in the ITAs' intelligibility, but because she included no uninstructed comparison group, it is unknown whether the changes were due to the instruction or to experience in an English-speaking environment for six months. In Chapter 3, we pointed out that the first year of residence in an L2 environment is the time when most naturalistic phonological change happens (a window of maximal opportunity), so in the case of Perlmutter's study, we might expect some degree of improvement even in the absence of instruction. A few years later, Champagne-Muzar, Schneiderman, and Bourdages (1993) carried out a controlled study of the effects of perception and production training on 34 learners' acquisition of French pronunciation, examining both segmental and suprasegmental properties. The findings of this innovative study showed improvement that could be attributed directly to instruction. This was, to our knowledge, the first study to confirm what pronunciation teachers had long believed: that a pedagogical focus on perception and production could have positive results for L2 students.

In an effort to identify the best approach to teaching pronunciation, MacDonald, Yule, and Powers (1994) compared four groups of ESL students, three of which received instruction under different conditions, while the fourth group served as a control. All the learners were required to produce target vocabulary in mini-lectures before (Time 1) and immediately after the interventions (Time 2) and, again, two days later (Time 3). The four instructional conditions were these:

1. a 10-minute "teacher-led vocabulary practice drill" (p. 79)
2. a 30-minute "self-study vocabulary practice with tape-recordings" (p. 79)
3. a 10-minute session "involving modified interaction with particular emphasis on vocabulary items" (p. 79)   in this condition, requests for clarification from the ESL students were made
4. a 10-minute non-intervention (the control), "[which allowed] time for self-reflection on, and/or practice of vocabulary" (p. 79).

The students' productions from each time point were then presented in a blind paired-comparison task to native listeners who indicated which of two utterances (either Time 1 vs. Time 2, or Time 1 vs. Time 3) sounded more native-like. Improvement was perceived in only the self-study group between Time 1 and Time 2, where 57% of the NS responses favoured Time 2. Although this study posed a very interesting question, some aspects of the procedure led to inconclusive results. First, although the authors designed the study to reflect what actually happens in language classrooms, a single 10-minute lesson can hardly be expected to have a lasting effect on students. Second, the time on task was not held constant across conditions. Notice that the only group that showed improvement was the self-study group who had 30 minutes to practice, and note further that the effect of the practice was not maintained by Time 3. Third, the listeners were required to choose which recordings sounded more native-like, rather than the ones that were easier to understand. In our view, a comprehensibility rating would have been preferable to an accent judgment. Despite its shortcomings, this study triggered interest in classroom-based pronunciation research, and in that regard it made an important contribution to the field.

Derwing, Munro, and Wiebe (1997) were interested to know whether pronunciation changes could be brought about in L2 speakers who had lived in an English setting for an extended period of time, well past the window of maximal opportunity that occurs during the first year of residence. They recorded the progress of a class of 13 students enrolled in a 'Clear Speaking' course. The average length of time the students had spent in English-speaking Canada was ten years, and all of the participants indicated that they had extensive daily conversations in English. The course was offered two evenings a week for 12 weeks. Because the students were from several different language backgrounds, the course was based on relatively broad aspects of speech that could affect intelligibility, and that would be shared across many of the students. Body language, volume, voice quality, speech rate, and suprasegmentals were the primary foci; segmentals received little attention, since few problems were shared across the range of L1s represented. The researchers recorded the participants reading a list of true/false sentences on the first and last nights of the course (e.g. 'Some people keep dogs as pets'; 'March has thirty-eight days'). Several sentence productions were chosen from this list for a pre- and post-instruction intelligibility task in which native listeners transcribed what they heard. The same native listeners also completed comprehensibility and accentedness rating tasks, in which they assigned scores on two Likert scales (1 = extremely easy to understand; 9 = extremely difficult to understand) and (1 = very little accent; 9 = very strong accent) respectively, to sentences collected before and after the intervention. The listeners found the post-instruction sentences, both true and false, to be significantly more intelligible than those recorded pre-instruction; that is, they were able to transcribe the sentences produced after pronunciation teaching much more accurately than the 'before' sentences. Furthermore, the listeners rated the comprehensibility and accentedness of the true sentences significantly better over time; however, there was no change in the ratings of the false sentences. The authors concluded that the lack of improvement in the ratings of false sentences may have been related to the unpredictability of the content; true sentences often allow listeners to use their knowledge of the world to a certain extent to help them understand, but false sentences do not. Even though the listeners had actually understood the false sentences collected after the intervention better than those from before the pronunciation course, they did not perceive them as being easier to understand; that is, the false sentences took more effort to process than the true ones. Similar to the Perlmutter (1989) study, this classroom-based research did not include a control group, although given the 'fossilized' nature of the learners (that is, they had been speaking in an English environment for years and had not seen any improvement in their own productions over that time), it was assumed that any changes in just twelve weeks would be the result of instruction and not of the additional exposure to English gained in that very short period of time.

In a follow-up study, the same researchers assessed the effectiveness of segmental versus suprasegmental pronunciation instruction for adult L2 learners, in a controlled study (Derwing, Munro, & Wiebe, 1998). Forty-eight intermediate proficiency students from a range of L1 backgrounds, all of whom were studying ESL for 20 hours a week, participated in the study over the course of 10 weeks. Sixteen learners were assigned to a class which received 20 minutes of segmental instruction a day; another 16 were placed in a class in which suprasegmentals were taught for 20 minutes a day, and the remaining 16 students received no pronunciation-specific instruction. The participants were recorded reading a list of true and false sentences during the first week, and again at the end of the study. They also recorded a verbal account of a picture story about two hunters who were unsuccessful in their quest. These narratives were collected as samples of extemporaneous speech in which the learners produced the vocabulary and grammatical structures necessary to explain the story represented by the cartoons. This task was expected to be more representative of everyday speech than sentences that were read aloud. Once the 'before' and 'after' utterances from all three speaker groups were randomized, 48 native listeners rated the recorded sentences on 9-point Likert scales of comprehensibility and accentedness. Both the segmental and suprasegmental groups showed significant improvement in both comprehensibility and accentedness over time, but the control group demonstrated no change in either dimension. Forty-five second 'before' and 'after' excerpts from the picture narrative data from the same speakers were also assessed by six trained ESL teachers. They were asked to rate the speech samples on comprehensibility, accentedness, and fluency scales (1=native like fluency; 9=extremely dysfluent). Only the group that had received suprasegmental instruction showed significant improvement on any of the measures; their Time 2 excerpts received significantly better scores on both the comprehensibility and the fluency scales. No other comparisons in any of the groups were significant. The authors concluded that suprasegmental instruction has more influence on extemporaneously produced speech, but they surmised that segmental instruction is important, too, because in the case of a communication breakdown, L2 speakers who are aware of their own challenges will be able to focus on individual segments in a conversational repair.

Couper (2003, 2006, 2011) has carried out a series of classroom studies examining the effectiveness of pronunciation instruction. In each investigation, he chose particular aspects of L2 pronunciation on which to focus, based not on intelligibility, but on

A CLOSER LOOK: Choosing stimuli for pronunciation research

Researchers interested in the development of L2 phonological skills have used a range of stimuli to collect speech samples from L2 speakers. The classic approach when examining individual segments is to ask learners to listen and repeat a given word, often embedded in a sentence frame, such as "Now I say _____." (e.g. Munro & Derwing, 2008). Other researchers favour reading passages, such as the Rainbow passage, originally developed for speech language pathology (e.g. Munro & Mann, 2005) or the Stella passage (Weinberger, 2015), both of which have been constructed to include a wide range of phonemes and intonation patterns in English. Another approach is to have L2 speakers read sentences aloud (Munro & Derwing, 1995). The primary benefit of read-aloud tasks is the control over content, so that listener-judges will not be affected by grammar and vocabulary errors and can direct their focus on L2 pronunciation alone. A disadvantage of reading-aloud tasks is that they are somewhat artificial and the outcome may not sound much like the natural productions of the learners when they have to access syntactic structures and the lexicon as well as organize their thoughts and speak on their own (see Levis & Barriuso, 2012, on reading aloud versus spontaneous speech). One approach to giving students some content support at the same time as encouraging extemporaneously-produced speech is the picture narrative task, which has been employed in many L2 pronunciation studies. Rossiter, Derwing, and Jones (2008) developed a list of 33 criteria for researchers to consider when selecting a picture story. Other researchers have used excerpts from monologues or interview data to obtain natural samples of L2 speech. When Derwing, Rossiter, Munro, and Thomson (2004) compared low proficiency L2 speakers' fluency on picture narratives, monologues, and speech samples from conversations, they found that the learners were judged to be more fluent on the latter two tasks than on narratives, possibly because they had more control of the content and could avoid vocabulary or structures that might cause them problems. Foster and Skehan (1996) also compared task types and demonstrated that the degree of cognitive load contributes to learners' performance.

error frequency across speakers of different L1s. He measured the students' productions prior to and after the pronunciation courses, counting the number of errors and determining whether there were changes in the students' speech. Not only did Couper demonstrate that the foci of the interventions were successfully altered, but in his 2006 study, he also conducted a delayed post-test showing that the beneficial effects of the instruction were maintained 12 weeks after the course ended. Among other errors, Couper chose to address two problem types that cause a disruption of syllable structure: epenthesis – the insertion of a vowel where one doesn't belong, (/sətɔɹi/ for 'story') and absence or omission – the reduction of a consonant cluster or the elimination of a final consonant (/tɛts/ for 'texts' and /fæs/ for 'fast'). Although Couper did not measure intelligibility, other studies have shown that the disruption of syllable structure sometimes interferes with listeners' comprehension. In the 2011 study, with epenthesis in syllable CODA position as the primary issue, Couper conducted a listening discrimination task in addition to speaking tasks, and determined that the instruction resulted in improved comprehension and production. He employed four conditions to teach 45-minute lessons to try to identify the aspects of the lessons that made a positive impact on the students. He determined that "socially constructed metalanguage" (SCM) or "students working together with the teacher using already understood first language (L1) concepts to help in the formation of target language phonological concepts" (p. 159) and "critical listening" (CL) or "listening and contrasting to learn phonological categories and their boundaries" (p. 159) were both helpful. In the speaking tasks, significant improvement occurred when students had co-created metalanguage to describe the pronunciation phenomenon of epenthesis, whereas the results of the listening discrimination task were boosted significantly by the critical listening instruction. Couper suggests not only that pronunciation instruction should be explicit to facilitate change in learners' perceptions and productions, but also that the students themselves should participate in deciding how to describe the phonological factors which are the focus of concern, following Fraser's (2006) cognitive approach to pronunciation. For instance, Couper contrasts a standard teacher response to the insertion of a vowel where there shouldn't be one with an SCM response: "when the student says 'thinker' instead of 'think', the teacher would say, 'try not to add an extra syllable', whereas with SCM the teacher might say 'make the "k" quieter and shorter'" (p. 164) (note that in New Zealand English, 'thinker' is pronounced with a SCHWA in word-final position).

While MacDonald et al. (1994) compared four conditions for pronunciation improvement, and Couper's (2011) research revealed differences in effectiveness of pronunciation instruction depending on the inclusion of socially constructed metalanguage and critical listening, Saito and Lyster (2012) studied the potential benefits of FORM-FOCUSED INSTRUCTION (FFI) (see Spada, 1997, 2011) with and without CORRECTIVE FEEDBACK on pronunciation learning. Their concern was the well-documented difficulty that Japanese speakers often experience in producing English /ɹ/. The researchers recruited 65 Japanese learners of English and placed them in one control and two experimental groups. The teacher in the first experimental group (Group 1) provided 4 hours of FFI to her students, by seeding her lesson with numerous instances of words that required English /ɹ/. Group 2 received the same FFI, supplemented with corrective feedback (CF); each time a student made an error in the production of /ɹ/, he or she received a RECAST from the teacher (i.e. the teacher repeated the word in question, but with an appropriate rendition of English /ɹ/). Group 3, the control, also received four hours of instruction, but their focus was on vowels. The participants were tested both pre- and post-instruction with word and sentence reading tasks, and a picture description task. In the post-test session, they also completed a generalizability task to determine whether any changes in /ɹ/ had transferred to new contexts. The FFI + CF condition, that is, Group 2, showed significant improvement; Group 1, which received FFI alone, did not improve to the same extent, and the control group showed no differences over time at all. The authors concluded that CF in combination with FFI is an optimum approach for teaching pronunciation contrasts. In other words, explicit feedback seemed to have an optimal effect. Unfortunately, neither of the experimental conditions appeared to generalize to improved English /ɹ/ in new contexts; however, the instruction time was short, and there was a trend in the expected direction. In a study similar to Saito and Lyster's, also focusing on the effects of implicit versus explicit feedback, Dlaska and Krekeler (2013) compared students' immediate responses after receiving feedback. Although a single session does not suggest that the students "learned" a new pronunciation pattern, it was clear that the explicit feedback was significantly better at raising students' awareness of their errors than was implicit feedback.

On a methodological point, Saito and Lyster's (2012) study involved both listener judgments and acoustic measurements to determine whether Japanese learners of English changed their production of English /ɹ/. Derwing and Munro (2005, 2009), and Derwing and Munro (2013) have argued that the gold standard for measuring pronunciation improvement is listener data-either comprehensibility ratings or intelligibility measures. Although acoustic measures can provide evidence of a shift in speakers' productions, they do not necessarily reveal which changes listeners actually attend to. As a result, they do not indicate whether speech intelligibility has actually improved. Ultimately, L2 speakers who communicate with others have to make themselves understood to human interlocutors-thus human listeners in pronunciation studies are the best reflection of how individuals' pronunciation will be received in natural settings.

Lord (2010) conducted an interesting study comparing English L1 study-abroad students who had received Spanish pronunciation instruction with students who had not. All eight students spent two months in Mexico, where they received L2 instruction and lived with host families. Both groups produced more instances of appropriate fricative allophones of Spanish stops after the study-abroad experience, but those who had received instruction prior to leaving showed significantly greater gains in accuracy than the immersion only group. This suggests that the instruction heightened the learners' awareness of a particular accent feature. Awareness-raising also seemed to play an important role in Saalfeld's (2012) study of the perception of Spanish stress patterns. Two groups of learners completed a pre-test containing no distractor items. Several weeks later, both the instructed and the control groups showed improvement on the post-test. Oddly, however, the control group appeared to make more gains than the students who had received pronunciation instruction. This finding may have been the result of differential aptitude.

Whether pronunciation instruction can be effective with L2 speakers who have deeply entrenched accents was partially addressed in Derwing, Munro, and Wiebe (1997). In that study, as indicated above, the average length of residence in the L2 environment was 10 years. However, recently, Derwing, Munro, Foote, Waugh, and Fleming (2014) conducted a study with seven L2 speakers who had been living in an English-speaking city for an average of 19 years. With a mean age of 43 years, these speakers were older than the college students in many of the other studies addressed in this section. All had at least a high school education in their countries of origin (Vietnam [6] and Cambodia [1]). The researchers were approached by a local factory to provide some pronunciation support to several middle management employees, whose work skills were excellent, but whose oral communications were frequently hampered by a lack of intelligibility. On average, the participants had enrolled in eight months of ESL when they first arrived in Canada, but none reported receiving any pronunciation-specific instruction. All had started working in the factory, along with many compatriots who spoke their L1. These individuals, however, continued to be promoted to positions requiring better communication skills in English. The factory owners agreed to a workplace-based pronunciation course: participants were given a half hour three times a week to attend class, and were expected to do at least ten minutes of homework each day on their own time. All told, the class received 17 hours of instruction in both listening and speaking tasks over the course of three months. A comparison of pre- and post-test results showed that both the participants' own perception of speech in English and their productions, in terms of intelligibility and comprehensibility, improved significantly. This study makes a further contribution to the growing body of research that suggests that pronunciation instruction can bring about change in speakers' productions, even when the L2 users' speech patterns are heavily entrenched.

Sardegna's (2011) study compared the accuracy of LINKING in passages read aloud by 38 ITAs before instruction began, again at the end of the course four months later, then again at a third testing time between an additional 5–25 months, and finally, yet another 9 months later. The students showed significant improvement, and despite some backsliding at the third testing point, the linking measures were still significantly better than they were prior to instruction. The students who were available for testing at the final time maintained the changes to their pronunciation. Like an earlier unpublished study of stress (Hahn, 2002), this study shows that, at some level, instruction resulted in relatively permanent restructuring of the students' phonological systems. Whether this particular finding extends to spontaneous speech, as well as reading aloud, was not determined. McGregor and Sardegna (2014), in a more extensive study of pronunciation instruction, integrated language awareness into an oral proficiency course, by introducing learners of English to specific pronunciation features. An aspect of the study that learners found to be very helpful was a video component, in which

A CLOSER LOOK: Comparing pronunciation instruction methods

MacDonald, Yule, and Powers (1994) attempted to compare different approaches to teaching pronunciation, but their interventions were too short to yield conclusive outcomes. Derwing et al.'s (1998) classroom study was not a comparison of 'methods' *per se*. Rather, the study compared two distinct foci (segmentals vs. suprasegmentals); in other words, there was a difference in content. However, the same pedagogical principles were emphasized by the instructors, and many of the same activities were used in both conditions, such as modeling and repetition. The difference in the instruction had to do with *what* was taught, not *how* it was taught. Couper's (2011) study compared four conditions of instruction including socially constructed metalanguage and critical listening components, and found that when neither were present, students' inappropriate use of epenthesis was not curtailed. Again, though, these were 45-minute interventions, which are unlikely to become generalized. In other words, the students may have been able to produce certain words that were explicitly taught using SCM and CL, but they may not have learned to avoid epenthesis in general. Saito and Lyster's (2012) study is a true methods experiment, in that FFI alone, FFI +CF, and a control group were compared. Though the results for FFI +CF were promising, this was essentially a laboratory study. A true classroom study over a period of several weeks comparing different methods of teaching several aspects of pronunciation (in other words, settings which reflect what happens in existing L2 programs) would make a significant new contribution to the field. Such studies are notoriously difficult to carry out, and controlling for factors such as the teacher, the proficiency level of the students, the L1 backgrounds and ages of the students, in addition to the inevitable cancellation of classes for field trips, bad weather, and general program testing make classroom-based research a major challenge.

they viewed themselves presenting in English, and then reflected on their own pronunciation. Students also reported that the most helpful strategy in improving their pronunciation was recording, revising, and re-recording oral homework for submission to the instructor, who then provided feedback. The authors observed significant improvement in all the areas they measured: intonation, primary stress, linking, and unstressed vowel reduction.

Other studies have shown that learners' perception and production of individual segments can be enhanced with instruction delivered through technology. Ron Thomson, for instance, developed a computer game in which learners practiced discriminating vowels. Not only did their perception improve (Thomson, 2012a), but their productions also became more target-like (Thomson, 2011). These studies will be discussed at greater length in Chapter 7.

Although the research is still somewhat limited, it seems clear that pronunciation-specific instruction can be effective. Yet it is also clear from the surveys and classroom observation data cited above that pronunciation does not have a prominent place in communicative classrooms. The Foote et al. (2013) study, in particular, indicated that the actual teaching time devoted to pronunciation in a Grade 6 classroom was about 10%, compared to 20% on grammar and 70% on vocabulary; moreover, most of that instruction was incidental, in reaction to student errors. Survey data provide little reason to expect different patterns in adult classes. Given these findings, a question worth exploring is whether general communicative L2 classrooms as opposed to pronunciation-specific classes are beneficial in terms of improving students' pronunciation.

Trofimovich, Lightbown, Halter, and Song (2009) conducted a longitudinal study which suggests that even the relatively little pronunciation instruction students receive from regular L2 classroom teachers is of some benefit. Francophone ESL students were assessed at the end of Grade 3 and again when they finished Grade 4. One of the tests the students completed was a sentence repetition task. Trained raters assigned an accent score based on segmental errors alone (only one error was coded per word, so the score was a conservative representation of the students' productions). The sentences were also played to listeners, who judged them on Likert scales for both comprehensibility and fluency. What is especially interesting about this study is that 12 of the classes received regular audiolingual instruction with a teacher, which included the four language skills (listening, speaking, reading and writing), while 8 other classes were restricted to listening and reading. The latter students worked autonomously, could choose whatever they wanted to do, and had access to a full range of materials; what they did not have was a teacher or another speaker with whom they could interact or from whom they could receive feedback. Trofimovich et al. were curious to know "whether, and to what extent, sustained, long-term comprehension practice in both listening and reading (without structured classroom activities, oral interaction, teacher input, or tests and in the virtual absence of any language exposure outside the classroom) can help develop young learners' L2 pronunciation ability" (p. 615). It turned out that the empirical measures (number of phonological errors and speech rate) were not significantly different between groups, although both sets of students showed improvement from Grade 3 to Grade 4. However, the comprehensibility and fluency ratings at the end of Grade 4 were significantly higher for the students enrolled in regular programming with a teacher. Thus we may infer that the small amount of pronunciation correction that the learners received from their teachers may actually have helped them. However, for those students who have serious intelligibility problems, such feedback is likely insufficient.

Not all pronunciation-specific courses have positive effects, though in some cases we might not hear about courses with negative outcomes because of a general bias against negative findings in research journals. Ordinarily, if a study has a non-significant outcome, it does not qualify for publication, in part because it is often impossible to determine why no change occurred as a result of instruction. So many variables can influence oral language behaviour, including student motivation, the nature of the instruction (focus, length of time, task-type, materials, etc.), aptitude of the students, variability in terms of experience with the L2, and the students' ages, that a non-significant result cannot be traced to a single factor. However, some studies with negative outcomes may still provide useful insights when they include additional data that help clarify the results. This was the case for Kennedy and Trofimovich (2010), who compared L2 performance before and after a pronunciation course for university students from a range of L1 backgrounds. The students' pre- and post-instruction recordings were rated on scales of accentedness, comprehensibility, and fluency by 10 listeners. The researchers found no significant differences over time on any of the three dimensions when comparing grouped data. Their study, then, might not have been published if it were not for other data that contributed some interesting insights into their overall results. The L2 students had been asked to keep a language journal throughout their course, in which they were to reflect on what they were learning in their pronunciation course, and on their own behaviours. The purpose of the journals was to determine whether degree of language awareness had any relationship to L2 pronunciation. Indeed there was evidence of what the authors called a 'Matthew effect', such that students whose pronunciation and fluency was best at the outset were the ones who showed the most improvement, while the students whose pronunciation and fluency were the weakest at the beginning of the course did not improve at all. In other words, there appeared to be an aural comprehension threshold; those people whose listening comprehension was beyond a certain level could analyze and make use of input to a greater degree than those whose listening skills were weaker. The comments in the students' language journals supported this view. Those whose journals showed evidence of qualitative reflections (that is, who saw their task as extracting meaning from an unfamiliar context) as opposed to quantitative comments (they viewed language in an itemized fashion: words/sounds/rules to be practiced and memorized) showed more improvement in the rating data, when examined individually. The authors concluded that the approach the students took to learning pronunciation might have influenced their performance. They suggested that teachers encourage their students to find opportunities to listen to their L2 outside of class to enhance their aural comprehension skills, which might, at the same time, enhance their ability to benefit from pronunciation instruction. For a summary of the classroom-based pronunciation intervention studies discussed here, see Table 5.1.

It has been encouraging to see a much greater focus on pronunciation instruction research over the last decade than in the preceding years. In a meta-analysis of 86 studies (both published and unpublished), Lee, Jang and Plonsky (2014) succeeded in locating only 26 studies in the period between 1982 and 2005, but noted a substantial upswing in the ten years that followed. Lee et al.'s results also seem encouraging in that they identified a relatively strong positive effect of instruction overall; however, they observed a moderating effect of outcome measures, such that studies involving

Table 5.1. Summary of selected intervention studies

Study	Linguistic foci	Speakers	Length	Comments
Perlmutter (1989)	Global intelligibility	24 ITAs mixed L1s	6 months	No control group, but significant improvement in intelligibility at end of study.
Champagne-Muzar et al. (1993)	Perception and production of French segmentals and suprasegmentals	34 English L1	22 1-hour sessions over 1 semester	Included control group; only experimental group showed improvement in both perception and production (intelligibility not measured, but proximity to native target)
MacDonald et al. (1994)	Global accent	23 Chinese	10–30 min	Compared effectiveness of different techniques, but results were inconclusive, in part because of limited time, and uncontrolled aspects of the study
Derwing, Munro, & Wiebe (1997)	Suprasegmentals	13 mixed L1s	12 weeks @ 3 hours/week	Examined effectiveness of instruction for 'fossilized' learners with mean LOR = 10 years; no control group; learners were significantly more intelligible, and comprehensible at end of study
Derwing, Munro, & Wiebe (1998)	Suprasegmentals and segmentals	48 mixed L1s	10 weeks @ 20 min/day	Compared suprasegmental vs segmental instruction with a control; significant improvement in comprehensibility in instructed groups when reading aloud; only suprasegmental group improved in comprehensibility in extemporaneous speech.
Couper (2003)	Various	15 mixed L1s	16 weeks @ 2 hours/week	Evaluated post-test productions of errors targeted on the basis of pre-test findings; significantly fewer errors; no measure of intelligibility or comprehensibility.
Couper (2006)	Epenthesis and absence (omission)	21 mixed L1s	12 sessions @ 30 minutes each	Pre-test, post-test, and delayed post-test; compared to a control group; showed significant improvement – i.e. fewer epenthesis and absence errors
Couper (2011)	Epenthesis in syllable codas		45 minutes	Examined effects of socially constructed metalanguage and critical listening

(*Continued*)

Table 5.1. (Continued)

Study	Linguistic foci	Speakers	Length	Comments
Kennedy & Trofimovich (2010)	Suprasegmentals	10 mixed L1s	3 hours/week for 11 weeks	Accentedness, comprehensibility & fluency – no change in group analysis; individual students' language awareness was correlated with ratings.
Sardegna (2011)	Linking	38 ITAs, mixed L1s	40 hours (50 m × 3 days/wk)	Linking, covert rehearsal model pronunciation strategies, significant improvement maintained long after intervention; no control group
Lord (2010)	Fricative allophones of Spanish stops	8 learners of Spanish; L1 English; 4 received instruction	1 semester of Spanish phonology; 8 weeks study abroad in Mexico	Immersion-only students improved significantly (although marginally), but those who had pronunciation instruction before study abroad made much greater gains; Nativeness Principle-difference from a NS target.
Saalfeld (2012)	Spanish word stress	32 students of Spanish; L1 English	10 hours/wk × 4 wks	Instructed group & control group – perception task; both improved; author suggests that the pretest served as an awareness-raising activity
Saito & Lyster (2012)	English /ɹ/	65 Japanese	2 hours/week for 2 weeks	Compared form-focused instruction with and without corrective feedback; found significant improvement as a result of corrective feedback
Dlaska & Krekeler 2013	Segmentals and suprasegmentals	169 learners of German, mixed L1s	1 time only immediate feedback	Compared effects of implicit vs. explicit feedback on comprehensibility; explicit corrective feedback was significantly more effective than implicit feedback; no control group
McGregor & Sardegna (2014)	Intonation, PRIMARY STRESS, linking & reduction	30 mixed L1s; English was the L2	15 week oral proficiency course	Pronunciation awareness and scaffolding activities; before & after read-aloud test; significant improvement on all measures; no control group
Derwing et al. (2014)	Segmentals and suprasegmentals	6 Vietnamese 1 Cambodian	17 hours (30 min × 3 days/week)	'Plateaued' learners with LOR M =19 years; no control group; significant improvement in learners' perception and production (intelligibility, comprehensibility)

very controlled responses showed stronger positive results than those that were more open-ended (and likely more similar to learners' natural productions). Thomson and Derwing (2014) examined many of the same studies in a narrative review. They also concluded that pronunciation instruction has been shown to have a significant positive effect, but expressed caution in interpreting the results of instruction studies. They noted that the majority of researchers measured a change in accent, rather than improvement in comprehensibility or intelligibility. As they pointed out, and as we have indicated repeatedly in this volume, a change to accent does not ensure an improvement in communication effectiveness.

Curriculum issues

Is pronunciation better taught in stand-alone or integrated classrooms?

The decision whether to offer L2 pronunciation as a specific course or to include it in a general skills course is usually made by program directors or policy makers, rather than individual instructors. As we have seen, in Finland, pronunciation is mandated in the public schools as a part of the students' English language training (Tergujeff, 2012). Similarly, in Quebec, Canada, ESL courses for elementary students incorporate pronunciation within the larger curriculum, although teachers have been observed to do very little pre-planning, relying instead on corrective feedback (Foote et al., 2013). In L2 programs intended for adults, instructors appear to view pronunciation as somewhat important, but the surveys reviewed above (e.g. Foote et al., 2011) suggest that when teachers in general skills programs attempt to include pronunciation, they do not spend much time on it, and are often unsure where to start. This is particularly challenging for those teaching heterogeneous classes, where it is difficult to know how to make the experience valuable to speakers of different L1s. If curricular frameworks and curricula do not provide adequate support to instructors, teachers in communicative classrooms are unlikely to incorporate pronunciation much beyond correcting their students' most obvious errors or giving them software materials to practice in the language lab. Levis and Grant (2003) have proffered three principles for instructors in communicative classrooms to follow: they suggest focusing primarily on suprasegmentals (e.g. THOUGHT GROUPS, intonation, contrastive stress) with some attention to segmentals; ensuring that speaking is the main focus in the class; and ensuring that pronunciation activities are commensurate with the nature of the task (for example, including both planned and unplanned activities for formal and informal speech acts, respectively). Levis and Grant give examples of several activities that could be utilized in classes focusing on speaking and listening "in ways that link features of speech with their communicative functions rather than ways that promote noncontextualized or irrelevant work on the sound system." (p. 14). Thus, the authors suggest that even in a stand-alone pronunciation class, the emphasis should be on genuine communication skills, rather than isolated practice of individual phonological units.

Stand-alone pronunciation courses are generally designed for adults, sometimes in large post-secondary institutions, but also in for-profit contexts. Students usually self-select for such courses, either in recognition of the fact that their pronunciation is holding them back from communicating effectively, or under pressure from their employers, who have indicated that their pronunciation is problematic. Courses dedicated to pronunciation should, as Levis and Grant (2003) have suggested, be geared to enhancing speaking and listening skills in context. However, as we will discuss in Chapter 9, while a plethora of accent reduction programs is available to L2 speakers seeking assistance with pronunciation, the quality of these courses varies widely, and many focus on individual sounds (Derwing, 2008) or aim to eliminate or "reduce" accent *per se*, rather than to improve intelligibility (Thomson, 2013).

A CLOSER LOOK: Who decides what is taught? A Canadian case

The Canadian federal government funds an adult ESL program called LINC (Language Instruction for Newcomers to Canada). This program and several provincially-funded ESL programs adhere to the Canadian Language Benchmarks (CLBs), a comprehensive description of proficiency levels for Speaking, Listening, Reading and Writing. Although the CLBs were first piloted in 1996, and finalized in 2000, it was only in 2012 that pronunciation instruction was acknowledged in a companion document, The CLB Support Kit (Centre for Canadian Language Benchmarks). The CLBs themselves, which were revised and reissued in 2012, give short shrift to pronunciation in the descriptors of each of the levels. Furthermore, there is a presumed linear order of acquisition that is not supported by research findings. What follows are the CLB characterizations of English pronunciation development: Benchmarks 1 & 2: pronunciation difficulties may significantly impede communication. Benchmarks 3 & 4: pronunciation difficulties may impede communication. Benchmark 5: pronunciation difficulties sometimes impede communication. Benchmark 6: pronunciation difficulties may sometimes impede communication. Benchmark 7: pronunciation difficulties may occasionally impede communication. Benchmark 8: pronunciation difficulties seldom impede communication. Benchmark 9: pronunciation rarely impedes communication. Benchmark 10: pronunciation very rarely impedes communication. Benchmarks 11 & 12: pronunciation does not impede communication. There is little other mention of pronunciation in the primary document, leaving the distinct impression that pronunciation will take care of itself. Thus, at a policy level it has been indirectly determined that pronunciation is not important to language program curricula. The short guide for pronunciation instruction in the Support Kit is excellent as far as it goes, but insufficient for providing teachers with the information they need to incorporate pronunciation effectively in their classrooms.

Should pronunciation instruction be offered in shared L1 or mixed L1 classes?

As with integrated versus stand-alone classes, instructors or program directors often have no influence over the composition of a class. In foreign language settings, the majority of students nearly always share the same L1 background, while in ESL and English as an International Language (EIL) contexts, it is not normally feasible (or even desirable) to limit a class to a particular L1. An advantage of a shared L1 is that the students might be expected to share certain problems at both the segmental and suprasegmental levels. Note, however, that as we pointed out in Chapter 3, many issues may be idiosyncratic-not all speakers of even the same dialect of a given L1 will necessarily experience the same pronunciation problems. Students may also have a somewhat inflated notion of their intelligibility if the only L2 speakers with whom they communicate share the same L1 background. Bent and Bradlow (2003) have presented evidence of an interlanguage speech intelligibility benefit, such that in some circumstances, L2 users who speak the same L1 find it easier to understand each other than L2 speakers from different L1 backgrounds. This benefit, however, appears to be minor. Other studies have shown that some L2 speakers do not understand any more of another speaker's productions where the L1 is shared than listeners from other L1 backgrounds (Munro, Derwing & Morton, 2006). On the other hand, if students share difficulties, their awareness can be raised to the point where they can listen for certain features that interfere with intelligibility in their classmates' speech and then peer-correct (Derwing et al., 2014). Mixed L1 pronunciation classes have the advantage of putting students in a position where their communication skills (both speaking and listening) may be pushed to more challenging levels, because they have to interact with students from a range of L1 backgrounds and thus have more difficulties with some accents than others. Encouragingly, as can be seen in Table 5.1, classes of both same L1 and mixed L1s have been shown to make significant improvement as a result of pronunciation instruction.

When should pronunciation be introduced?

Pronunciation is an integral part of language. Given its importance to communication, there is no reason for pronunciation to be held back until learners achieve higher proficiency levels. In fact, learners' phonological development seems to be most active during the first six months to a year of intensive language training and/or exposure to the L2 (Flege, 1988; Munro & Derwing, 2008). In other words, as we saw in Chapter 4, there appears to be a window of maximal opportunity to develop L2 phonological skills that will result in clear, comprehensible L2 speech. Darcy, Ewert, and Lidster (2012) offer excellent suggestions for a progression of foci related to proficiency level, such as having teachers focus on segmentals, spelling, and basic intonation in beginner level classes, when students have little language to work with. At intermediate levels of proficiency, teachers might then provide instruction on additional prosodic aspects of language, such as PHONOTACTICS, word stress and sentence stress, while at more advanced levels, teachers could focus on REGISTER awareness in addition to segmental and suprasegmental instruction. Not every L2 learner has intelligibility problems; some are highly intelligible right from the start, perhaps because of a high aptitude for pronouncing the L2 (see discussion of aptitude in Chapter 3). Even these learners, however, may benefit from some explicit instruction of phenomena that differ in their L1.

Zielinski and Yates (2014) cite an example of a teacher whose beginner-level students indicated on course evaluations that "they wanted to *learn how to speak in their daily lives*" (emphasis in the original). The instructor took that to mean that the students needed more opportunities to speak, so she added community contact activities to her course, in addition to more speaking assignments in class, but the students still asked for lessons on learning to speak in their daily lives. As Zielinski and Yates point out, the students wanted to know "*how* to speak." As soon as the instructor added explicit pronunciation as a regular component of the class, the students no longer requested lessons on how to speak. The benefits of starting early include confidence-building and enhanced comprehensibility. Students' confidence can be compromised if they are worried about their intelligibility (Zielinski, 2012), but it is clear from action research studies carried out in Australia that beginner-level students are able to learn basic metalinguistic vocabulary to talk about pronunciation. For example, they can use some IPA symbols, understand the difference between letters and sounds, count syllables and listen for word stress, and their increased awareness can lead to improved production (Zielinski & Yates, 2014).

Curriculum development

In this section we will address a number of classroom-related topics that are under-researched. Much of what we recommend here comes either from general education principles, or from our own experience as pronunciation instructors.

Curriculum development follows a somewhat cyclical pattern of needs analysis, goal-setting, syllabus design, materials development, instructional planning and implementation, as well as formative and summative assessment, which may result in additional needs analysis, followed by changes to goals, materials, and instruction. In the case of pronunciation, some preliminary negotiation and discussion with the students would be useful to help teachers understand their motivations, as well as to explain concepts and terminology useful for the course. Distinctions among terms such as 'intelligibility' and 'accent' should be discussed, as well as matters such as accent discrimination, and the roles and expectations of interlocutors in conversations.

A CLOSER LOOK: Won't practice make perfect? The role of exposure

What if we left well enough alone and just let pronunciation improve over time as the learners gain more exposure to the language? Won't some of their initial problems just go away? Yes, no, and maybe. Degree of exposure does make a difference. French, Collins, Gagné and Guay (2014) in an ingenious revisiting of data, examined the productions of 42 Grade 6 students who had taken intensive English, and 39 who had traditional 'drip-feed' English in Grade 6. These students were now in Grade 10. French et al. matched the two groups on academic performance in math and French, and assessed aspects of their English abilities. Speech ratings from picture narratives were assigned on 9-point scales for accentedness, fluency, and comprehensibility. Although there were no significant differences between the two groups for accent, the students who had received intensive English in Grade 6 were judged to be significantly more fluent and more comprehensible by the time they reached Grade 10. Thus the intensive English program, although limited in time, had long-term benefits for the speakers' oral skills. It was as though they reached a critical threshold that allowed them to maintain their improved comprehensibility and fluency long after they returned to traditional classrooms.

Adults also show some signs of improvement in the absence of instruction, but generally the changes are most marked in the first year of intensive exposure to the L2. Derwing and Munro (2013) examined the fluency, comprehensibility and accentedness of Mandarin and Slavic language speakers participating in a longitudinal study. Overall, the Slavic language speakers continued to make significant progress in comprehensibility as a result of exposure to English in a wide range of interactions, whereas most of the Mandarin speakers did not. The latter group reported several reasons for their lack of exposure (see Derwing, Munro & Thomson 2008). Some of them would probably have benefited from targeted pronunciation training, because as we have seen from some of the studies reported above, until L2 speakers are made aware of their difficulties, they do not know where to begin. Obviously, not everyone needs pronunciation instruction, but for those who have difficulty being understood, it is clearly called for.

Students' own perceptions of their pronunciation difficulties should also be reviewed and noted. Although they may be unable to pinpoint their own specific problems, many L2 students are aware that their pronunciation sometimes interferes with intelligibility (Derwing, 2003).

Needs analysis

Teachers are normally in the unenviable position of having to make decisions about what to include or exclude in terms of pronunciation content without assistance from others (aside from the students' own reflections); thus a needs analysis takes on tremendous importance. Repeated listening to recordings of students allows the teacher to carefully consider which aspects of L2 pronunciation seem to have the greatest effect on intelligibility and comprehensibility; where students' own perceptions of L2 phonology are weakest; which problems are shared by the majority of students; and which segmentals pose the most difficulties for individuals. Several textbooks have diagnostic tools for assessment purposes (e.g. Gilbert, 2012) to determine where students' perception and production difficulties lie. Table 5.2 shows the basic steps for classroom assessment of students' pronunciation.

Table 5.2. Steps for classroom assessment of pronunciation

Step	Details
Elicit samples of read and extemporaneous speech	Record students reading some simple utterances and ask them to describe what they did yesterday – or some other easily retrievable topic
Assess globally through multiple listenings	Listen several times to the recordings while attending to prosody, effectiveness, comprehensibility
Assess analytically (individual characteristics)	Listen again for individual factors: rhythm, intonation, word stress, segments
Assess student perception	Administer a cloze, dictation, or forced-choice task to determine whether students can perceive the distinctions they were unable to produce
Determine priorities according to hierarchy of importance (Functional Load, etc.)	Plan instruction with a focus on intelligibility and comprehensibility

It is best to elicit samples of both reading aloud and spontaneous speech, because as Levis and Barriuso (2012) have shown, different issues may emerge, depending on the sample type. Munro and Mann (2005) compared accent ratings of individual words, read sentences, a modified version of the Rainbow passage (a reading passage first constructed for speech pathology to determine where articulation problems occur in disordered speech) and a picture description task. They recommended that sentences give the best overall representation of accent. There are pros and cons to asking people to read aloud, because reading aloud is a somewhat specialized skill, and with L2 speakers, there is a possibility that reading passages may be somewhat beyond their own proficiency levels. To circumvent this problem, Munro and Derwing (1994) asked L2 speakers to produce picture narratives, which were then transcribed into standard orthography. The transcribed material was returned to the same participants a week later to read aloud, thereby ensuring control of proficiency levels. In a subsequent listening task, native raters did not distinguish between the spontaneously produced narratives and their read-aloud versions. However, in most reading tasks, especially ones that have been written to capture as many phonemes and intonation patterns as possible in as brief a passage as possible (e.g. the Rainbow passage or the Stella passage from the *Speech Accent Archive* [Weinberger, 2015]), even native speaker readers occasionally stumble over some of the constructions. Although L2 speakers may make grammatical and lexical choice errors in a picture description task, their narratives more closely approximate their usual spontaneous productions. A good compromise, then, is a test that consists of sentences containing high frequency vocabulary, a range of intonation patterns and phonemes that have a high functional load, as well as a picture description task. In addition, listening tasks such as odd-one-out, identification, discrimination and cloze or a short dictation exercise can be used to assess students' perceptions (see Table 6.1 in Chapter 6). Although usually focused on segments, tasks such as these can be adapted to ask students to mark sentence stress and basic intonation, as well.

Goal-setting

Once teachers have identified areas that would most benefit their students in terms of increasing intelligibility and comprehensibility, they can decide what is best covered in class, and what can be assigned as homework. Teachers are advised to discuss the overall outcomes of the perception and production tests with the students, outlining the results and explaining how the most critical elements will be covered throughout the course. Students' responses should be elicited at this time. It is our view that students who are well-informed of the intent of the teaching tasks, and who have been consulted for their input are more likely to invest in activities designed to help them. Goal-setting at this stage, before the actual teaching begins, is best done in concert; with some classes it may be possible for students to help each other if they know what their classmates' goals are. Peer feedback must be handled carefully, and it is at the teacher's discretion to assess the supportiveness of the classroom climate, but the more helpful feedback students receive, the better. Depending on their proficiency level, students' goals may include choosing a model speaker whose style they would like to emulate. Meyers (2013) has suggested that audiovisual recordings from high proficiency, highly intelligible NNSs who share the students' L1 backgrounds are ideal candidates. Allowing students to choose their own models gives them some additional control in making decisions about how they want to sound.

Syllabus design, materials development and resource selection

Whether incorporating pronunciation into a general skills class or teaching a stand-alone course, teachers need to carry out preplanning based on the outcomes of the needs analysis and goal-setting exercises. Typically, several students from different L1 backgrounds share suprasegmental needs but have some idiosyncratic segmental problems (Derwing, Munro, & Wiebe, 1997). It is well worthwhile to consider how consequential each sound contrast is. Recall that in Chapter 3 we discussed the concept of Functional Load as a way to determine the importance of a particular contrast. In deciding which segments students should work on, the Functional Load hierarchy can provide some guidance. Segments lend themselves well to perceptual training with technology (Thomson, 2012a), which can also result in improved production (Thomson, 2011); thus segmental practice can be beneficially assigned as homework. However, the teacher should assist students in understanding where their own segmental problems lie, and it would be useful to do some initial perception practice in small groups that share similar problems, while other students work independently on something else. L2 students can be pointed in the direction of useful websites where they can practice segmentals; but they should also be assigned homework that gives them more exposure to the L2. In a study of adult L2 learners, Derwing, Munro & Thomson (2008) found that greater exposure and interaction in the L2 was tied to greater gains in comprehensibility and fluency. Thus homework that involves contact activities, and even active listening to the radio or podcasts may benefit students.

Selecting suprasegmentals on which to focus should be informed by research and by the degree to which students share certain problems. Although there is a need for far more research on the relationship among prosodic features and intelligibility, we do know in the case of English that prominence (given/new information; emphatic and contrastive stress) is important (Hahn, 2004), as is word stress (Field, 2005; Zielinski, 2008). In recent years, it has been suggested that helping students use 'thought groups' is a good starting point to the introduction of suprasegmentals (Gilbert, 2010). However, one over-arching rule that can guide the instructor is to start instruction with those aspects of oral production that have the greatest effect on intelligibility, and 'zoom in' on lesser components later (Firth, 1992). For instance, if a student cannot be heard because of insufficient volume when speaking the L2, it doesn't really matter how intelligible other aspects of the speech are. Inadequate speech volume (or loudness), or talking with a hand in front of one's mouth, which results in a lack of clarity, are the first things to be addressed because without overcoming these problems, the students will continue to have communication trouble regardless of other interventions.

A variety of print and web-based materials may prove useful in class. For example, textbooks such as *Well Said* (Grant, 2010) and *Sound Concepts* (Reed & Michaud, 2005) and online programs such as Richard Cauldwell's (2005) *Streaming Speech* ⟨www.speechinaction.com⟩ are specifically geared to pronunciation concerns, while *YouTube* videos unrelated to pronunciation *per se* may offer excellent examples of natural speech for classroom use. Teachers may also have to develop their own original materials focusing on the aspects of pronunciation most important to their students, while still covering content prescribed by their language program.

Although general skills textbooks often claim to offer pronunciation activities, a review by Derwing, Diepenbroek, and Foote (2012) of 12 popular ESL series (consisting of 48 textbooks) indicated that an average of only 5% of total content was devoted to pronunciation (range = 0.4%–15%). Several series showed considerable disparity of activities at different proficiency levels, such that some texts had several foci, whereas others in the same series had very few. Some of the series did a poor job of spiraling material, such that students would not be provided with review of pronunciation concepts as they advanced through the series. Clearly, judicious selection of materials on the part of the teacher is necessary. Instructors may wish to refer to books developed for ESL teachers by Celce-Murcia, Brinton, and Goodwin (with Griner) (2010), Hewings (2004), or Yates and Zielinski (2009) for supplementary activities that can be incorporated into either a stand-alone or an integrated skills class.

Instructional planning and implementation

The amount of attention teachers give to pronunciation instruction is partially determined by the program in which they teach. For general skills instruction, pronunciation commonly falls within the speaking and listening components of the course. Depending on program constraints and the identified needs of the students, teachers should aim to find time each day for some preplanned activities, as well as regular corrective feedback on aspects of students' pronunciation that are problematic for intelligibility or comprehensibility. The expectation of homework should be reinforced; one possibility is to ask students to track their progress in an online journal. Homework should not be overwhelming-ten minutes a day each day is far preferable to an hour once a week. If students are assigned practice on websites such as *English Accent Coach* (Thomson, 2012b) or *Phonetics: The Sounds of American English* (University of Iowa, 2001), they should keep the instructor informed of their activities on these sites. The instructor may also choose to assign other homework, for example, recording a SHADOWING activity. Sound editing and recording software such as *Audacity*, which is freely available and easy to use, make it possible for students and teachers to send sound files back and forth. *Audacity* supports 50 languages other than English, so it can be utilized in many non-English settings for the teaching of pronunciation of other languages as well. Teachers can also set up wikis to allow students to send and retrieve homework. The effort spent on developing a wiki is well worth the convenience of having all the homework in one place and not having to keep track of physical recordings.

The activities that teachers choose to implement during class-time should have high interest for the class as a whole. Any number of speaking activities can take on a pronunciation focus. Goodwin (2013) lists several techniques and sources of activities that L2 teachers may find useful. Incorporating audio or audiovisual materials that include a range of voices and dialects is useful to learners (see Harding, 2011), particularly for perception tasks, because ultimately, students may be exposed to many accents as L2 users. Using tongue twisters is one activity that we strongly advise against, despite its appearance in many textbooks on pronunciation. This activity focuses on utterances that have been made deliberately difficult for NSs to produce-consequently it may lead to extreme frustration for struggling learners. For instance, /s/ versus /ʃ/ may be exceptionally difficult for a Cantonese speaker, so until the learner has a modicum of control over these two segments, it would be inappropriate to ask for a rendition of *She sells seashells by the seashore*. We know of no evidence that this type of exercise offers any benefits. Table 5.3 provides a list of popular pronunciation activities and possible foci.

Table 5.3. Popular classroom activities and related foci

Activity	Focus
Shadowing (imitation of a speech model, either simultaneously or slightly after)	Prosody
Mirroring (exact imitation of speech and body movements)	Prosody, body language, general speech habits
Dictation cloze	Perception (final Cs & CCs; Vs; stress)
Short dictation	Perception
Dialogues	Intonation
Self/peer monitoring using video	Multiple aspects of pronunciation

Assessment

Although it seems obvious, it bears pointing out that a fundamental principle of progress assessment is that teachers should test what they have taught. Whether assessment is formal or informal, it should be closely related to the lessons or interventions planned by the instructor. The notion of formative assessment is crucial to determining the direction of the class. Students' perception of minimal pair segments should be checked regularly (easily done on some software which students can then report). A little time each week devoted to language produced in front of the class (either from mirroring or shadowing assignments or practiced dialogues, or short planned talks on a topic of interest) can give the teacher a sense of what seems to be improving and what the next steps should be. Video recording (or audio if video recording is not possible) is invaluable in the language class. Full class presentations should be watched by everyone-they can all see what has improved and what still needs to be worked on, in terms of pronunciation, pragmatics, and body movement. In our experience (Derwing et al., 2014), students can provide their peers with helpful feedback, while at the same time heightening their own awareness of issues that they themselves need to work on. The aspects of pronunciation that have been the focus of attention in class may require additional work, or may be set aside for a week or so to allow a new focus. However, teachers should recycle both the tasks that students liked and that seemed to produce positive results, and features of pronunciation that present ongoing challenges for students. The development of a particular pronunciation feature does not necessarily follow a linear course. Rather, considerable evidence from naturalistic circumstances, at least, shows that some aspects of language are of the "two-steps-forward, one-step-back" variety. In order to ensure that students' progress is significant and lasting, the instructor must attempt to revisit difficult points regularly.

Revision

In programs where students progress to a higher general skills class, the instructor should provide the next teacher with a summary of each students' challenges and progress over the term, as well as the results of a summative assessment. This will make it easier for the next instructor's initial first steps, and will provide continuity for the students. The final or summative assessment should be similar to the pre-teaching tasks to determine where the students have made progress, and what the next steps should be. Both the instructor of the course and the students' next instructor will benefit from identifying tasks that worked best for the students, in terms of (1) bringing their attention to particular aspects of pronunciation, (2) facilitating change (which early on may simply be the destabilization of an erroneous fixed form), and (3) engaging the students. Those aspects of the course that did not seem to be effective should be withdrawn and replaced with new activities.

Preparing students for standardized tests

In the less common context of preparing students for the spoken component of standardized tests, the teacher should have some familiarity with the nature of the test, and, if possible, some experience as an assessor to gain insights into what assessors are expected to do in conjunction with making decisions about pronunciation.

A full discussion of the issues involved with the assessment of pronunciation by standardized tests is beyond the scope of this chapter, but interested readers are directed to Yates, Zielinski, and Pryor's (2011) research report on the newly revised IELTS. Harding's (2011) book on accent and listening assessment is also a fine resource that addresses testing from a variety of viewpoints, exposing the complexity of factors involved in assessing L2 pronunciation, particularly when the voices used in the assessment tool are accented. Pronunciation assessment in general will be discussed in Chapter 6.

Summary

In this chapter, we have reviewed much of the research on L2 pronunciation that has dealt directly with teachers, materials, foci, and outcomes for L2 students' pronunciation. We have seen that L2 pronunciation instruction can be effective, in that L2 speakers' perception and production can improve significantly as a direct result of teaching. While many lacunae remain, the tremendous upswing in interest in L2 pronunciation in the last few years is encouraging.

CHAPTER 6

Assessment of L2 pronunciation

We once taught in a language program where the director put a premium on assessment. All tests had to be vetted by either the director or the co-director, and all students had to be tested at the end of every semester. Strangely enough, speaking skills in general, and pronunciation in particular, were required to be assessed in a written test. The teachers had to be creative to come up with exam questions that supposedly accessed students' speaking skills in writing! Clearly, pronunciation assessment should involve aural/oral skills. It is possible, using recordings, to devise reasonable written assessments of perception skills, but pronunciation itself has to be assessed via oral tasks. In this chapter, we will address some of the issues associated with the assessment of L2 pronunciation.

Introduction

Testing is a very large subfield of applied linguistics. Although pronunciation testing has received far less attention than the evaluation of other aspects of L2 development (Isaacs, 2014), it has recently come to the fore in SLA research (Carey, Mannell, & Dunn, 2011; Harding, 2011, 2013; Isaacs & Thomson, 2013; Yates, Zielinski & Pryor, 2011). Our focus in this chapter will be on pronunciation assessment in some commonly-used standardized tests as well as assessment issues faced by classroom teachers. Since our goal is to provide a basic introduction to the topic, we will not cover many of the issues that arise in testing in general.[1]

Texts on language assessment commonly classify tests into a variety of subtypes including diagnostic, achievement, and proficiency tests. The first two of these are typically used in the classroom, while proficiency tests are often employed by educational institutions for admission purposes, e.g. *IELTS* (International English Language Testing System); *TOEFL* (Test of English as a Foreign Language); *TOEIC* (Test of English for International Communication).

---

1. Readers looking for a more comprehensive overview of testing should consult a survey textbook such as Bachman and Palmer's (2010) *Language Assessment in Practice: Developing Language Assessments and Justifying their Use in the Real World.* For more detail on testing pronunciation and listening in particular, we recommend Harding's (2011) book, *Accent and Listening Assessment.*

Testing pronunciation in the classroom

As we noted in Chapter 4, students in any given class may differ widely in their pronunciation needs, even if they come from similar L1 backgrounds. Some may have
only minor difficulties in producing intelligible speech, while others may be constantly
frustrated by unsuccessful attempts to get their ideas across to others. Moreover, they
may be unable to pinpoint the sources of their difficulties themselves. In a study of
advanced German learners, Dlaska and Krekeler (2008) reported that "even experienced L2 learners seem to find it difficult to self-assess correctly their pronunciation
skills" (p. 506). Similarly, when Derwing (2003) interviewed 100 adult students of
intermediate level English from mixed L1 backgrounds, she found that over half of
them attributed communication problems directly to their pronunciation, yet when
she asked them to specify their difficulties, over a third were unable to so, and those
who did mention individual issues cited a small set of salient segments, 26 of which
were "th", and 12 were the infamous /l/ – /ɹ/ distinction. Only 11% of the responses
pertained to prosody. These findings suggest that many learners require guidance
from their instructors in the selection of specific pronunciation foci to improve their
overall communicative effectiveness. In other cases, they may simply need reassurance
that their speech patterns are highly intelligible and comprehensible. The purpose of
assessment is not solely to identify what one does wrong – it is about what matters for
communication.

Most teachers are likely familiar with the three types of tests that are most typical
of the language classroom: initial NEEDS ASSESSMENT, ongoing FORMATIVE ASSESS-
MENTS and SUMMATIVE ASSESSMENTS. However, as we saw in Chapter 5, a number
of instructor surveys have shown a general discomfort with teaching pronunciation
altogether, which suggests that many instructors may not feel at ease developing
and implementing testing instruments (Breitkreutz et al., 2001; Burns, 2006; Darcy
et al. 2012; Foote et al., 2011; Henderson et al., 2012; MacDonald, 2002). They may
choose to ignore pronunciation testing altogether and to rely on commercially pack-
aged materials for pronunciation instruction, if they teach pronunciation at all beyond
unsystematic provision of corrective feedback.

Needs assessment

A needs assessment is a type of diagnostic test, commonly administered at the beginning of a course of instruction. Its goal is to identify the students' current capabilities and to determine directions for instruction over the semester. Although many
language programs have a curriculum in place, a needs assessment is valuable for
tuning instruction to the individual needs of the learners. Regardless of whether a
teacher is assigned to a stand-alone pronunciation class, a speaking class with a rich

pronunciation component, or a general skills language class, a needs assessment provides a basis for the development of lesson plans and suitable activities that will address each student's needs.

What makes a good initial needs assessment? We recognize that instructors are often constrained by time and institutional requirements, but, ideally, each student should be assessed by the instructor on an individual basis. Below we give our desiderata for a well-designed needs assessment.

Fast implementation. To facilitate individual testing, the instrument should be relatively brief, and easy to use. A checklist approach in which the evaluator marks certain features on a score sheet can help achieve this goal.

Recording. Given the technology now available, teachers can digitally record their learners easily. This serves a two-fold purpose. On the one hand, it allows the teacher to listen to the learners' productions as many times as necessary in an offline setting. On the other hand, the initial recording can be played back to students for awareness-raising purposes, as a means of pointing out areas that need work. This can be done individually by sending the students sound files, using freely available software such as *Audacity* (see Chapter 7 for more information on the use of technology in the classroom). Furthermore, the initial needs assessment recording can be used at the end of term to show the students their progress.

Multiple elicitations. Levis and Barriuso (2012) demonstrated that the nature of the speaking task affects the kinds of errors that L2 learners produce. They found large differences in vowel and consonant errors produced in conversational speech as opposed to speech that was read aloud. In assessment, teachers need to recognize the tradeoffs that come with choosing one elicitation method versus another. Reading tasks offer the advantage of requiring speakers to produce particular segments, words, and grammatical constructions, but they sacrifice the naturalness of unrehearsed oral production. Extemporaneous speech elicited through interviews and picture narratives may give a very different picture of the students' capabilities. However, such tasks don't allow an assessor to target particular items for evaluation. For these reasons, we suggest that a combination of elicitation methods be used (see Chapter 5). If students are asked to read a short passage or set of sentences, the vocabulary and grammatical structures should be of high frequency and should correspond to idiomatic spoken language, as opposed to the complex, "bookish" structures found in some written texts.

Issues known to be important for intelligibility. Although research has not completely described which aspects of pronunciation are most important for intelligibility, we now have some indication of aspects of accent that compromise listener understanding. To be as comprehensive as possible, the test should cover prosodic elements, segmentals, and global speaking habits. Within these categories we know that prominence (or what Hahn, 2004, called primary stress), word stress, high functional load segments, vocal projection, and speech rate all affect comprehension.

Perception. The ability to accurately perceive segmental and prosodic phenomena in the L2 is related to production ability. To establish the source of a student's difficulty, it is necessary to test perception. If the learner cannot distinguish phonologically important aspects of the L2, then work on perception is called for; however, often a learner will be able to perceive a given segment or prosodic element but will be unable to produce it. The instructor's course of action will be determined, in part, by the results of the perception tasks on the test.

Outcomes. It should be possible to translate the results of a good needs analysis into specific recommendations for classroom practice and activities, providing students with personal feedback on their performance, and, in some instances, recommendations for homework that could benefit their perception and production.

Formative assessment

The chief purpose of formative assessment or progress testing is to determine whether the instruction provided has been beneficial and whether goals have been achieved. If they have, the test gives the instructor an opportunity to set new goals, and to determine whether other problems have developed. If the original goals have not been met, then the teacher can decide whether to try different instructional techniques. Progress tests need not be dramatically different from needs assessments, except that their scope is typically narrower; that is, they normally focus on the concerns that have previously been identified.

Summative assessments

Summative assessments are usually intended to determine a student's attainment at the end of a course of instruction. These tests are often used to decide whether a student will move on to another level or will remain at the current level. Apart from their higher stakes status, summative tests differ little from progress tests.

Test materials

When assessing students, instructors have the choice of using tools available in pronunciation textbooks, developing their own instruments, or employing a combination of the two. Resources such as Celce-Murcia et al.'s (2010) *Teaching Pronunciation* and Gilbert's (2012) *Clear Speech Teacher's Resource and Assessment Book* "both offer test content (such as diagnostic reading passages) and rubrics to guide testing, such as the *Speaking Performance Scale for UCLA Oral Proficiency Test for Nonnative TAs*" (Celce-Murcia et al. 2010, p. 486). Teachers can also develop an eclectic set of materials tuned to the needs of their students and their institution. In-house tests should include items that are not identical to practice materials used throughout the term, in order

A CLOSER LOOK: Testing pronunciation through written tests?

In a book on language testing, Robert Lado, one of the 20th century's most influential L2 teaching specialists, proposed that pronunciation skills could be evaluated using pen and paper tests when it was impractical to obtain oral productions (Lado, 1961). While Lado did not claim that this indirect testing was perfectly equivalent to oral assessment, the very idea of a written pronunciation test may seem ludicrous in principle; in other words it lacks FACE VALIDITY. However, perhaps because of convenience and low cost, Lado's idea took hold in some EFL programs-particularly in Japan, where several major colleges even incorporated the tests into their entrance examinations. Only a handful of researchers have ever taken an interest in investigating whether these tests are actually of any use. One of these was Gary Buck, who published an empirical study entitled "Written tests of pronunciation: Do they work?" (Buck, 1989). Buck's questions, all taken from published tests used in Japan at the time, required EFL learners to perform a variety of tasks, including matching sounds with different spellings (*Which word contains the same sound as the underlined letters in least?*), identifying stressed syllables (*What is the number of the stressed syllable in curiosity?*), and selecting the odd item out (*In which of the following words is the qu spelling pronounced differently than in the others?*). For comparison purposes Buck recorded the test-takers reading aloud the words used on the written test, as well as several sentences, and some extemporaneous speech. Then the recordings were rated for accuracy. The results were definitive. First, the written tests were unreliable: different versions of the test gave wildly different results. The three types of oral test (words, sentences and extemporaneous speech), however, were moderately reliable, such that scores on one of the tests were correlated with scores on the other two. Second, the written tests did not provide a valid assessment of oral skills: correlations between the results on the two test types were low. While Buck couldn't rule out the possibility that better designed written tests might give higher reliability and greater validity, his findings indicate that relying on quick pen and paper evaluations of pronunciation is misguided.

to determine whether instruction has transferred beyond the items taught. Instructors may wish to use electronic sources for some of the perceptual tasks, particularly segments, such as the *English Accent Coach* (Thomson, 2014), which can be administered in a computer lab.

Once the initial assessments have been completed, the instructor should look for class commonalities that are high priority to best utilize class-time. Wherever possible, students should be provided with individual feedback and given advice about independent study opportunities. Finally, teachers may find it advantageous to work cooperatively in the collection of recordings and subsequent analysis to achieve consensus judgments. Such collaboration promotes professional development in that less experienced teachers can benefit from the expertise of their colleagues.

What does the instructor need to know to evaluate effectively?

Assessing and teaching pronunciation requires a reasonably good familiarity with the sound inventory of the language being taught, and the associated phonetic symbols. A clear understanding of the nature of L2 articulations provides instructors with the tools they need to explain how to modify segmental productions. For example, they may instruct students to round the lips, move the tongue farther ahead, touch the lower lip to the upper teeth, or move the tongue back from an /s/ position to produce /ʃ/. These simple instructions require an understanding of the articulatory relationships among sounds in the target language. Such knowledge is needed to establish how students are actually using their articulators and to help them produce more intelligible utterances in the L2.

The instructor should also understand the nature of prosodic elements; weaknesses in English stress, rhythm, and intonation can all interfere with intelligibility. To assist learners in these areas, the teacher should have a comfortable familiarity with prosodic patterns. Accurate pronunciation assessment also requires an ability to approach L2 speech analytically. Such a skill can be developed through experience listening to foreign-accented productions while focusing on specific elements of the speech such as vowels, consonants, stress, and intonation. *The Speech Accent Archive* (Weinberger, 2015) is a particularly useful source of speech material for practice with a wide range of accents. Finally, it is important to have insights into the pronunciation learning process. Most speakers are unlikely to become nativelike, but for learners with intelligibility issues, classroom instruction can indeed be beneficial. Not every L2 speaker needs work on intelligibility; in fact many learners are highly comprehensible and intelligible right from the beginning. Depending on the learning context, they may need no pronunciation instruction at all. However, some learners in this position may choose to work on their pronunciation, nonetheless. As long as intelligibility issues have been addressed, we see no harm in helping learners with any additional aspects of pronunciation that they wish to pursue. Another aspect of the learning process that it is important to be aware of is the Window of Maximal Opportunity during the beginning stages of language learning in the L2 environment. Because pronunciation is most amenable to change during the first several months of acquisition, the sooner learners receive pronunciation feedback, the better. Finally, it is important for teachers to recognize that individuals will exhibit different learning trajectories, even when they share the same L1 background.

Testing pronunciation beyond the classroom

Pronunciation is increasingly a factor in high-stakes proficiency testing carried out by large organizations, such as *Educational Testing Service* (ETS); *The British Council*

A CLOSER LOOK: Classroom test content

The types of speech materials suitable for classroom testing are similar to many of those used in pronunciation research (Derwing & Munro, 2005a). For perception testing, teachers may opt to produce utterances aloud themselves or to use recorded materials. A danger in the first case is that the instructor may be inconsistent in producing the items or may hyper-articulate, giving the students unnatural models. Recordings take time to prepare, but provide consistency and can be used across multiple test sessions. The most common listening tasks include discrimination (recognizing differences between sounds, words, or longer utterances), identification (indicating which of two or more sounds, words, or longer utterances has been presented), odd-one-out, cloze (fill in the missing words in a written narrative as the audio version is played), dictation (write utterances in standard orthography), and multiple choice match the meaning (choose a synonymous item from a list). Table 6.1 provides examples of each of these. Notice that virtually any task type is suitable for any type of target.

Table 6.1. Examples of tasks for testing perception

Target	Task type	Students hear	Students' task is to
vowels	discrimination	/biɫ/ /bɪɫ/	say whether the words are the same or different
consonants	identification	/naɪt/	say whether they heard *night* or *light*
lexical stress	odd-one-out	/ɹɪˈkɔɹd/ /ɹɪˈkɔɹd/ /ˈɹɛkɪd/	say which item is different from the others
final consonants	cloze	He loved to watch the cars.	fill in the missing words in *He loved to __ the __.*
general listening	dictation	A short passage selected by the tester	write the entire passage in standard orthography
contrastive stress	match the meaning	*John went to the office yesterday.* (contrastive stress is placed on one of the nouns)	choose among a) John, not Fred. b) office, not store. c) yesterday, not today.

For production, it is advisable, though not entirely necessary, to record test-takers to allow later analysis. Production assessment instruments are available in pronunciation textbooks. Both reading (to target specific phonetic details) and extemporaneous speech (to assess fluency and other properties of more naturally-produced speech) should be elicited when possible. As we mention in Chapter 5, it is advisable to have students read aloud sentence-length utterances and then provide an extemporaneous speech sample. The read-aloud material should target sounds and connected speech patterns that are likely to challenge L2 learners and to have an impact on intelligibility. Extemporaneous speech may consist of monologues addressing simple questions such as "What did you do yesterday?/ What was the best day of your life?" Beginner-level students who need additional support in providing a speech sample may be asked to describe a simple picture or picture story. It is also advisable to record an actual conversation with the tester, an approach that provides the most ecologically valid window on the learner's oral skills. The recorded production material may be used not only for pronunciation assessment, but also for other aspects of oral production such as grammar and vocabulary.

IDP: IELTS Australia, Cambridge English Language Assessment; The Canadian Centre for Language Benchmarks; and *Pearson.* Similar tests are available for other languages as well, such as the Diplôme d'études en langue française (DELF) for French, administered by the *International Centre for French Studies. The German Adult Education Association,* using the Common European Framework, has developed proficiency tests for ten languages, collectively referred to as the TELC (The European Language Certificates). Pronunciation assessment is often implemented as part of a more general speaking assessment, and may not always be a clearly separable component. None of the widely used English tests, for instance, reports a pronunciation score to test-takers. This tendency may reflect the difficulty in isolating pronunciation skills from other aspects of speaking proficiency such as grammatical accuracy, fluency, vocabulary use, discourse markers and pragmatics. Even when assessing pronunciation using a formalized rubric, examiners can differ widely both in their assignment of scores and the aspects of speech to which they attend most closely. The demands on the assessor are especially evident in real-time high-stakes evaluations such as the IELTS. For instance, in a study of assessor reliability, Yates, Zielinski and Pryor (2011) reported that only 30% of assessments matched the IELTS-assigned score of Band 7. Furthermore, the assessors were more likely to incorrectly assign lower rather than higher scores to Band 7 speakers. The consequences of such inconsistencies and biases can be quite dramatic, given that IELTS scores are frequently used in decisions regarding admission into academic programs, awarding of professional qualifications, and vetting of visa applications from potential immigrants to such countries as Australia and Canada.

Reliability and validity

RELIABILITY and CONSTRUCT VALIDITY are two fundamental concepts in testing. The first broadly refers to the likelihood of obtaining the same results when a test is administered more than once. In a well-designed test, this must be the case, regardless of who carries out the assessment and irrespective of geographical location. While there

A CLOSER LOOK: Sound relationships

Although we do not believe that pronunciation teachers need to be expert phoneticians, we are quite convinced that a basic knowledge of articulatory phonetics is indispensible. An example of the usefulness of recognizing the articulatory relationships among sounds comes from our early days as ESL teachers. One of our colleagues complained that her Vietnamese students tended to 'drop' final /t/ from words like *feet* (/fit/). However, when she worked on this problem with them, they started to produce /s/ at the end of the words (i.e. /fis/). She was distraught, believing that she had unwittingly taught them to replace one error with another. What she failed to recognize was that the students' /fs/ pronunciations were actually closer to /fit/ than their original productions of /fi/. In fact, in terms of segments, the revised pronunciation was 2/3 correct. They had perceived and produced a final consonant that was produced in the right (alveolar) place of articulation and was voiceless. All that remained was to teach them to produce a stop rather than a fricative. Had she made use of this bit of phonetic knowledge, she would have known what to do next and would have gained more confidence in her teaching skills.

are many types of validity, the essence of the concept is whether or not a test measures what it purports to measure. Although reliability is one necessary condition for validity, many other conditions must be satisfied to ensure a valid test. These matters are covered in detail in many introductory textbooks on testing and assessment.

Problems with reliability can occur in pronunciation testing because of the heavy demands placed on human evaluators. Real time testing, which refers to carrying out an evaluation in a live situation, as opposed to listening to a recording which can be played multiple times, is taxing, even for the most skilled assessors. It is impossible to attend equally to all aspects of the L2 speaker's speech simultaneously, and therefore giving an accurate assessment of each dimension is extremely difficult. Another reliability issue is the variability across test-takers in the language content they choose, which makes fair comparisons across candidates challenging. Different testers may differ in terms of degree of experience with particular accents, which in some studies has been shown to influence their scoring (Carey et al., 2011; Winke, Gass & Myford, 2013), although other researchers have not found an influence of familiarity (Isaacs & Thomson, 2013). Still one other reliability concern is that of differences across human assessors, aside from their familiarity with accents. Assessors will not always agree about a given speech sample, perhaps because they have attended to different features of the sample, or because they interacted slightly differently with candidates in live situations, even when following identical scripts. The chief method that testing organizations use to overcome reliability problems is to train evaluators rigorously and require them to recalibrate periodically. However, even with these precautions, the degree of reliability in a test may fall short of a desired criterion.

A CLOSER LOOK: The nature of pronunciation tests

Harding (2012) uses two dimensions to characterize tests. The *holistic-analytic* dimension refers to the degree to which the evaluation aims at a global description of the speaker's capabilities, while *analytic* evaluation zeroes in on specific details of the speaker's pronunciation. Harding also uses a scale ranging from *impressionistic*, which focuses on ratings, to *objective*, which may entail acoustic measurements, automated scoring, or transcription by a human listener. Of course, most tests will fall somewhere on the continua represented by the scales. For classroom purposes, teachers may assess both holistically and analytically, though they are most likely to rely on impressionistic rather than objective aspects of assessment. In our experience, the use of acoustic measurement in classroom contexts is very rare if it occurs at all.

Technology and assessment

An emerging approach to general language testing, aimed at removing the human variability factor from assessment, is the application of language technology. Tests such as *Pearson* (formerly *Versant*) use artificial intelligence developed on the basis of rating corpora from many humans to score aspects of oral language proficiency. Tests such as these are likely to be reliable, since the system should give the same outcome when presented with a given speech sample multiple times. However, as Isaacs (2014) points out, it is improbable that "the automated system is sensitive to the same properties of speech that human raters attend to when rating" (p. 11). Furthermore, the test's validity depends on many of the same factors that influence human-administered tests. If the speech material is elicited under contrived conditions (e.g. a recording with no interlocutor present) there is no guarantee that it reflects the speaker's typical communicative abilities. The best automatic testing system is one that gives the same results as a reliable cohort of human raters judging a truly communicative speech sample. Currently, most evaluation, whether human or machine based, is carried out on somewhat contrived speech samples that are not naturally communicative. Even so, automatic testing systems vary in their ability to match human judges on the various dimensions of speech. Such systems have not proven sufficiently accurate to be adopted in the most prominent tests such as *TOEFL* and *IELTS*. For instance, Kibishi, Hirabayashi, and Nakagawa's (2014) acoustically-based method yielded significant correlations with human ratings for global pronunciation (which appears to be an accent rating), but relationships for intelligibility, though significant, were noticeably lower. While this work is promising, we note that the Kibishi et al. (2014) study included only speakers with fairly high levels of intelligibility. In addition, their use of scores for native speakers of English as part of their calculations may have distorted the correlations. Not only is there a need for a broader range of intelligibility, but improvements in the accuracy of the automated scoring are necessary for the test to be valid.

Summary

Pronunciation testing remains an underdeveloped aspect of language assessment in general. The relatively limited progress in this area is due to the complexities involved in collecting speech samples that reflect genuine communicative output and in evaluating them in a way that focuses on the key components of intelligibility and comprehensibility that we emphasize throughout this book. For classroom purposes, teachers can make use of a growing set of published resources, both print-based and electronic, to assist them with needs assessments, formative assessments and summative assessments. However, they cannot do without knowledge of the articulatory, prosodic, and perceptual aspects of speech, as well as a willingness to improvise according to the needs of their students. In high-stakes testing, technology appears to offer some promise as means of reducing the heavy demands on language assessors. It remains to be seen, however, the degree to which automatic assessment can be trusted to provide accurate, fair evaluations of learners' oral productions.

CHAPTER 7

Technology in L2 pronunciation instruction

In pronunciation teaching, technology can be a double-edged sword. Several years ago, the authors attended a lecture given by Bernard Rochet, a phonetician and instructor of French. While demonstrating some commercial software that promised speech recognition for learners of French, he showed that it was possible to severely mispronounce a word in several different ways, yet receive feedback each time from the software indicating that the utterance was correct. Rochet argued that any speech recognition software used for pronunciation purposes has to be tailored to the specific needs of the learners. Years later, we undertook a study with our colleague, Mike Carbonaro. We wanted to know whether a program such as Dragon Naturally Speaking dictation software would identify the same intelligibility problems in L2 accented speech as human listeners do. We piloted the experiment with a relatively proficient speaker of Cantonese-accented English. The training component of the program took her three times as long to complete as the pilot native speaker. Both our research assistant and the L2 participant were close to tears by the end, out of sheer frustration. When we submitted our request to the ethics research board for approval for this study, we had not anticipated just how difficult it would be for our L2 participants. Technology can be a great resource and supplement to the teacher's lessons, but any software program's value should be carefully assessed before it is recommended to language learners.

Introduction

Let's begin this chapter with an exercise in fantasy. Imagine a future time when technology has evolved far beyond its current capabilities. If you were a language learner, what sort of help would you want to get from a computer? Your answer to that question will depend to a great extent on how you feel about interacting with computers in general. If you are a technophile, you might imagine a computer that you can speak to effortlessly, that "understands" what you are trying to say and that responds to you in a very personal way. Like Theodore Twombly, the lead character in the movie *Her* (2013), perhaps you would be happy to spend a great deal of time interacting with it and would judge your experiences to be worthwhile. You might be excited by a system that could do the following:

a. evaluate your speech intelligibility and comprehensibility automatically.
b. identify prosodic and segmental problems in your productions that compromise effective communication.

c.   prevent you from making humiliating errors, and spare you the embarrassment of having your errors corrected in person.

d.   provide you with a series of interesting exercises with feedback to help you with the difficulties identified in (b) and (c).

e.   monitor your learning, providing you with regular progress measures and a pronunciation skills assessment at the end of instruction.

Of course, not everyone feels so enthusiastic about learning via computers, and your own personal expectations may range from 'somewhat skeptical' to nearly the opposite of what is described above. Language is, after all, a social tool that we use to develop and enhance our relationships with other humans. Some people find interacting with computers unsatisfying, time-consuming, and even alienating. This is not surprising given that current technological capabilities do not even come close to matching the implementations described above. AUTOMATIC SPEECH RECOGNITION (ASR) systems used on customer service telephone lines, for example, sometimes perform poorly, leaving users frustrated and anxious to talk to a living human being. In the classroom, 'technical glitches' seem to happen far more often than they are supposed to, resulting in wasted time and abandoned lesson plans. And many learners who have tried commercial CALL packages become disappointed with them when they find them to be repetitive and mechanical.

To give us some perspective on the role of technology in the classroom, let us consider some technological advances from the last century. The ballpoint pen, the portable tape recorder, the photocopier, and the laptop computer were all innovations that revolutionized learning. And all of them entailed periods of adjustment. The ballpoint, for instance, had existed for decades before becoming a commercially viable product. Early designs leaked profusely, became clogged, and distributed ink unevenly-so much that the original developer eventually abandoned his patent. However, improvements eventually led to writing instruments that were far superior to the nib pens commonly used before. (If you don't know what those were like, there are good reasons!) We have no expectation that technological change will be any different for teachers, learners, and researchers in the future. More than likely all of us will find ourselves adjusting to new technologies for the rest of our lives. This does not mean, however, that consumers of educational technology should settle for hardware and software that fail to deliver their promised advantages. Rather, language teaching specialists need to critically consider the merits and drawbacks of new products. In the sections that follow we identify several technological trends that either have an impact on pronunciation teaching now, or promise to do so in the future. We point out some of their advantages and current limitations.

Implementing technology in classroom pedagogy

Perhaps the best promise technology offers with respect to pronunciation has to do with individualized assessment and instruction-a pedagogical approach much valued by Pierre Delattre, as mentioned in Chapter 2. Below, we expand on some of the directions such individualization is taking; however, it is currently up to the teacher to decide how to individualize lessons for L2 students. A realistic expectation for contemporary classrooms is that teachers monitor and assess students' pronunciation difficulties and direct learners to appropriate technological resources and content for self-study, in addition to designing classroom activities to address problems shared by the majority of students.

Current technology allows for easy access to activities that could be conducted in the past, but only with considerable effort on the part the instructor. Goodwin (2013) for instance, discusses the use of shadowing (imitating a spoken model either at the same time or slightly after) and mirroring (imitating both speech and body movements) with *YouTube* or other readily available digital multimedia tools. Although imitation activities have been the cornerstone of pronunciation classes for decades, perhaps centuries, they have been roundly criticized for being boring and demotivating. Technology cannot solve these problems, but it has made it much easier to find natural, diverse, and interesting content for imitation purposes. For example, Meyers (2013) discussed a multi-step mirroring project, in which comprehensibility problems were first identified for ITAs. Then the students chose a proficient speaker to emulate (either native or nonnative) using a *YouTube* clip in a multi-week imitation task. All the ITAs gave a presentation both before and after their mirroring experiences. Meyers reported on one student's progress, concluding that she improved in her problem areas as a result of mirroring. The student had chosen a highly intelligible nonnative speaker who shared her ethnic background to serve as a model. Her final one-minute 18 second presentation, which can be viewed online (Meyers, 2013), showed evidence of improved focal stress and pitch, as well as better nonverbal body language.

Another benefit of technology is that it offers more possibilities for dual-purpose activities, as Goodwin (2008) illustrated in her discussion of classes for ITAs. When she assigned deep listening activities, including transcription, marking of intonation and stress, as well as shadowing, she had the ITAs listen to interviews with undergraduates. The interviews dealt with the day-to-day lives of the NS students, their motives for their choice of study, their work habits, and their other interests. Since the ITAs were from other cultures, this information was of real value to them from a sociocultural and teaching perspective. Thus, the language the ITAs were focused on for pronunciation purposes was authentic, and its content was of high interest.

In both integrated skills and stand-alone pronunciation classrooms, teachers can post audio and video clips, links, and other exercises to a wiki or other website so that students can practice material covered in class and retrieve and submit individual homework assignments. One advantage of such postings is that teachers can ask students to focus on their own problem areas, rather than taking up valuable class time addressing an issue that affects only one or two students. This represents a major step forward over traditional language labs, because it offers students the freedom to determine when and where they do their assignments, and how long to spend on them. The availability of inexpensive but good quality digital recording devices, including smartphones, has added to the convenience of downloading and uploading audio files for such a purpose.

An advantage offered by contemporary synchronous audio-video software, such as *Skype*, is the ease with which interactions can be set up with speakers of the learners' L2. Just as students can correspond with penpals for L2 writing practice, learners have the opportunity to interact orally in the L2 in a relatively authentic way. As observed by Bueno Alastuey (2010) in an investigation of voice chats among language learners (both with NSs and NNSs), communication breakdowns as a result of pronunciation difficulties occurred, giving learners the chance to recognize some of their recurring problems. Improvements in Internet bandwidth and speed and in the audiovisual capabilities of computers have made such interactions more accessible and much easier for an instructor to organize.

Both web-based software and dedicated smartphone apps are emerging as resources for individual pronunciation learning. When Foote and Smith (2013) surveyed 51 applications available for smartphones and tablets (25 for iOS and 26 for Android, with only 6 in common), they found widely varying quality. Also, the majority of apps required a certain amount of prior knowledge on the part of the user to be at all effective. There was a strong focus on individual segments. Although apps offer potentially viable opportunities for pronunciation practice with both perception and production, teachers are advised to read reviews and recommendations from authoritative sources and then to screen apps carefully before recommending them to students.

Using digitized speech

As we noted in Chapter 2, the commercial availability of analog recording equipment, such as tape recorders and record players, was one of the most important technological innovations in language teaching during the 1900s. However, the 21st century digital capabilities of computers, tablets, and smartphones reflect another giant leap for the field. Because digital recordings can be replayed without having to locate a particular

A CLOSER LOOK: Radio for L2 English users

Sometimes old technology has been "rediscovered" as a way of teaching English to learners. In Canada, the Canadian Broadcasting Corporation (CBC) and the Government of the province of Manitoba agreed to broadcast current news stories in English written at an intermediate level. In 2010, the Government of the province of Alberta decided to emulate Manitoba's project, thinking that it would be an effective cost-savings to produce podcasts for the whole province and to provide accompanying lessons on a website. Initially, it was assumed that any newcomer would benefit from the radio shows, despite the fact that the weekly lessons would be offered for L2 learners at a single proficiency level (CLB 4), and that the monthly lessons would be offered at CLB 6 (see A Closer Look: Who decides what is taught? in Chapter 5 for a description of the CLBs). Although government authorities promised accountability at every turn, they were convinced that broadcasting into the ether would be the best way to reach learners, possibly allowing for the phasing out of provincially-funded ESL classrooms altogether. In February of 2011, the release of *Learning English with CBC* was announced at a press conference. For the very first time, it was stated publicly by an elected official that *Learning English with CBC* would be a superb classroom tool, which it has turned out to be. Many teachers now use this program and tie in pronunciation lessons to the weekly newscasts. However, the number of independent listeners who have opted to study on their own is unknown, and practically speaking, unknowable.

spot on a tape or record (a feature known as "random access"), it is far easier to select very specific pieces of speech material to be used for listening and repetition purposes. Digital recordings are also of higher quality and can be replicated for redistribution and backup purposes with no loss of fidelity, whereas analog recordings degrade every time they are reproduced. This is important because both analog recordings, such as tapes, and digital media, such as CDs and hard drives, are subject to failure. Because perfect backups of digital files can be made, it is possible for such recordings to remain available indefinitely. Some specific implementations of digital recording for L2 learners include talking dictionaries, which can give learners an accurate rendition of individual words, sometimes with more than one speaking voice. Teachers may need to provide support, however, for words that have more than one rendition because of dialectal variation.

A more advanced use of digital recording is audio feedback training, which is available on both smart phone and computer apps. An example of this is the *English Accent Coach* (Thomson, 2012b), distinguished from many other programs by the use of multiple voices to implement HIGH VARIABILITY TRAINING, which has been found to be effective in empirical studies. The software plays words containing target sounds for a learner to identify, and then provides feedback on the learner's perception. This approach helps develop knowledge about the boundaries of segmental categories.

Preliminary evaluation of the software (Thomson, 2012a) suggests that perception of L2 sounds can improve significantly through the use of this tool.

Currently-available software does not generally take advantage of all that is known about effective L2 perceptual training. For instance, phonetics research has shown that manipulation of speech to enhance particular acoustic features, thereby making them more salient, can improve perception if the learners are gradually exposed to more natural stimuli (Guion & Pederson, 2007; Iverson, Hazan, & Bannister, 2005; Jamieson & Morosan, 1986). Of course, teachers have always used exaggeration to model difficult sounds and even prosodics, but software can achieve the same goal more systematically and can taper off the exaggerated forms more effectively than humans can. Wang and Munro (2004) observed that Mandarin speakers of English mistakenly regarded the distinction between /i/ and /ɪ/ as a length difference, when in North American English it is primarily a vowel quality distinction. Using synthetic speech, they exposed learners to tokens of these vowels that were designed to refocus their attention to quality rather than length. By gradually adding more natural vowels to the training regimen, the authors found that the learners were eventually able to identify the two vowels much more accurately than at the outset of the study.

Digital recording continues to become more sophisticated, but at the same time more convenient and easy to use. Freeware such as *Audacity* and *Pocket WavePad* are readily available to instructors and students for straightforward recording and playback. Although these programs have the capacity to do much more, the recording function alone makes them valuable as a supplement to the language classroom.

Visual representations of speech

As mentioned in Chapter 2, early speech scientists looked for ways to represent the acoustic properties of speech on the printed page. At that time it was expected that visual depictions of speech might help learners to match the productions of a native-speaker model. While dedicated sound spectrographs were once used for visual speech analysis in laboratory settings, speech technology has advanced to the point that waveforms and spectrograms can be generated by any user on nearly any type of computer platform. Inexpensive or freely-available software, such as *Praat* (Boersma & Weenink, 2014) produces displays such as the one in Figure 7.1, which can be highly informative to phoneticians. Waveforms show the time-varying amplitude of the speech: large upward and downward peaks indicate louder parts such as vowels like /ɑ/, while flat areas indicate silences during pauses or stop consonant closures. The dark areas on spectrograms show the frequencies where acoustic energy is concentrated.

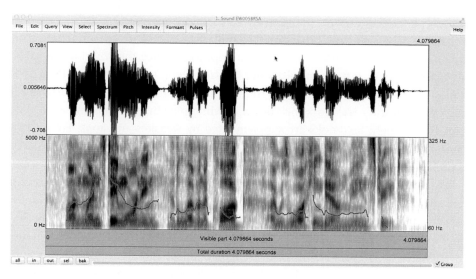

Figure 7.1. *Praat* (Boersma & Weenink, 2014) window showing a waveform display (upper panel) and spectrogram with superimposed pitch track (lower panel)

Reading and correctly interpreting spectrograms requires considerable expertise in phonetics. For that reason these representations are unlikely to be of much use in the classroom: the time required to give students the necessary technical training would be prohibitive. However, as Chun, Hardison, and Pennington (2008) point out, certain types of visual speech analysis are known to provide effective feedback in the teaching of prosody. One type of traditional analysis, the PITCH TRACK, has been available commercially in the form of the *Visipitch* (by Kay Elemetrics) and other software. Pitch is a relatively straightforward concept, and pitch displays are fairly easy for learners to interpret (Chun et al., 2008) by associating the rises and falls in visual patterns with pitch changes in another speaker's (or the learner's own) voice. A number of other studies have also demonstrated the pedagogical effectiveness of visual pitch displays (e.g. de Bot & Mailfert, 1982; Hardison 2004).

In a slightly different use of pitch information, Hincks and Edlund (2009) provided visual feedback to Chinese students of English based on their oral productions. Students' utterances produced with flat pitch were met with a display of yellow lights, while more variable, and therefore more expressive pitch resulted in a display of green lights. This user-friendly feedback was found to increase vocal expressiveness in learners who used it.

The application of speech analysis to segmental productions appears to be more difficult and less well-developed than the prosodic implementations discussed above. No simple acoustic representations of vowels or consonants would be likely to help L2 learners. Instead, developers have aimed at transforming acoustic information into representations that are more intuitively accessible. *Sona-Match* by Kay Elemetrics, for instance, displays a vowel space on the computer screen corresponding to learners' individual vowel productions. Learners attempt to produce the vowel in the correct part of the space to match a model voice. In *HearSay* (Dalby & Kewley-Port, 2008), a computer-based speech training system developed using principles derived from research, the learner tries to knock down bowling pins by pronouncing a word correctly. Increasingly, textbooks are supplemented by websites and apps. For example, Gilbert's (2011) *Clear Speech* offers a ball toss, a basketball game, a push the blob into the wall and a stop the flow game for different aspects of speech.

Animations have been available on websites for some time and have recently been adapted for use on smartphones. The University of Iowa ⟨http://www.uiowa.edu/~acadtech/phonetics/⟩ offers the *Sounds of Speech* app for iOS and Android. It provides two-dimensional representations of the vocal tract, along with animations and audiovisual samples for all of the English consonants and vowels. This app is based on the website that has offered the same animations for several years. In related work, Massaro (2003) reported on a 3-D animated talking head which later was developed into iBaldi, an "embodied conversational agent" modeled after Baldi (and later, a female version, Baldette) on the ⟨http://freapp.com/apps/ios/504464546/⟩ website.

Computer-assisted pronunciation training

Strictly speaking, COMPUTER-ASSISTED PRONUNCIATION TRAINING (CAPT) refers to a range of ways of using computers to teach pronunciation; however it is most often understood as the application of automatic speech recognition (ASR) to provide pronunciation feedback to learners. Levis (2007) discusses some of the capabilities and limitations of CAPT, most of which still hold true today: "The central question in CAPT feedback is whether ASR can effectively provide immediate feedback that allows learners to know which parts of their pronunciation are correct and which are not" (p. 192). Clearly this criterion is not met by off-the-shelf dictation software, which was designed for an entirely different purpose, although some sources (e.g. Sustarsic, 2003) have attempted to promote pedagogical use of dictation apps. In our study of an early version of *Dragon Systems Naturally Speaking* (Derwing, Munro & Carbonaro, 2000), we compared the performance of the speech recognition software on Cantonese and Spanish accented English with that of human listeners. Our chief finding was that the transcriptions of the humans bore little resemblance to the computer output; furthermore, the humans were far more accurate. In other words, they were less adversely affected by L2 speech than was the software. Inspection of the transcriptions indicated that the listening errors made by the humans made logical sense in terms of the phonetic aspects of the speakers' productions. The computer output, however, appeared arbitrary and highly unlikely to provide any significant help to L2 speakers. In fact, it could seriously mislead them with regard to their speech errors.

We don't mean to imply that ASR is inherently unsatisfactory for providing feedback to learners. Cucchiarini, Neri and Strik (2009) reported success when they tailored an ASR system to learners of Dutch. The criteria they used in developing the software were "common across speakers of various L1s; perceptually salient; potentially hampering communication; frequent; persistent; suitable for robust, automatic detection" (p. 854). Although their system was not perfect in detecting errors, the constraints listed above allowed it to provide learners with sufficiently rich feedback so that they outperformed a comparison group that had received pronunciation practice without ASR, and a control group. Research in this vein will be helpful in the future streamlining of ASR software for pedagogical purposes, but except in instances such as Cucchiarini et al.'s work, where the system has already been carefully calibrated to meet the needs of the learners, L2 classrooms are not currently able to successfully implement ASR systems.

The internet and language teaching

The last decade has seen a radical shift in language teaching (and other types of instruction) toward increased use of online resources, in either blended or strictly online courses. Part of this movement is motivated by cost-savings; in addition, learners in remote areas benefit from immediate access. Many traditional language programs now deliver at least some courses through online audiovisual materials, virtual classrooms and individual instruction. The Center for Advanced Research on Language Acquisition (CARLA) at the University of Minnesota offers courses to help language teachers transition to teaching online.

For language learners seeking individual on-line help, *YouTube* and other repositories offer pronunciation lessons. Some commercial enterprises have set up one-on-one instructional programs, the quality of which is variable because there is little or no regulation. In principle, anyone – with or without credentials – can claim to be an accent coach or pronunciation specialist and promise to eliminate clients' foreign accents. Lippi-Green (2012) likens this situation to that of hucksters who "claim to have developed a miracle diet and charge money for it" (p. 229). We discuss some of the ethical issues that arise in connection with this problem in Chapter 9.

Software that allows oral social interaction over the Internet has revolutionized learners' opportunities to interact in their L2. Participants in virtual worlds such as *Second Life* may choose to take formal language lessons online, including pronunciation, where they go to class, do homework assignments and receive feedback and even grades. In addition, students can get extensive oral/aural practice by going to other virtual locations where speakers of the L2 congregate. Virtual worlds offer exposure to spoken language that some students would not be able to access in any other way. In fact, the use of *Second Life* for language learning has been popular enough to spawn annual conferences dedicated to learning L2s in a virtual world. As with all language instruction, the quality varies widely in online settings. The currently limited research in such contexts is certain to expand as the popularity of this type of software grows.

Summary

The benefits of technological advances for pronunciation learning and teaching are indeed exciting; at the same time, several caveats need to be highlighted. On the positive side, we can point to four particularly compelling strengths of the current status of pronunciation teaching and technology. First, perception skills can be heightened using high variability training, presenting stimuli that zero in precisely on target issues, and enhancing perceptual cues to redirect learners' attention. Second, technology offers high interest content that can be integrated into pronunciation instruction. Third, technology provides unprecedented opportunities for learners to interact orally in their L2. Finally, emerging resources and techniques can facilitate individualized instruction with higher-quality feedback than has traditionally been possible.

In spite of these benefits, we take a skeptical view of some aspects of the current push toward more use of technology in language instruction in general, and pronunciation in particular. Some providers of instruction see technology primarily as a cost-saver, irrespective of its pedagogical merits and limitations. In fact, as has been reiterated many times in the CALL literature, technology cannot replace teachers, nor is it *necessarily* better than, or even as good as, traditional instructional methods. Its effectiveness depends on how it is implemented as a support to well-developed, evidence-based teaching approaches. If implemented without due attention to principles of pronunciation that are rooted in research evidence, they may not benefit the student. For instance, software packages that merely take learners through the entire inventory of segments in their L2, with no prioritization or individualization, are guaranteed to waste the learners' time. Another concern is the limits of the technology itself. As we have seen above, off-the-shelf ASR technology is of little use in identifying production problems because it is unable to distinguish accent features that do and do not affect intelligibility.

In our view, it is crucial for teachers to treat technology as one tool among others to enhance their learners' L2 pronunciation. To do this effectively, the teacher must have a good understanding of the foundations of pronunciation research and the pedagogical knowledge to exploit the benefits that technology has to offer.

CHAPTER 8

Social aspects of accent

In a review of Canadian legal cases pertaining to accent discrimination, Murray Munro (2003) discovered documentation of an interesting human rights proceeding. A tribunal had ruled on the case of a Polish L1 substitute teacher, Mirek Gajecki, who had been told that his employer, a school district in British Columbia, had concerns about his accent. A note had been placed in Gajecki's file indicating that he "did not speak English" despite the fact that he had been teaching successfully for several years, and had been evaluated as a competent instructor. Once the note was removed from his file, Gajecki was called to substitute every day of the next school year. The tribunal judged that the school district had discriminated against Gajecki and ordered compensation both for lost wages and for the indignity he suffered. Accent carries a lot of baggage; people tend to make assumptions, often unwarranted, based on very little evidence.

Only very rarely are foreigners or first-generation immigrants allowed to be nice people in American films. Those with an accent are bad guys. – Max von Sydow (humanaccents.com)

Introduction

Language is the most human of all animal behaviours. Other species certainly communicate. In fact, Washoe and other chimps, dolphins, and even dogs and cats seem to have made greater progress learning and responding to a human L2 than we have made learning the communication systems of their species. However, they do not interact with speech, nor do they write novels, Shakespearean-style plays, or manuals on how to use the latest version of an electronic device. They do not consult their smartphones at every opportunity to check their latest texts, and they do not follow even a single person or organization on Twitter. They don't have TV shows and magazines devoted to idle gossip. In short, other species seem to communicate necessary information such as danger warnings, mating calls, directions, and soothing sounds for their young, but they are not dependent on language in the way that human beings are. Not all societies are literate, nor are all individuals within a given society literate; but barring some unfortunate disability or disease, all humans communicate far more than is necessary simply to survive. Language is our means of connecting with each other and our way of determining if someone shares our values. In most cultures it is the primary delivery mechanism for education. It is through language that we express our own selves – our identities. Language is so central to our essence that one of the most devastating punishments humans have devised is solitary confinement, whether through imprisonment or through a timeout in the corner for a three-year-old. We are social beings, and language is a key (although certainly not the only) means of judging whether someone new to us is someone we would like to get to know, or someone with whom we'll choose to have little or no contact. The importance of social factors is highlighted in Schumann's (2013) article on "workarounds" for adult second language acquisition: "[H]umans are both a monolingual and multilingual species and it is the way social contexts interact with motivation/attachment, ability/aptitude, and opportunity that produces either a monolingual or a bilingual human" (p. 206). In this chapter, we will review some of the social aspects of language, paying particular attention to the role of accent in conveying information to an interlocutor. We will examine sociolinguistic aspects of an L2 accent in three domains: attitudes; identity; and, related to each of these categories, context. Finally, we will outline some pedagogical implications, taking into consideration the sociolinguistic aspects of an L2 accent.

The importance of accent

People have reacted viscerally to accented speech for as long as there has been intergroup contact (Weinreich, 1953). Even the Bible offers an example of the negative consequences of an accent in the description of the dispute between the Ephraimites and the Gileadites:

> In order to keep the Ephraimites from escaping, the Gileadites captured the places where the river Jordan could be crossed. When any Ephraimite who was trying to escape would ask permission to cross, the men of Gilead would ask, "Are you an Ephraimite?" If he said "No," they would tell him to say "Shibboleth." But he would say "Sibboleth" because he could not pronounce it correctly. Then they would grab him and kill him there at one of the Jordan river crossings. At that time, forty-two thousand of the Ephraimites were killed.   Judges 12.4–6
> The Good News Bible

This barbaric example may seem to represent only the distant past, but as we mentioned in Chapter 1, accent can be a factor in life-and-death situations even today. The speech of refugee claimants, or asylum seekers, as they are also called, is often analyzed for aspects of accent to determine whether they will be granted refugee status, or sent back to their countries of origin, which, in some instances, may result in their deaths (Derwing, Fraser, Kang & Thomson, 2014). The results of Language Analysis for Determination of Origin (LADO) are used in Australia, Canada, and several western European countries; the governments in these countries contract companies that specialize in identifying shibboleths that will give away a refugee's country of origin. Unfortunately, in some instances, the investigators who make the linguistic determination are not linguistically trained and may use unreliable methods (Fraser, 2013). Although a set of ethical guidelines for LADO has been developed by the International Association of Forensic Linguists, some practitioners choose not to follow them. For an extensive discussion of this issue, see Eades (2005). Suffice it to say here that L2 pronunciation can still have an extraordinary impact on a person's life, many centuries after the death of 42,000 Ephraimites.

Attitudes towards accented speech

In the second half of the last century, psychologists and sociolinguists showed great interest in both regional and foreign accents, as well as in listeners' attitudes and reactions to them (Bradac, 1990; Brennan & Brennan, 1981a, b; Giles, 1970; Honey, 1989; Ryan & Carranza, 1975; Ryan, Carranza & Moffie, 1977; Preston, 1999). For a comprehensive review of this literature, see Gluszek and Dovidio (2010). In several of these studies, especially the foreign accent attitude research, listeners have assigned scalar evaluations based on personality and behavioural descriptions, such as unfriendly/friendly, lazy/hardworking, and so on. Repeatedly, researchers have found that listeners employ STEREOTYPES to ascribe features to unseen speakers, solely on the basis of their accents.

To give a sense of how views of foreign accents have ranged, without a clear consensus, over the last 90 years in SLA and L2 teaching, examine Table 8.1. Greene and Wells (1927) were speech-language pathologists (SLPs), who interpreted foreign accents to be defective speech, and therefore in need of treatment as a pathology.

Abercrombie (1949), a pedagogical specialist, expressed the view that L2 speech should simply be intelligible, not native-like, echoing the arguments of Henry Sweet (1900) nearly 50 years before. Griffen's (1980) take on L2 accents is reminiscent of Greene and Wells, in that he saw accents as a deviance from clinical normalcy. As a linguist, he advocated accent eradication. Porter and Garvin (1989) on the other hand, were reporting comments from language teachers who took an extremely strong view in the other direction, arguing that it was immoral to change anyone's pronunciation. To determine whether teachers' views differed from those of learners, Porter and Garvin conducted a survey, concluding that learners were more concerned with obtaining a native-like accent than their teachers, but that most people saw striving for more than intelligibility to be a waste of time. Morley (1991) argued that it would be unprofessional for language teachers to ignore pronunciation difficulties experienced by their students. Golombek and Rehn Jordan (2005) downplayed the importance of

Table 8.1. Views of foreign accents

Source	Opinion
Greene & Wells (1927)	Foreign accent, being of the nature of imperfect or defective speech, is the result of incorrect articulation and enunciation and is therefore classified, from our therapeutic viewpoint, as stammering speech. (p. 24)
Abercrombie (1949)	I believe that pronunciation teaching should have, not a goal which must of necessity be normally an unrealised ideal, but a *limited* purpose which will be completely fulfilled; the attainment of intelligibility. (p. 120)
Griffen (1980)	The goal of instruction in pronunciation is that the student (or patient) should learn to speak the language as naturally as possible, free of any indication that the speaker is not a clinically normal native. (p. 85)
Porter & Garvin (1989)	(reporting the views of some teachers) To seek to change someone's pronunciation – whether of the L1 or of an L2 – is to tamper with their self-image and is thus unethical – morally wrong. (p. 8)
Morley (1991)	[I]gnoring students' pronunciation needs is an abrogation of professional responsibility. (p. 489)
Golombek & Rehn-Jordan (2005)	(reporting the views of some teachers) For L2 speakers, intelligibility is an illusion if it is simply operationalized as a set of skills located within an individual that can be easily manipulated or changed. (p. 529)
Rajagopalan (2010)	[T]he adjective intelligible is analogous to others such as beautiful, ugly, easy, difficult, primitive, civilized, and so forth, which are also sometimes used with respect to languages, and which we have long learned to regard with suspicion on the grounds that they invariably presuppose the standpoint of someone who furtively manages to remain invisible. (p. 465)

intelligibility and saw it as only peripheral in developing nonnative language teachers' identity. Similarly, as recently as 2010, Rajagopalan made the argument that intelligibility is merely an evaluation or judgment; he appears to deny the possibility that some L2 speakers' speech is not understandable to others despite considerable evidence to the contrary. At present controversies still flare over whether L2 pronunciation should be taught at all, and even among those who support changing L2 learners' speech, there are also divides. In a recent review of 75 L2 pronunciation intervention studies, Thomson and Derwing (2014) determined that 63% were guided by the Nativeness Principle, 24% fell under the Intelligibility Principle, and the remaining 13% had elements of both. Many of these studies did not overtly claim to be aligned with a given theoretical model, but the types of assessments they used to measure the success of the intervention suggested that they were looking for native-like productions (Nativeness Principle) or an overall improvement in comprehensibility (Intelligibility Principle).

Given the lack of consensus in researchers' approaches to L2 pronunciation, and the limited number of programs offering pronunciation instruction (Foote, Holtby, & Derwing, 2011), it is not surprising that students themselves receive mixed messages about what is important. For those residing in a country where their L2 is the majority language, they receive feedback, both implicit and explicit, from members of the public. It is the reactions of those interlocutors we will examine in more depth here.

The stigma of a foreign accent

Gluszek and Dovidio (2010) reviewed several decades of social psychology research probing native speakers' attitudes towards L2 accented speech. Many of these studies were conducted using a MATCHED GUISE technique, in which a highly proficient compound bilingual speaker provides speech samples with and without an L2 accent. These studies generally found negative attitudes towards accented speech such that a speaker in the accented condition was judged less intelligent, less competent, and less proficient in the L2 than the *same person* speaking with a "nativelike" accent. Lippi-Green (2012), in discussing L2 English, has highlighted the strong connection between race and accent discrimination. She observed that speakers from nonwhite backgrounds are discriminated against in the US, but that "there are no documented cases of native speakers of Swedish or Dutch or Gaelic being turned away from jobs because of communication difficulties, although these adult speakers face the same challenge as native speakers of Spanish, Rumanian, Thai or Urdu" (p. 253). Accent, like physical appearance, often evokes an immediate reaction, some aspects of which may be subconscious. Moreover, negative attitudes towards L2 accented speech can have serious consequences: Dávila, Bohara and Saenz (1993) determined that the strength of Mexican Americans' accents correlated negatively with their incomes, and Kalin and Rayko (1978) found that English native speakers perceived L2 accented speakers to be better suited to low status jobs than high status positions. In an examination of reports of human rights cases involving accented speech in Canada, Munro (2003) categorized three types of accent discrimination: hiring decisions in which accent is equated with language proficiency (as in the anecdote at the start of this chapter); employment and housing discrimination; and harassment of an individual in which accent is the target. He found several instances of each through the *Canadian Human Rights Reporter,* a publication that provides the details of human rights cases on which tribunals have ruled. Some of the cases reported were relatively egregious situations that disturbed the complainants enough to provoke them to appeal to Human Rights Commissions, because of both financial and personal costs associated with accent discrimination.

Globalization has introduced L2 accents into previously homogeneous settings through the outsourcing of call centres (Pickering, Menjo, & Bouchard, 2012). This phenomenon has become so prevalent that there is even a Hollywood comedy about it (*Outsourced*, 2006). However, some of what happens over the telephone lines is nothing to laugh about. In 2005, *The Telegraph* reported a story about two young Britons, both born and raised in England, working in a call centre in India. Their job was to convince customers in Britain to switch from one telecommunications service to another. They were shocked at the responses at the other end of the line. One of them, Ian Hussey, recounted a call in which the customer asked him where he was located. In Ian's words: "I told him India and he just said 'F***off, you job-stealing Paki,' and slammed the phone down…. I can appreciate it's annoying being cold-called by someone trying to sell stuff, so I don't really mind being told to 'sod off', but it's another thing to get a mouthful of racist abuse" (Foster, 2005). When Ian asked his Indian co-workers what their experiences had been, they indicated their L2 accents elicited racial epithets nearly every day. The other Briton at the call centre, Hasmita Patel, was of Indian heritage, but spoke with a native British accent. She had been asked to intervene when an Indian co-worker was having difficulty with a customer. The woman recognized her English accent, and said she wanted to deal with no one else from then on "because I want to speak with English only." Hasmita wondered if the customer would want to talk with her if she could see her skin. It is little wonder that an entire industry has been built to train call centre employees to "neutralize" their L2 accents (Wang, Arndt, Singh, Biernat & Liu, 2013).

Wang et al. (2013) conducted a fascinating study of call centre encounters. They recorded four deliberately-staged service interactions. An American native speaker of English and a speaker of Indian English each recorded interactions with either a favourable or an unfavourable outcome for the listeners. These were played to 122 American undergraduates, who were instructed to take the perspective of the customer as they heard the interactions. They were told that the purpose of the study was to improve employee service and were asked to rate the call centre employees' accents on a 7-point scale. Interestingly, when the service outcome was favourable, "employee accent had no impact on the description of employee contribution" (p. 188), but when the outcome was unfavourable, "respondents in the Indian accent condition described the employee contribution in more detail" (p. 188) than those in the American accent condition. The authors concluded that the listeners were able to suppress accent bias when an outcome was satisfactory, but allowed their prejudices to come to the fore when the service outcome was unfavourable. They recommended that call centre employers consider giving L2 accented employees jobs likely to have a positive outcome (e.g. activating a new account, or providing good news), and suggested that the delivery of bad news be carried out by employees who share the same accent as the customer.

Most businesses see their primary goal as making money, and anything that detracts from that is a concern. Mai and Hoffman (2014) have proposed a model for the role of accents in business communication. While much of it is speculative, and several of the research findings they use to support their claims are rooted in dialect studies, rather than L2 accent research, it is nonetheless interesting to see how economists interpret the effects of L2 accents in business. The authors propose a *vampire effect*, such that L2 accents bleed the customer's attention away from the message to be conveyed, bringing the focus to the effort of listening to the accent itself. They recommend that employers recognize that the customer's bias, rather than an employee's accent per se, compromises service encounters, but they encourage employers to find "speech training" for individuals with "very strong regional and foreign accents" (p. 152).

Accent discrimination is not limited to call centres, of course, and occurs in many forms of employment (Lippi-Green, 2012), but it is especially apparent in the field of language teaching. As Moussu and Llurda (2008) have observed, in many parts of the world advertisements for language teachers (and English teachers in particular) typically specify that "NSs [native speakers] need only apply." The preference for native speaker English teachers (NESTs) over non-native English speaking teachers (NNESTS) is not limited to English as a Foreign Language (EFL) contexts; Clark and Paran (2007) and Mahboob, Uhrig, Newman and Hartford (2004) have demonstrated a hiring bias against NNESTs in both the UK and the USA. In recent years there has been considerable controversy over who should teach English, and who has ownership of the language. There is no question that unequal treatment occurs. For instance, native-English-speaking "backpackers" in EFL contexts, who often have no academic preparation for language teaching, sometimes earn more money than well-trained local NNESTS. From our standpoint, however, the question of native speaker status should be irrelevant (Derwing & Munro, 2005b). In making hiring decisions, we propose a list of questions to be considered for prospective language teachers, regardless of whether they are NESTS or NNESTS:

1. Is the applicant proficient in the language to be taught? Clearly proficiency is a necessary but not sufficient requirement to teach a language.
2. Does the prospective instructor have sufficient metalinguistic knowledge of the language being taught (e.g. a good grasp of grammatical structures, the phonological inventory of the language, pragmatics, and idiosyncrasies that will need to be explained to learners)? Unless they have had specific training, many NESTs do not have explicit awareness of how their own language works, while many NNESTs, because of their own experiences in acquiring their L2, have an excellent declarative grasp of the L2's grammatical and phonological systems and of other issues that may prove difficult for learners.
3. Does the applicant have strong pedagogical skills? As in all educational situations, good pedagogical skills enhance the learning experiences of students. Neither NESTs nor NNESTs have an inherent advantage here – but students should expect strong teaching skills from their instructors.

4.   Finally, does the instructor have a clear understanding of the contexts (both narrow and broad) in which students will use the L2, and the flexibility to adjust the content of the course in which the L2 is embedded accordingly? In other words, can the instructor set the stage for learners to become participants in the language communities they will enter? The narrow interpretation entails teaching specialized vocabulary and pragmatics to learners for a specific role such as a medical practitioner; see for example, Dahm and Yates (2013) and Yates (2007). The broader context is the students' role in society. Language teachers can help to interpret the choices students can make to frame their own identities, and help them to see whether they want to "invest" in a new language and culture (Norton Peirce, 1995). They can also foster students' awareness of what awaits them, both positive and negative. Morgan (2009) describes a program for language teachers designed to help them become "transformative practitioners," that is, teachers who can utilize critical pedagogy to inform their students in ways that may give them agency in developing both their L2 skills and strategies for dealing with marginalization or discrimination.

In sum, it should matter little whether a language teacher is a NEST or a NNEST; what is critical is whether the instructor has the requisite skills, both linguistic and pedagogical, to provide students with a quality learning experience.

An interesting twist on accent discrimination is what Rubin (2012) and Kang and Rubin (2009; 2014) have called REVERSE LINGUISTIC STEREOTYPING: a phenomenon in which listeners persuade themselves that they hear an L2 accent where none exists. Rubin (1992) carried out an innovative study in which two groups of college students listened to a recorded mini-lecture while viewing a picture of the lecturer and then responded to comprehension questions. Both groups heard exactly the same recording, spoken by a native speaker of the same dialect of English that the students used. The sole difference in the two conditions was that one group saw a picture of a Caucasian woman at a podium while the other saw a picture of a Chinese woman of similar age, height, and level of attractiveness in the same context. Rubin found that the students in the latter group allowed the visual information to interfere with their listening perception to such an extent that they actually understood less of the lectures. As he (2012) pointed out: "In reverse linguistic stereotyping, listeners "hear" the pronunciation they expect to hear, sometimes with little regard to the actual properties of the acoustic signal (p. 11)." The study has been replicated in several contexts, including a nursing home with elderly patients – a real life context where L2 accents are common. Kang has tested the Reverse Linguistic Stereotyping technique on several classes of university students, and each time has obtained findings similar to those in the original experiment (Kang & Rubin, 2014). Students who assume that the Asian face projected in front of them is Japanese report hearing

/ɹ/ and /l/ confusions, even though the recording is in a familiar American English accent. It is important to be aware of this type of visual bias, because no pronunciation instruction for L2 speakers would conceivably remedy the problem. We will revisit this point later in the chapter when we discuss the role of the interlocutor and pedagogical implications.

L2 accent and identity

John Levis once remarked that pronunciation is the "face" of language. How one presents oneself to the world through speech is evident not only in what one says but also in how one says it. Adults have their own L1 identities (multiple roles), but when they start to learn an L2, they may find it impossible to present their true selves because of linguistic limitations in grammar, vocabulary, pragmatics, and, of course, pronunciation. Marx (2002), an Anglophone Canadian living in Germany, was concerned that she not be taken for an American (from the USA). Because General Canadian accents closely resemble General American accents, Marx deliberately appropriated a French accent when speaking in German, in part to prevent her interlocutors from switching to English, and in part to avoid being categorized as an American. She changed her way of dressing to conform culturally, and she stayed away from other native English speakers to give herself as much exposure to German as possible. After about a year, Marx started to aim for "accent-free" German. She had built up significant expertise in her L2, and reported that she was delighted "at not being 'caught' as a foreigner when speaking with strangers" (p. 272). A similar sentiment is echoed in Piller (2002), who interviewed L2 spouses of native speakers living in the L2 environment. Some indicated that they enjoyed passing as a native speaker in service transactions and other first encounters with strangers. One of Piller's participants pointed out, though, that in extended interactions, she would reveal her L2 status, despite her excellent pronunciation of German, because "If I don't, some reference to something every German knows will come up, and I won't understand, and they'll think I'm stupid" (p. 195). Piller described this reaction as a trade-off between one aspect of the L2 speaker's identity (intelligent, informed) for another (being able to pass as a native speaker). Interestingly, Marx (2002), after mastering the pronunciation of the local dialect of German, moved back to North America, where she taught German in the USA. She was again in an L1 context, but her accent had been influenced by both German and aspects of a British accent, which she interpreted as "resist[ing] membership, staying on the periphery" (p. 275). Although Marx had participated in German culture, and had become very proficient, she still saw herself as a foreigner, and this identity extended to her stay in the USA. After about three months, however, Marx interacted more often in English, and her L1 accent reverted to her original Canadian way of speaking.

Both Marx's and Piller's (2002) studies are indicative of the extent to which we are concerned with self-presentation to others, and with protection of our own identities even as they shift, sometimes through conscious decisions and sometimes subconsciously. Morgan (2010) described learning as a process of "acquiring an identity, of becoming someone or something" (p. 35), but it is not always possible to acquire the identity one might wish for, particularly in the case of L2 pronunciation. However, some aspects of pronunciation are volitional. Cutler (2014) studied American immigrant youth from East European backgrounds who adopted features of African American Vernacular English (AAVE) in their L2 pronunciation, despite very little exposure to African Americans. She argues that "Their pronunciation choices are not about a desire to pass as African American or Latino, but rather to signal their feelings of otherness and alienation which may be a result of direct experiences they have had, or may stem from resentment about the difficulties that African American and other ethnic groups have experienced" (p. 159). In other words, Cutler makes the point that L2 speakers can adopt versions of an 'other' dialect to express their identity. She cautions language teachers to take into consideration these volitional aspects of pronunciation.

Gatbonton, Trofimovich and Segalowitz (2011) have also documented aspects of L2 pronunciation tied to social relations and solidarity within a particular group. The authors had adult Francophone Canadians read an English passage seeded with 70 instances of /ð/, a low Functional Load but highly frequent phoneme that does not exist in French. The participants also answered a number of questions designed to determine their degree of ethnic group affiliation (EGA), including their political leanings and their beliefs about the links between language and identity; they also reported how regularly they used English. The results indicated that speakers who used /ð/ the least had stronger EGA, and particularly stronger political aspirations. However, those who used /ð/ less also had more limited interactions in the L2. Thus the extent to which the participants used this English phoneme may have had more to do with lack of contact than as a marker of solidarity, though both factors may have been involved.

Derwing (2003) interviewed 100 immigrants to English-speaking Canada about their experiences learning their L2, and their attitudes towards their L2 accented speech. When asked whether they would like to pronounce English like a native speaker, an overwhelming majority of 95 said that they would. The participants were also asked whether they would feel a loss of identity if they were to speak English with a Canadian accent. The majority indicated that they would still have full use of their mother tongue, and that their identity was tied to that; speaking English without an L2 accent was viewed as an asset because it would allow the participants to hide their L2 status (similar to Piller's (2002) interviewees who "passed" in short encounters with strangers). Several of them complained about being asked repeatedly how long they had been in Canada, where they were from, and so on; they wanted to be treated in the same way that they perceived Canadian-born people were treated. Derwing (2003) pointed out that these individuals were living in a city where the majority speaks a single variety of English, although many minority ethnic communities use other languages. The participants, unlike Marx (2002), had chosen to spend the rest of their lives in an L2 environment; several had already taken out Canadian citizenship, and although they used their L1s with family and friends, they wanted to belong to the larger society as well. This points to the role of context: where one lives and why one chooses to learn an L2 both have a major impact on identity and issues of pronunciation.

The role of context

The influence of context and contact on language learning has been of interest for many decades (e.g. Weinreich, 1953). In his seminal article, Schumann (1976) attributed the degree of SOCIAL DISTANCE between two language groups to such factors as group dominance ("politically, culturally, technically or economically dominant, non-dominant or subordinate" (p 136)); group size and cohesion; degree of desire for preservation of group traditions; degree of enclosure (e.g. do the groups live in the same neighbourhoods, or are they confined to distinct areas?); congruence of the cultures involved; and attitudes toward the other group. Schumann proposed that in situations where the groups have relatively equal dominance and size, positive attitudes towards each other, low levels of enclosure, and congruent cultures-in other words, low social distance-language learning should be unimpeded by social factors. On the other hand, if the groups have negative attitudes towards each other, quite distinct cultures, segregated neighbourhoods, and strong inclinations towards preservation of group traditions, language learning will be hindered. Findings from a recent investigation by Thomas (2014) illustrate this. In a case study of a town near San Antonio, Texas, Thomas interviewed the oldest group of native-English-speaking Mexican Americans as well as the oldest group of Anglos. The language samples were examined for several pronunciation variables. Ethnicity proved to be the strongest independent variable, as opposed to sex, year of birth, or educational attainment, all of which made much more limited contributions. Thomas suggests that the degree of social tension between the two groups led to the Mexican Americans' choice to avoid emulating Anglo speech.

Another indication of the role of context is evident in Timmis's (2002) survey of 400 students in 14 countries, who were asked whether they would prefer to have a nativelike accent or to simply speak intelligibly. Two thirds of the students opted for a nativelike accent, but of those from South Africa, Pakistan, and India (all colonized countries where English is now an official language), 64% said that intelligible

English, rather than native-like status, was their goal. In each of these countries, other languages are also official languages, and English, although deeply-entrenched, has been influenced significantly by local L1s and local social conventions. According to Timmis, this finding suggests that attitudes towards L2 accents are "context-sensitive" (p. 242). Although he does not identify the other countries in the survey, it seems plausible that many were English as a Foreign Language (EFL) environments (for instance, China is mentioned several times), whereas the three countries that differed in responses from the others were all places in which a variety of English that differs from a "native speaker" norm was well-established. One might ask several questions about this survey. First, to which dialect of English did "native speaker" refer? This was left to the survey respondents to interpret as they wished. Second, to what extent did the question reflect the students' actual take on possible realities versus wishes for an unattainable but, for them, ideal outcome? Timmis also surveyed English teachers, who showed a greater preference for intelligibility versus nativelike speech than did the students, but who appeared, in some cases, to see intelligibility as the "more *realistic*, rather than the more *desirable* outcome"(p. 243). The author concluded that some students want a native speaker model, in spite of the arguments for a model that reflects EIL, that is, varieties of English that may differ from those of Inner Circle countries, but which have currency as a LINGUA FRANCA.

World Englishes and English as a lingua franca

Although many aspects of pronunciation instruction and research discussed thus far have some application to teaching in general, regardless of the languages involved, the majority of research on and discussion of pronunciation teaching entails L2 users of English. The fact that there are far more nonnative speakers of English (estimates range from 500,000,000 to 1 billion, Crystal, 2003) than there are native speakers (320–380 million, Crystal, 2003) is testament to the influence of this language. Kachru (1985; 1991) has famously discussed the status of English in terms of Inner, Outer, and Expanding Circle countries. As a major colonizer, Britain took English to many parts of the world, and in some cases it overwhelmed the local languages almost completely (e.g. Australia, Canada, New Zealand, the USA). These are categorized, along with Britain, as part of the Inner Circle. Other former colonies have been left with a legacy of English, particularly in educational and government contexts (e.g. India, Singapore, Hong Kong, many African states), while locally spoken languages have continued to thrive; Kachru classifies these as Outer Circle countries. Finally, the Expanding Circle comprises countries in which English has no particular status, but is popular as a second language for economic reasons (e.g. China, Japan, most of Europe, Russia, some African countries). Controversies have raged for decades about which type of English should be taught in these environments. Typically, there is little argument over learners in Inner Circle countries acquiring the local variety of English; in most cases, learners are immigrants who have chosen to move to their new country. They want to understand and be understood by their neighbours and coworkers. Although some of their teachers may be from L2 backgrounds themselves, or from a dialect region distinct from that of the majority in a given location, L2 immigrant students generally have the opportunity to hear a wide range of accents, but especially that of the local region. Many immigrants choose to speak in a way that is as close to the local dialect as possible (Derwing, 2003), but in some instances, as we have discussed above, they choose to distinguish their accents from "standard" varieties for social reasons, (Cutler, 2014), albeit in ways that are intelligible to the larger society.

In Outer and Expanding Circle countries, the situation is quite different. As McArthur (2001) noted in a state of the art review, World Englishes comprise all the "varieties of English (standard, dialect, national, regional, creole, hybrid, 'broken', etc.) throughout the world" (p. 5). Scholars such as Braj Kachru and Larry E. Smith had earlier brought World Englishes to the attention of linguists through conferences and a position paper in 1981 outlining the need for research and, in particular, the need to distinguish between English for internal purposes (as in India) and English

A CLOSER LOOK: Will students accept non-native teachers in an inner circle country?

Nuzhat Amin (2004) was a Toronto teacher and graduate student of Pakistani heritage. She interviewed visible minority instructors who taught English in a government-funded language program for adult immigrants. We can assume that their employers felt that they were qualified to teach and did not see their accents, their race, or their country of origin as obstacles, or they would not have hired them. Amin reported that some of the learners objected to her interviewees on the grounds that they wanted native speakers as their instructors. She was interested in knowing how the notion of 'native speaker' was present in ESL classes and how visible minority teachers "negotiated nativism and the native speaker construct" (p. 64). The women she interviewed were asked whether immigrant students ever requested that the school director move them to a class with a native speaker teacher. As one of her interviewees stated:

> Yes. True. But eventually not so many of them do that. These are adult students, and they are looking for a good teacher to help them with their language difficulties. They soon realize that it's not just the color of the skin [that they should go by]. Is she a good teacher? That is the bottom line. Your reputation gets around. If you are a dedicated teacher and you are doing a good job, then the word gets around and then there will be no problem. (p. 72)

as a lingua franca (as in Japan). Since that time, both the journal *World Englishes* and the International Association for World Englishes have been established. One of the principal concerns for World Englishes in general (which tend to be relatively stable within a given context), and English as a lingua franca (ELF) in particular, is mutual intelligibility. To this end, Jenkins (2002) proposed a 'lingua franca core' of features that she argued should be adopted and taught internationally to ensure intelligibility across varieties of English. Her core consists of most consonants within RP, with the exception of the interdental fricatives; RHOTIC /ɹ/ (as in General American English); English /t/ in medial position rather than a flap; and subphonemic variation. She also argued for aspiration of initial voiceless stops; shorter vowels before voiceless consonants than before their VOICED counterparts; no cluster reduction in word initial position; reduction in medial and final clusters, but only according to typical standard English patterns; no reduction of /t/ in word medial /nt/ combinations, such as 'winter.' Oddly, she claimed that epenthesis is acceptable, giving the example of the word 'product' pronounced as /pəɹˈʊdʌkʊtɔ/. The evidence in favour of greater intelligibility of a word of 5 syllables versus 2 is slim, to say the least, and the use of full vowels as opposed to a reduced schwa would surely cause difficulty for some listeners. Far more evidence is necessary from a wide range of listeners to give credence to her claim. As for vowel sounds, Jenkins allows for regional variation, as long as speakers are consistent. The only prosodic variable in the core is CONTRASTIVE STRESS. As Prodromou (2007) points out, Jenkins' conception of ELF (2006) excludes native speakers from the equation; there is an unspoken sense that lingua franca speakers will not talk to native speakers, and if they do, native speakers will be obliged to use the core, rather than their own dialects. Certainly, when motivated to communicate across distinct accents, people generally make an effort to align, as Giles (1970) proposed in his accommodation theory. However, Jenkins' approach seems highly prescriptive, and is based on very little evidence. In a comprehensive volume on pronunciation in EFL instruction, Szpyra-Kozłowska (2015) explored several of the benefits of Jenkins' lingua franca core outlined by Walker (2011); in particular, she noted that although on the surface the lingua franca core has appeal, in fact, at the level of implementation, many dilemmas become evident. She also pointed out that since "the majority of English learners in the Expanding Circle already use English pronunciation based on some native model, EFL users might have problems not only communicating with native speakers, but also with non-native speakers" (p. 21). As Isaacs (2014) has argued, " the inclusion criteria for speech samples in the English as a lingua franca corpus that Jenkins and her colleagues frequently cite have not been clarified (e.g. Seidlhofer, 2010). Therefore, substantially more empirical evidence is needed before the lingua franca core can be generalized across instructional contexts or adopted as a standard for assessment" (p. 8).

Regardless of the accuracy of the lingua franca core, Jenkins' claims have given impetus to considerable research on both World Englishes and ELF. Although it is still too early to make definitive arguments for changes to pedagogy in light of this research, there is no question that students are interested in learning varieties that are transferable. McArthur (2001) cites an article written in 1995 by a Japanese executive in the *International Herald Tribune* entitled *Dear English Speakers: Please Drop the Dialects*. In the article, Mikie Kiyoi argues that "Native English speakers who are international civil servants cannot fulfill their international responsibilities if they speak as if they were addressing only fellow natives" (McArthur, 2001, p. 10). This brings us to our next topic, the role of the native speaker interlocutor.

Role of the interlocutor

The interlocutor's contributions to communication with an L2 speaker have recently become an area of research interest, particularly in Inner Circle contexts, but also in international contexts involving native speaker-nonnative speaker communication. We have seen that interlocutors can be swayed by the visual appearance of a speaker to the point of imagining a foreign accent that doesn't exist (Rubin 1992). This raises the question of whether they can be taught to be better listeners. Derwing, Rossiter, and Munro (2002) explored this notion in an experiment in which NSs of English were trained to listen to L2 accented speech. Three classes of students in the first year of a social work program took part. One group (the control) took only the pre- and post-tests, while another (the familiarity group) were exposed to Vietnamese-accented English in several different contexts, all related to their coursework. The final group (Accent Instruction) received exactly the same amount of exposure to Vietnamese-accented speech as the familiarity group, as well as explicit instruction about the features of the speech (e.g. reduced consonant clusters, especially at the ends of words; epenthetic /s/, and so on). Comparisons were made between the phonology of Vietnamese and English. For example, English allows over 150 final consonants and final consonant clusters, versus six to eight singleton consonants in Vietnamese. Our colleague Ron Smyth once taught a field methods course to linguistics students using Vietnamese as the language of investigation. The class's informant said that she could not understand why "English keeps going at the end of the word." We related stories such as these to the Accent Instruction group to help them understand the challenges faced by Vietnamese speakers. We also provided them with exercises in predicting how a Vietnamese speaker might produce certain words.

Our assessment of the listening comprehension of the three groups of social work students before and after the interventions suggested that the test itself may have been a source of learning. Both the Control and Familiarity groups made small gains, while the Accent Instruction group improved by a much larger margin. In the post-test, we included some scalar-response attitudinal questions about ability to understand foreign accents in general, and confidence in understanding someone who speaks with an accent. The gain scores in the Accent Instruction group were notably greater than those of the other groups. Most telling were their reflections in an open-ended comment section of the test. Several students reported having better listening skills: "I can pick out words now when the last consonant is dropped. I am more aware of the words made by clusters.... I tend to listen and give myself time to listen and understand. I appreciate the difficulties that people have speaking with an accent. I am not quick to dismiss or turn away from people who I don't understand.... I feel more confident about interacting with people with accents. I seem to be able to recognize the dialect better. I listen more attentively. I am more patient and want to understand" (Derwing, Rossiter, & Munro, 2002, p. 254).

A limitation of this study was that, for institutional reasons, the social work students could not be assigned randomly to the three conditions. Instead we were compelled to use three intact classes, all taking the same course. By chance, the students in the Accent Instruction class happened to be at a much lower starting place than the other two groups. However, their dramatic improvement in confidence (and ability to understand) was all the more impressive for this. It is our contention that people

A CLOSER LOOK: A little knowledge can be a dangerous thing

As we have seen, it is possible to help interlocutors become more familiar with accented speech, and as a consequence, they may become better listeners. However, we would not recommend, as Cho and Reich (2008) have, that teachers alter their speech to mimic that of their learners in an effort to make it more comprehensible to them. These Social Studies teachers advised their colleagues to do the following:

> Adjust speech rate and enunciation. While English is a stress-timed language, many other languages, including Spanish, are syllable-timed languages. English tends to stress one or two syllables and slur the rest of the word or sentence. This means that English sounds are often unclear to some speakers of other languages. Thus, pronouncing equally stressed words or sentences many increase students' comprehension along with adjusted speech rate. (p. 239)

With lower proficiency students, some adjustment to the teacher's speech rate, lexical choice, and grammatical complexity may be necessary and helpful, but giving equal stress to every syllable or even every word would grossly distort the patterns that learners are expected to understand outside the classroom. Experts on second language listening (e.g. Vandergrift & Goh, 2012) would argue that slowing one's speech is unnecessary, and likely does L2 students few favours in preparing them to listen to authentic speech.

who plan careers working with the public, like the social workers here, police officers, teachers, and other professionals, should be given both cultural awareness and accent instruction in their training programs. One student from the Accent Instruction group called her social work instructor 16 months after this study was complete. She had been a part of a team investigation of elder abuse involving a Vietnamese grand-mother. The social work student was the only team member able to communicate with the woman. She credited her experiences during the study with her ability to both elicit the necessary information and understand it.

Weyant (2007) conducted an interesting study in which four groups of college students heard recordings of either a Spanish-accented or a native-English speaker (both women). The speakers read from the same script to control the language used. According to the author, the Spanish speaker was fluent in English and highly com-prehensible, but had a noticeable accent. After hearing the recording, students wrote a paragraph describing a typical day for the speaker. Half of them were told to write from the perspective of the speaker; in other words, they were to put themselves in the shoes of the speaker (either the native speaker or the Spanish-accented speaker, depending on which recording they had heard). The other students were not directed to take on the speaker's perspective. Subsequently, the students filled out their impressions of the speaker using 7-point scales, covering such dimensions as 'unintelligent/intelligent,' 'competent/incompetent,' 'successful/unsuccessful,' and so on. Weyant found that the students writing from the perspective of the Spanish-accented speaker rated her sig-nificantly more favourably on the attitudinal dimensions than the students who did not take a first person perspective. The ratings of the native speaker were not affected by perspective-taking. This finding has implications for intercultural training in the workplace, and for educational institutions. It is heartening that a relatively simple task could have such beneficial effects.

In another intervention involving NSs of English, Kang and Rubin (2012) devised a study in which undergraduate students rated international teaching assistants (ITAs) both before and after a contact activity in which the students and the ITAs met to solve puzzles together, while sharing pizzas. The students from the contact condition rated the ITAs as having higher levels of instructional competence after the intervention than did members of a control group; they also judged the ITAs' speech to be more comprehensible. The one-on-one contact activity encouraged the undergraduate stu-dents to see their ITAs as individual persons, not just talking heads at the front of the room. The contact seemed to instill a willingness to listen.

Willingness to communicate

Peter MacIntyre and his colleagues (MacIntyre, Clément, Dörnyei, & Noels, 1998; MacIntyre, 2007) have proposed the Willingness to Communicate (WTC) framework to describe L2 learners' propensity to interact in their new language. The WTC was originally designed to describe NS-NS interactions, and the factors that contribute to individuals' willingness to initiate a conversation. MacIntyre and colleagues' adapted model accounts for an L2 speaker's willingness to speak in the L2 based on psychological, sociological, and contextual factors. Issues such as anxiety, motivation, confidence, communicative competence, attitudes towards a given interlocutor or group of interlocutors, and personality all underlie an L2 speaker's decision to communicate with another person. The importance of WTC is its contribution to interaction in the L2, which has been shown to lead to greater facility in the language. Obviously, L2 users vary in their own WTC, particularly in terms of personality traits, but as MacIntyre et al. (1998) observed, "certain groups may be more homogeneous than others with respect to certain traits or profiles. As well, groups may show different average or baseline levels of a given trait" (p. 558). Derwing, Munro and Thomson (2008) found evidence of group differences in WTC when they examined two immigrant groups in Canada: Mandarin speakers and speakers of Slavic languages (primarily Russian). Their study entailed listeners' ratings of the L2 speakers' comprehensibility and fluency at three times over a period of two years. They also examined the learners' reported frequency of interactions in English, as well as their perceptions of opportunities to use their L2 at work and in the community. The researchers found that the Mandarin speakers made no significant improvement over the two-year period in either comprehensibility or fluency, while the Slavic language speakers were significantly better on both dimensions at the one-year and two-year points than they were at the outset. Furthermore, they noted that the Slavic language speakers had significantly more interactions in English over the course of a week than did the Mandarin speakers. Even more compelling, though, was the interview data, in which the two groups reported very different approaches to initiating interactions. The Mandarin respondents had less self-confidence, and seemed reluctant to start conversations, while the Slavic language speakers were more optimistic about being able to communicate, regardless of their own limitations. The Slavic speakers' gains in pronunciation were primarily made in the first year (an apparent Window of Maximal Opportunity for some aspects of intelligible speech), but WTC seemed to have benefited them in changing their productions in the absence of any formal pronunciation instruction, while the Mandarin speakers' lack of access to interlocutors hindered their progress.

The social, psychological, and contextual factors that led these two groups to differential success prompted the authors to make several recommendations for language programs to enhance opportunities for interaction in English outside the classroom. First, they suggested that workplaces hiring large numbers of immigrants be provided with cross-cultural workshops and training regarding communication with people who may still be learning English. As noted above, native speakers are sometimes reluctant to interact with L2 speakers, but in some instances, their reservations can be overcome with brief training modules. Second, the authors advised language instructors to provide their students with "strategies for small talk; background information on issues of topical interest; and motivation" (p. 376). Several of the Mandarin speakers had little awareness at the two-year point of high interest "water cooler" topics at the time. One of these was the finals of the Stanley Cup hockey tournament, which involved the Calgary Flames-a team in the same province where the immigrants lived. Another topical concern of which the Mandarin speakers appeared to be unaware was an upcoming Canadian federal election. The Slavic language speakers, on the other hand, had an advantage, because most of them followed hockey and shared a penchant with many Canadians for complaining about politicians. Contrary to stereotypes, not all Canadians watch hockey or even care about it, but when a Canadian team makes the finals, someone who is unaware comes across as 'out of it.' Hockey is a defining feature of Canadian life, as evidenced by the fact that it is very often in the news section as well as the sports pages of Canadian newspapers. And although voter turnout is generally low in elections, complaining about politicians is a favourite Canadian pastime. To be unaware of the names of the political parties and their leaders at the time of an election is likely to be interpreted as a lack of 'with-it-ness' that would discourage interaction with others. Language instructors would do their students a great service to impress upon them how important it is to be able to make small talk about more than the weather in order to establish some common ground and ongoing potential for in-depth interactions. The chief goal is to encourage a sense of belonging, but a side effect is improved language skills, including comprehensibility. As Moyer (2014) points out, "one of the ironies of L2 pronunciation is that those who have mastered it reasonably well tend to have greater confidence in their language abilities overall and to seek out contact with native speakers in order to build social networks" (p. 23).

Pedagogical implications

To this point, we have considered attitudes towards accent, factors that influence identity, and the different social contexts in which second languages are learned, including the role of interlocutors. All of these have implications for instruction, some directly related to the learners' perception and production, and others one or two steps removed.

LeVelle and Levis (2014) offer some suggestions for a 'sociolinguistic core' for pronunciation to be applied in Inner Circle contexts. Their recommendations are intended to help learners gain access to interlocutors and thereby increase opportunities to practice newly-learned patterns. Furthermore, the authors suggest discussing negative attitudes towards accent and ways in which learners might confront such attitudes. The core elements are as follows:

1. Interacting outside the comfort zone
2. Using interactional strategies that match the targeted social group
3. Judiciously using sociolinguistic markers in pronunciation
4. Looking the part
5. Being realistic about both the stigma of accent and long-term outcomes in pronunciation. (p. 111)

These behaviours can serve as ways for L2 speakers to increase their opportunities for interacting and gaining social acceptance, while at the same time improving their pronunciation. As the authors point out, the first of these is an obvious means of eliciting additional input. Language students often complain that they have few opportunities to interact with highly proficient speakers of the L2, but this is often because it is difficult to break with their normal life routines. Derwing et al. (2008) reported on two learners faced with this dilemma:

> It's not easy to find native speakers to talk to. Yesterday, I talk to my husband, I said, "We should found the opportunity to speak to native people." My husband also say "It's difficult. Where can we found native people who can, who can talk with us?" (p. 372).

This couple realized that they would have to leave their comfort zone to find interlocutors. Their first attempt was at a church, but it turned out that most of the parishioners were roughly four decades older than they were, and had little in common with the couple. Teachers may be able to smooth the way by identifying some initial contacts and by explaining to their learners how important it is to motivate themselves to talk to others. Levelle and Levis (2014) suggest that the second and third strategies may help a speaker gain entrance into a target community. They cite Miller's (2003) example of high school students appropriating words such as 'like' because they are in-group markers in that context. Similarly, employing local pronunciation markers can make learners sound more like the interlocutors with whom they want to communicate. When Tracey Derwing was first learning Spanish, she was immersed in an Andalusian context, but was taught Castilian pronunciation in her formal lessons (Spanish approved by the Real Academia Española). Although she was well aware of the "official" pronunciation, she deliberately altered her speech when spending time with her new friends, none of whom employed final plural markers, for instance, and whose speech was notably different from that taught in the classroom. To her, it just seemed to make sense to try to sound like the people who were willing to talk to her, especially given her limited proficiency.

Levelle and Levis's next strategy, looking the part, in some respects seems to overstep the mark in terms of pedagogy. Clearly some learners make clothing choices to look as much as they can like the people around them in order to fit in (e.g. Marx

2002), but this choice is not feasible for everyone, and it strikes us as something that is not the teacher's business to even bring up as a point for discussion. Self-presentation is a private matter that can be tied to variables outside the learner's control (e.g. religious restrictions, financial considerations, and modesty). Part of this same strategy suggested by Levelle and Levis includes body language and gestures. Here we concur that it would be useful for instructors to talk about culturally distinct conventions that learners might not notice on their own.

The final strategy suggested by the Levelle and Levis (2014) is being realistic about stigma and about progress. As Derwing (2003) indicated, "the politics of accent should be explored with second language students. An understanding of the interrelationship of language, accent and social factors may help learners to be more realistic in their goals" (p. 562) as well as more cognizant that some communication breakdowns have absolutely nothing to do with their pronunciation. Rubin's (1992) study is a perfect introduction to a classroom discussion about interlocutors' own contributions to misunderstanding. While globalization may eventually help to change such unconscious influences on perception, in the meantime it is definitely worth discussing the two-way nature of communication with L2 pronunciation students. Levelle and Levis (2014) offer a story of one of their students who was laughed at in a service encounter because of her accent. She reprimanded the clerks and received an apology. Derwing (2003) indicated that learners' own responses to accent discrimination, such as the one Levelle and Levis recounted, are good ways to open discussions on what to do when faced firsthand with accent discrimination.

It is not always easy to convince native speakers to make an effort when talking with L2 speakers, but pronunciation teachers are well positioned to attempt to do so, given their insights into the affective consequences of discrimination or avoidance. Teachers' principal role is to help students become more intelligible and comprehensible, but whenever an opportunity arises to raise awareness of the subconscious assumptions native speakers sometimes make, it behooves them to take advantage of it. This can be done in both formal and informal venues. Intercultural training programs for corporations or government employees, which typically focus on pragmatics, could also introduce research findings about listening to L2 accented speech. Even informal conversations with acquaintances can make a difference. For instance, one of our colleagues, Leila Ranta, told her brother about the Derwing, Rossiter and Munro (2002) training study. She explained that part of the training entailed pointing out common features of Vietnamese-accented English, including reduced consonant clusters and final consonant deletion. Her brother, who worked with a Vietnamese speaker, reported back to his sister a few weeks later that just knowing those two things helped him understand his co-worker's speech. Ultimately, we hope that native speakers and L2 speakers alike can increase their WTC. Surely the responsibility for successful communication rests with both parties in any interaction.

Summary

In this chapter, we have observed that the social impact of speaking with an L2 accent is related to listeners' attitudes, which often involve stereotyping. Evidence of accent discrimination is readily found in the workplace, where visceral reactions to perceived "foreignness" can interfere with perception to the extent that interlocutors can sometimes imagine an L2 accent where none exists. Accent is also a crucial factor in one's self-presentation, as it indicates in-group or out-group status. Furthermore, the context in which an L2 user speaks has a significant role in determining access to other speakers of the L2. Research on the role of the interlocutor has focused almost entirely on NSs of the L2 and has shown that NS reactions to L2 accented speech can be mitigated through training, perspective-taking exercises, and carefully managed contact activities. Finally, the WTC framework, which has been applied to both NS and NNS interlocutors, is a useful account of many of the variables that determine whether an individual will choose to speak to another person.

CHAPTER 9

The ethics of second language accent reduction

In the film, The King's Speech (2010), a biography of King George VI, the main character has a severe stammer. One of the popular treatments of the day is depicted in the movie: a doctor asks the soon-to-be King to fill his mouth with marbles, and to then read a passage from a book. He makes an attempt, and then, exasperated at the complete inef-fectiveness of the method, spits the marbles out, saying, "I nearly swallowed the bloody things." The film makes it obvious that the marbles technique is a worthless gimmick. Interestingly, though, other equally bizarre techniques are currently in use to reduce a foreign accent. (The marbles scene can be found on YouTube ⟨http://www.youtube.com/watch?v=Z-k_beKOFLM⟩)

Introduction

It may seem odd that we are bringing up the notion of ethics in a book on the applica-tion of research to L2 pronunciation instruction. How do ethical considerations even enter the picture? Is there a set of values or principles for L2 pronunciation that differ from L2 teaching in general? Some have argued that altering another person's speech patterns is unethical, because, they say, it is tantamount to altering his or her identity. Porter and Garvin (1989), for example, reported that many teachers feel that "To seek to change someone's pronunciation – whether of the L1 or of an L2 – is to tamper with their self-image and is thus unethical – morally wrong" (p. 8). Golombek and Rehn Jordan (2005), in an article about L2 preservice teachers who plan to instruct EFL, also objected to changing L2 speakers' pronunciation in the name of intelligibility; they argued that "a decentering of the primacy of intelligibility as a skill is necessary if preservice teachers are to make informed decisions about how best to establish their credibility as speakers and teachers of English" (p. 529). There are, no doubt, others who also believe that it is unethical to help L2 speakers change their pronunciation, in case it adversely affects their personal identity. It is our view, however, that if an indi-vidual is unable to communicate in the L2 in a way that interlocutors can understand, the expression of personal identity is threatened far more than by any changes pro-nunciation instruction may bring about. This sentiment was supported in a large study of adult L2 immigrants to Canada, who were asked whether their identities would be threatened by speaking English with a native Canadian English accent. Derwing (2003) found that 95% of respondents would opt to speak with a native accent if they could, and that their identities lay with their mastery of their L1, not their L2. From our standpoint, then, L2 pronunciation teaching is ethical provided that (a) the instruction is from language teachers who have formal training about pronunciation teaching approaches grounded in evidence-based research, (b) the instruction addresses the students' intelligibility and comprehensibility needs, (c) the instruction is based on accurate principles, and (d) the instruction does not exploit the L2 speaker, either financially or through fear tactics or false promises. Until now, we have used the terms 'pronunciation teaching' and 'pronunciation instruction' interchangeably, with the assumption that we are addressing a readership that is largely composed of pronunciation researchers, ESL teachers, students in TESL or applied linguistics programs, or students who intend to conduct research in the area of L2 pronunciation. However, applied linguists and language teachers are not the only ones interested in working with L2 speakers when it comes to aspects of accented speech.

'Accent reduction,' 'foreign accent modification,' and 'pronunciation teaching' all refer to approaches to changing a speaker's productions in the L2, but they are typically employed by three distinct groups of providers: entrepreneurs, speech language pathologists (SLPs), and language instructors, respectively (Derwing & Munro, 2009). Although many people assume that accent reduction and accent modification are the same as pronunciation teaching, in fact, they can be quite dissimilar. In addition, as Thomson (2014) points out, some blurring can occur across the three models, such that some SLPs set up private businesses to specialize in foreign accent modification, as do some language teachers (although on a much smaller scale).

Thomson (2014) evaluated the top 50 Google hits for "accent instruction" and "accent modification," as well as 50 sites that offered pronunciation assistance, to compare mode of delivery, educational background, and cost. Providers of accent reduction and accent modification tend to use face-to-face or Skype lessons, in addition to selling printed or recorded materials, while those sites offering pronunciation instruction are primarily intended as supplementary resources either for teachers or for any L2 speaker who wants to access them. As Thomson points out, face-to-face delivery within the education model of pronunciation instruction happens more often in language classrooms.

Accent reduction – The business model

Accent reduction is the term most often used by entrepreneurs who view L2 speakers as clients who want to sound more like native speakers. Some such providers are known for outrageous assertions, such as the common claim that they can "eliminate" a foreign accent. Although some entrepreneurs may have professional training, others do not. Nor is there any regulation of the accent reduction business; anyone can claim to be an accent reduction expert, regardless of educational background or experience (Thomson, 2013a). Lippi-Green (2012) actually likens the claims of many accent reduction entrepreneurs to those who assert that they "have developed a miracle diet and charge money for it" (p. 229). Anyone with a lot of hubris who can come up with a website and make arrangements for credit card payments has the basis for an accent reduction business.

Often accent reductionists have a prominent presence on the web, offering sample lessons, in addition to advertising their services. A visit to such sites is eye-opening, indeed. For example, "Coach" Andy Krieger, an accent reduction businessman based in Vancouver, Canada, states in a sample web lesson that "In American English there are no syllables" ⟨http://www.youtube.com/watch?v=nUGAgES2BUY⟩. From a linguistic standpoint, this is an absurd assertion, and a claim that simply isn't true. Even kindergarten children can grasp the notion of 'syllable' and can count and manipulate syllables in American English (Liberman, Shankweiler, Fischer, & Carter, 1974). Ironically, the intention of the lesson seemed to have been a directive to stress the first syllable of bi- and tri-syllabic words, "not the middle, not the end."

Krieger offers other advice on his website, such as "Speak more slowly to allow youself (sic) time to get your tongue and lips into an EXACT POSITION, to make every word have a LONG VOWEL, AND ALWAYS MAKE YOU (sic) VOICE ALWAYS (sic) GO DOWN." "ALWAYS start with your MOUTH OPEN." (Emphasis in original; ⟨http://www.andykrieger.com/⟩. In just a few lines, we find several overgeneralizations that may seriously mislead students. Speaking more slowly, for instance, is not necessarily good advice, especially for L2 students who may already have difficulties with oral fluency. Munro and Derwing (1998) conducted a study in which Mandarin speakers of English produced utterances both at their normal speaking rate and at a slowed rate. In a subsequent evaluation task, NS listeners judged the slow L2 productions to be *less* comprehensible and *more* accented than the normal-rate speech. In a follow-up study which entailed both speeding up and slowing down natural L2 speech rates by 10 percent (Munro & Derwing, 2001), native listeners found that the optimal speech rate for comprehension was somewhat faster than L2 speakers' own natural rates, unless the L2 speakers were already very fast talkers. In other words, slowing down the speech rate of L2 speakers, whose normal L2 speaking rates are usually slower than NSs anyway, does not necessarily facilitate better comprehensibility, and may actually impede it.

The second piece of advice, that speakers should allow themselves to have time to get their "tongue and lips into an EXACT position" is also highly questionable. Not only is the speech stream continuous, precluding stopping and starting until the "exact" position is located, but also co-articulation, that is, the phenomenon of individual speech sounds being affected by the position of previous and following ones, means there is no EXACT position for a given sound in English. A hallmark of normal, highly-intelligible speech, then, is its lack of exactness. If one were to attempt to produce all segments as they are said in citation form (that is, in isolation), the resulting speech would be very odd indeed. In the early days of speech synthesis, researchers attempted to replicate human speech by joining individual sounds. However, they soon recognized that intelligible synthetic speech cannot be created by simply concatenating a series of independent phones, no matter how "exact" they are. Rather, Olive (1998) notes that it is essential to replicate the transitional movements of the articulators in order to obtain speech that is understandable. In sum, advising students to aim for exact positions would most likely result in greater- rather than less-accented speech, along with reduced intelligibility.

The third suggestion, to make every word have a long vowel, is also a misrepresentation of what happens in typical English. Function words, such as 'a', 'the', 'but', 'in', etc., have reduced vowels, except in situations of emphasis or contrast. If all such words were to be pronounced with long vowels (and it seems clear from the *YouTube* video cited above that 'long' is used in the temporal sense), the rhythm of an utterance would become highly distorted. Yet rhythm is an aspect of speech that helps listeners to process it effectively. The most likely effect of the recommended strategy would be a loss of comprehensibility.

The next piece of advice from the website, "ALWAYS MAKE YOU VOICE ALWAYS GO DOWN," is somewhat ambiguous: it either implies (incorrectly) that there is only one intonation pattern in English, or means that the volume or loudness should be reduced at the end of utterances. In either case, this is a severe distortion of the facts of English prosody, one that L2 speakers would be ill-advised to follow. Variable intonation patterns are fundamental to English, and loss of volume at the ends of utterances is almost certain to reduce intelligibility.

Finally, L2 speakers are counseled to "ALWAYS start with your MOUTH OPEN." This mysterious recommendation seems to have been made without regard for utterances beginning with labial consonants such as /m/, /b/, /p/, /v/, /f/, which, by their very nature, require closure of the mouth. The problems identified in a few lines on this website are not isolated phenomena – many accent reduction websites make similarly egregious misstatements.

We chose to feature this particular accent reductionist because of his high profile. In one widely publicized instance, Krieger was contracted by the Creighton Elementary School District in Arizona, to work with Hispanic-background teachers, to help reduce their accents (Lacey, 2011). This case is just one of many indications that the claims made by the accent reduction industry have a certain cachet with potential clients, who appear to have little awareness of the quality of the advice. Jordan, writing for the *Wall Street Journal* (April 30, 2010), reported that the Arizona Department of Education ordered school districts to remove teachers whose English was heavily accented or ungrammatical from classes containing ESL students. According to the *Wall Street Journal* account, state auditors objected to some teachers' use of forms such as 'biolet' for 'violet' and 'tink' for 'think' -clearly representing low Functional Load substitutions that are unlikely to interfere with comprehensibility. The teachers were unfairly targeted by an unethical policy; in fact, some of them were then asked to attend an accent reduction program. Both the Linguistic Society of America (LSA) and Teachers of English to Speakers of Other Languages (TESOL), professional organizations for scholars engaged in the scientific study of language and language teaching respectively, issued resolutions against Arizona's language policies. The LSA's statement criticized Arizona State's 'English Fluency Initiative' on the following points: "1. The policy is based on uninformed linguistic and educational assumptions about accents and the role of accents in language teaching and learning. ... 2. The policy has the potential to unfairly target Latina/o teachers, and their students, by removing the very teachers who may be best qualified to teach them. The policy therefore risks an overall decrease in the acquisition of English by ELL students. And 3. The policy communicates to students that foreign accented speech is 'bad' or 'harmful'. This is counterproductive to learning, and affirms pre-existing patterns of linguistic bias and harmful 'linguistic profiling' (LSA, 2010). The US Departments of Justice and Education eventually stepped in: "Facing a possible civil-rights lawsuit, Arizona has struck an agreement with federal officials to stop monitoring classrooms for mispronounced words" (Kossan, 2011).

Some accent reduction providers are eager to share their lucrative market with others by offering training for prospective accent coaches. AmericanAccent.com, ⟨http://www.americanaccent.com/instructor_training.html⟩, for example, offers a 5-week course (one hour a week) over *Skype* for $500. There seem to be no prerequisites, and no final assessment of knowledge or ability. According to the website, in the course, "you go through all of the aspects of teaching the American accent, including intonation, word connections, pronunciation, classroom management, teaching techniques, student assignments, tests and tracking, navigating the online program and exactly how to conduct the diagnostic analysis for a variety of nationalities."[1] This list describes a very ambitious program, particularly for those trainees who have no linguistics, TESL, or even general educational background. As Watt and Taplin (1997) and Thomson (2004) have argued, any training program for people who are planning

---

1.   The notion of a diagnostic analysis for a variety of "nationalities" doesn't make sense. Nationality has no direct connection with pronunciation issues; it is the learner's L1 and possibly other learned languages that influence a new language. Although nationality and L1 are correlated to a certain degree, there is no causal relationship between what is essentially a political/geographical phenomenon and language learning.

to instruct L2 learners should go beyond a minimum requirement of being able to pay the tuition; furthermore, they have pointed out that "[p]rograms must be able to demonstrate that students in the program are evaluated on their learning. In short, it must be possible to fail for reasons of inability" (Watt & Taplin, 1997, p. 73), which cannot happen in a program that has no assessment component.

Targetting clients over the Internet is not confined to a few isolated cases; thousands of sites promoting accent reduction appear on the web (at the time of writing, there were over 472,000 hits for 'accent reduction,' 8,150 for 'accent elimination' and 6,700 for accent modification). Consider the following:

> We will give you a sample lesson for FREE! Live 1 on 1 coaching using *Skype* or your telephone covering a specific area that you'd like to focus on 〈http://www. cleartalkmastery.com/accent-reduction-ticket/〉

One problem with such an ad is that L2 speakers are often unable to identify which aspects of their speech cause the greatest problems for intelligibility (Derwing, 2003). Learners may be aware of some of the most salient aspects of their accents (e.g. English learners often have difficulties producing /θ/ and /ð/ and know it), but cannot give guidance to an accent reduction coach regarding those elements that make them difficult to understand. In fact, the most serious problem with accent reduction generally is that its proponents often work on changing accents without regard for intelligibility and comprehensibility. As we saw in Chapter 1 and elsewhere, the three dimensions of speech, intelligibility, comprehensibility, and accentedness, although related, are partially independent. Thus it is quite possible to change one's accent without changing either of the other two dimensions. In worst-case scenarios, clients of accent reductionists can actually be encouraged to sound less intelligible (see A Closer Look: Joanna Tam, this chapter). Although many accent reduction businesses have testimonials on their websites, they offer no scientific evidence that their lessons actually help their clients. Instead, some use fear tactics to suggest that people may lose their jobs because of their accents, while others claim career benefits as a result of their courses. Private tuition is not cheap; one program we examined charges $125 for a 50-minute session, with a minimum of 10 sessions. This is typical of accent reduction sites in general.

The lack of regulation of accent reduction programs means that learners may be vulnerable to claims from providers who have no actual expertise or knowledge about phonetics, phonology, or even foreign accent. Consider, for example, a newspaper story (Stuparyk, 1996) highlighted in Derwing (2008) of an accent reductionist, based in Toronto, who asked learners to recite the tongue twister 'Peter Piper picked a peck of pickled peppers. How many pickled peppers did Peter Piper pick?' in order to improve their production of the phoneme /p/. The L2 speakers were expected to produce this sentence while holding a marshmallow between their upper and lower teeth, thus holding their lips open. Basic phonetics tells us that the production of

A CLOSER LOOK: Joanna Tam

In 2011, Joanna Tam, then a Master's student in Drama at Tufts University, developed an innovative study in which she recorded herself receiving Skype lessons in accent reduction from a so-called expert. Joanna produced a video, showing her lessons and her struggle to change her accent. Her accent in English comes from her first language, Cantonese, and the variety of English she learned in school in Hong Kong: British RP. The changes on which the coach chose to focus were towards a more North American accent; but, in almost every instance, Joanna's "American" productions were less intelligible than her original pronunciation. Her rendition of 'dentist' for example, was perfectly clear when she pronounced it the way she had learned it in Hong Kong, with a /t/ in the middle of the word. Her "corrected" version, with the help of her accent coach, sounded like 'Dennis.' She focused so hard on leaving out the medial /t/ that she unintentionally eliminated the final /t/ as well. Similar problems emerged with the shift in her production of 'disappointing' from /dɪsə'pɔɪntɪŋ/ to /dɪsə'pɔɪŋ/, where she went from an appropriate four syllables to a less comprehensible three, all in an effort to eliminate the /t/ which the coach found so un-American. Several other examples in Joanna's video demonstrated that her coach's efforts to get Joanna to sound "less foreign" ended up making her less intelligible-at least during her lessons. As Joanna said "my accent is not standard-that's what my coach told me. She also kept telling me that I'm too British. Ok, I didn't know that. I thought I was too Chinese. But I think it makes sense-I'm from Hong Kong after all. Schwa, tap /t/, held /t/, voiced consonants-I was bombarded with these terms for two months. All I remember now is that my coach wanted me to drop all my /t/s" (Tam, 2012). In the end, months after the intervention, Joanna found that her pronunciation during conversational speech had not changed at all. Fortunately, her coach's attempts to change her speech had not worked, or she would have become less comprehensible than she was prior to instruction.

word-initial /p/ requires closure of the lips, followed by a puff of air on release called aspiration. There are many reasons to question the merit of this exercise. First, because the learners were from diverse language backgrounds, some likely had no difficulty producing a recognizable /p/ and were thus wasting their time. Others may have had a shorter aspiration period—a distinguishing feature between /p/ and /b/–than is typically found in English /p/, but, as Munro, Derwing and Saito (2013) have shown, less aspiration doesn't necessarily interfere with intelligibility. Finally, and most troubling, even if some of the learners had trouble producing English /p/, this particular activity would probably not help them, since the marshmallow interferes with lip closure.

Misinformation about the English sound system abounds on the Internet. Consider the following discussion of /n/ from ⟨http://www.l2accent.com/blog/tag/foreign-accents/page/2/⟩: "When we first learn the English alphabet, we are taught that there is only one /n/. …The first [n] is what often comes to mind as the regular [n], such as the [n] in the words "nice", "never" and "knowledge". This [n] is a short and sweet sound that temporarily directs air through your nose before the next sound quickly redirects it back into your oral cavity. The second and perhaps more obscure pronunciation of the /n/ consonant is called the syllabic [n]. The syllabic [n] is very important in the production of the North American English accent and it is characterized by an elongated direction of air through the nose. In other terms, *the syllabic [n] is simply held for longer than the regular [n]. It is very easy to identify the syllabic [n], because it appears every time the [n]is the last sound in a word.* For example, *common words such as "phone", "mean" and "button" all contain the syllabic [n]"* (italics added). The site goes on to list another five words that purportedly have a syllabic [n̩], although only one of the words actually does. From the standpoint of articulatory phonetics, the description of syllabic [n̩] is incorrect. A better description is that /n/ in an unstressed position can take on the status of syllable in the absence of a vowel, as in the words 'rotten', 'buttoned', 'wouldn't'. Single syllable nouns and verbs ending in /n/ such as 'phone' and 'mean' do not have a syllabic [n̩], and neither do words with stress on the final syllable, such as 'complain,' one of the faulty examples given on the website. Furthermore, syllabic [n̩] is not restricted to word final position; although it can never occur in a stressed syllable, it can appear medially in words such as 'buttoning.' These facts are entirely missed in an account that misleads potential clients about the nature of English syllabic consonants.

This same accent reduction website offers several goods for sale, including "Speech Buddies," tools that were originally developed for speech-language pathologists to use with children who have articulation disorders. At the time of writing, a Speech Buddy kit with all five plastic tools (about the size and similar in shape to some dental instruments) was offered for $299 CAD plus tax, plus shipping and handling. The tools can also be bought separately for $149 each; individual tools have been designed for /tʃ/, /ʃ/, /s/, /l/ and /ɹ/. The website does not distinguish between LIGHT and DARK /l/, or syllable initial and syllable final /ɹ/, although these sounds are produced differently. That is, the website claims that the /l/ tool will help with "words like leap, lower and school" and that the /ɹ/ tool will allow one to "produce the R sound perfectly" in words such as "rain, ride and bird." A *YouTube* video intended for SLPs who work with speech disorders is available on the accent reduction website to assist L2 learners with the placement of the tools in the mouth. As with so many accent reduction claims, we know of no evidence that Speech Buddies actually improve L2 pronunciation, just unsubstantiated claims that they do.

We have deliberately focused on Canadian sites in this chapter, but that is not to say that there aren't English language accent reduction programs in other immigrant-receiving countries – for example, *Accent Solutions, Accent Coaching for New Kiwis* ⟨http://www.accentsolutions.co.nz/⟩ offers to "improve your employability" in New Zealand; the *Australia English Institute* ⟨http://www.australiaenglish.com/ accent-reduction/⟩ promises "at least 50% improvement in your accent" (with no indication of how improvement is measured); and *The International Society of Communication and Drama* (*Voice and Accent Reduction*) in Britain ⟨http://iscad.org.uk/voice-and-accent/⟩ offers a course intended for L2 speakers which includes "Essential pronunciation – "TH" sounds voiced & unvoiced; non-rhotic "R"; schwa sound; voiced consonants and more." As indicated in earlier chapters, /θ/ and /ð/ are hardly essential, and as Jenkins (2002) has argued, rhotic productions are likely more intelligible than non-rhotic varieties. Why voiced consonants would pose more of a problem than voiceless consonants is never explained, especially since the site does not pursue clients from particular L1 backgrounds. There don't appear to be any guiding principles in the focus of instruction. The strongest claims we found, however, were on an American website: *The Accent Reduction Institute* ⟨http://www.lessaccent.com/⟩. "We promise you'll communicate clearly, and retain your culture," "We have a 100% customer satisfaction record," and "We boast greater than 70% average improvement in English pronunciation." From our perspective, the operative word here is 'boast.' One of the ways in which the *Accent Reduction Institute* (ARI) measures its success is the number of articles that have appeared in the media about the company. This particular business operates on a greater scale than many others, because it mainly targets large organizations that can pay for multiple employees to receive accent reduction programming, both in the USA and abroad. ARI also maintains that it has "metrics based outcomes" such that it can produce "over 70% reduction in critical speech errors." The site does not state what the critical speech errors are, or how they were measured; thus we cannot determine what the contributions of these "critical speech errors" are to intelligibility or comprehensibility. In fact, we find these assertions troubling, given that in L2 acquisition research on pronunciation, it is still poorly understood how aspects of an L2 accent interact to affect intelligibility, and as yet, only a few variables have been investigated individually for their impact. Perhaps ARI has decided a priori which speech errors are critical, and has been able to assist people in reducing these errors, but as we have argued in this chapter and elsewhere, accent reduction does not necessarily result in increased intelligibility or comprehensibility.

Accent modification – The medical model

Another group of providers, speech language pathologists (SLPs), often use the term 'foreign accent modification,' or FAM, to describe their services. As a report in *The ASHA Leader* indicates, "Many speech-language pathologists in the United States are discovering a niche market that's been around for more than 40 years but is growing: assisting highly educated non-native English speakers with their English communication skills, including accent modification" (Feinstein-Whittaker, Wilner, & Sikorski, 2012). Given that accent modification "will be a part of almost all working caseloads, at least to some extent, in the future" (p. 128), Schmidt and Sullivan (2003) wanted to know what preparation SLPs receive to serve L2 clientele. In their examination of graduate training opportunities for SLPs across the USA, nearly a quarter of responding programs did not offer any FAM programming. Although both the American and Canadian SLP professional associations, ASHA and CASLPA respectively, state that accent should not be viewed as a disorder (Thomson, 2013a), half of the 76 clinics Schmidt and Sullivan (2003) surveyed used diagnostic tests intended to identify speech disorders in their accent modification programs. Twenty-five percent of program respondents considered NNSs to be speech impaired, despite the fact that they were enrolled only in accent modification programs (a much larger percentage of impairment than one would expect in the general population). Schmidt and Sullivan hypothesized that these SLPs do actually view accent as a disorder. In other words, some of the SLPs may agree with Griffen (1980), who argued that "The goal of instruction in pronunciation is that the student ... should learn to speak the language as naturally as possible, free of any indication that the speaker is not a clinically normal native" (p. 182). That is to say, they may view an L2 accent as an abnormality despite the statements of their professional associations to the contrary.

Irrespective of whether some SLPs actually do consider an L2 accent to be a medical affliction, the ways in which they market their services sometimes convey a medical message. For instance, at the University of Alberta, *The Institute for Stuttering Treatment and Research (ISTAR)* offered a one-day workshop in 2011 for "English as a second language learners who wish to increase their intelligibility through reduction of their accent. ... General instruction about how to produce the English sounds and how to reduce speech rate for improved intelligibility will be provided." The poster advertising this event was sent through university email accounts to all academic and nonacademic staff. The poster also indicated that the staff benefits agreements "provide speech therapy coverage through the Supplementary Health Benefits. Academic staff receive $1000 per year per covered person and support staff receive $1000 per benefit year per person. In addition, Academic staff may utilize their Health Spending Account Account (sic) to pay additional speech therapy costs. Our speech-language pathologists are registered practitioners in Alberta and Canada." The level of detail on how to recover the cost of the $300 workshop seems to belie the position of professional SLP organizations that an accent is not a medical disorder. Instead, the poster presented accent reduction as worthy of health benefit insurance claims. We note also that the poster was aimed at language learners in general, regardless of their intelligibility needs and that it focused on segmentals and speech rate, although we know from research that suprasegmentals are also implicated in intelligibility problems. It is troubling as well that speech rate was identified as the only nonsegmental feature, and that slowing down was advocated. As noted above, a reduction in speech rate is likely to be beneficial only for fast talkers; moreover, many L2 speakers talk at a slower rate than native speakers, and indeed, have difficulty with fluency (Derwing, Rossiter,

Munro, & Thomson, 2004; Gatbonton & Segalowitz, 2005; Munro & Derwing, 2001; Rossiter, 2009). Interestingly, one of the primary approaches to helping stutterers, ISTAR's main clientele, is to encourage slowing of their speech. Perhaps the institute staff drew a parallel between foreign accents and fluency disorders, a comparison that we unequivocally reject.

Standard #18 of the CASLPA code of ethics reads as follows:

> Members shall not exploit the client by: (a) providing unnecessary or futile services/ products where benefit or continued benefit cannot be reasonably expected. This does not preclude a member from providing a period of trial therapy or product trial to determine if benefit could occur. (p. 4)

While we are not in a position to judge how well particular institutions adhere to this standard, the evidence-based approach to pronunciation that we advocate offers a meaningful perspective on the ethical concern at issue. In particular, a benefit from pronunciation instruction can be established (even in a trial period) only if a satisfactory initial assessment is carried out. Without actual assessment of a client's needs it is simply not possible to propose and implement a suitable course of instruction. As we have pointed out throughout this volume, empirical evidence shows dramatic variability in individual pronunciation difficulties, even among speakers from very similar backgrounds. Consequently, effective instruction foci must be selected individually for learners, with due attention to the results of an assessment. It simply isn't possible to know in advance which learners may benefit from instruction on individual sounds, a modification of speech rate, or any other specific work. Therefore, providing instruction that does not match learners' needs constitutes offering "unnecessary or futile services." In our view, then, "one size fits all" programs run a very high risk of violating CALSPAs Standard #18.

A prominent FAM program ⟨http://speechscience.com/about-us/faqs/⟩ lists several frequently asked questions on its website. One of the questions given was the following: "Q: *How long will it take to improve my pronunciation and accent? A: You will start to improve after the first session. However it generally takes from 3 months to 1 year to make significant improvements.*" No evidence is provided for the time estimate in the answer. Research studies of pronunciation interventions generally cover no more than twelve to sixteen weeks, often because of the constraints of school semester/term structures. To our knowledge, no scientific study exists of instructed pronunciation improvement that requires a year before significant change can be identified. However, given the costs of short-term instruction advertised on many sites, a year of instruction in a private program would certainly be expensive. Interestingly, questions about cost do not appear on the web page. A prospective client must contact the program to determine what the associated expenses are. This is consistent with Thomson's (2014) findings that many FAM programs do not indicate prices up front. Another frequently asked question on the same site is also of interest: "Q: *Can I sound like a native English Speaking* (sic) *through your accent programs? A: If you work at it – you may be able to achieve this goal. However, it is our opinion that having an accent is part of your identity, culture and heritage. You can be proud of your accent!! – it shows people you are bi or tri lingual. We will teach you how to sound clear and confident in English at all times, so that pronunciation or intonation difficulty never becomes a barrier to your communication.*" The first part of this answer has no basis in research findings that we are aware of. Rather, the best available evidence suggests that even adult L2 speakers who work very hard to improve their pronunciation are unlikely to sound like native speakers; in fact, we know of no documented case of an L2 speaker who has achieved the equivalent of a native speaker accent as a direct result of accent reduction or foreign accent modification. This claim is an example of the hyperbole commonly associated with accent reduction and accent modification programs.

Pronunciation instructors

We recognize that numerous English language teachers (ELTs) are involved in pronunciation instruction in the absence of any formal training in the area. Some may feel impelled by good intentions to help learners, but may actually have unrealistic intuitions about what their learners need. In Chapter 5 we reported that many ESL/ EFL instructors feel inadequately trained, and are thus reluctant to teach pronunciation. Others have developed methods on their own, based on intuition and sometimes faulty hypotheses. For instance, Usher (1995) suggested that English /p/ and /b/ are distinguished by breathing, such that /p/ sounds are exhaled, while /b/ sounds are inhaled. He claimed to have taught his ESL students to produce /b/ by inhaling as they said the word 'baby'. This approach to distinguishing between /p/ and /b/ is repeated in a book entitled *English is Stupid* (Thompson, 2011), which targets both language teachers and students. Despite the repeated claim, linguistic descriptions of the English sound system confirm conclusively that normal production of English uses egressive air (i.e. it entails exhalation only; see Cruttenden, 1994); no systematic use of sounds produced during inhaling (ingressives) exists in English. Indeed, the only meaningful ingressive sounds occasionally used by English speakers are the alveolar and lateral clicks represented by 'tsk tsk' and the sound to get horses to move; these are not words in the usual sense, though they have semantic value. In another teacher publication, van Loon (2002) writes that he was able to improve his L2 learners' comprehensibility by having them pause after every noun and verb in a sentence or longer passage. There is no evidence other than the author's own report that this technique results in clearer comprehensibility (no measures were made, and the addition of pauses at places other than natural phrase or clause boundaries directly contradicts actual L2 fluency research, see, for example, Wennerstrom, 2000). Similarly, another instructor-developed technique in which students hold pencils between their noses and upper lips has been advocated as an all-purpose exercise for improving English pronunciation (Stuparyk, 1996). We know of no evidence, of course, that a "stiff upper lip" will increase an L2 speaker's intelligibility.

Thomson (2013b) surveyed English language teachers, asking them to indicate whether they agreed or disagreed with a number of statements that have been made regarding accent. Some statements were relatively uncontroversial (e.g. "Accents are caused by carrying over the sound systems from students' native languages to their second language," p. 227), while others were patently false (e.g. "The /r/ sound comes from your stomach. Your stomach moves in and you can feel it in your stomach," p. 228). Thomson found that many of his respondents were comfortable with notions that they had learned in TESL programs but noted that they were "unable to critically evaluate beliefs and practices they have not previously encountered. This makes them susceptible to following dubious advice found on the Internet and in other materials" (p. 231). Furthermore, even the respondents who reported having taken a course specifically designed to prepare them to teach pronunciation were relatively uncritical of suggestions that were poor reflections of reality. Thomson reported that "57% of these more qualified teachers agreed that pronunciation errors result from having speech muscles that are not properly toned, while 36% agreed that improper airflow caused a foreign accent. A total of 14% agreed that learners can strengthen their tongue by placing it on the roof of their mouth applying suction and releasing it to make a popping sound; 14% also agreed that an English /b/ is produced while breathing in" (p. 229). In fact none of these suggestions has been shown to have any merit. Taken together, Thomson's findings point to a need for L2 teachers to become more conversant with the ways sounds are produced, the nature of both segmentals and suprasegmentals, approaches to initial assessment of students' needs, and appropriate techniques and activities to develop improved perception and production.

Summary

Throughout this chapter, we have presented a negative perspective on accent reduction, accent modification, and misinformed practices in pronunciation teaching. Especially in the case of many companies operating in the fields of accent reduction and accent modification, the primary motivation appears to be financial, sometimes with little or no evidence of careful, evidence-based consideration of L2 speakers' outcomes. We question the ethics of such businesses, and moreover, we reiterate Derwing, Fraser, Kang, and Thomson's caution (2014, p. 73), that "it is no less unethical if the person providing pronunciation instruction honestly believes he or she is equipped to teach pronunciation by virtue of his/her occupation as an ELT or SLP" alone. Some SLPs and English language teachers do indeed have the requisite knowledge and skills to make a difference to the intelligibility and comprehensibility of their clients/students. They have taken it upon themselves to learn about L2 acquisition, to read the research on intelligibility, and to avail themselves of training in teaching L2 pronunciation. Others, however, have not been so conscientious. The evidence of the use of fear tactics, promises of better career options, and testimonials (with no contact information) on some websites have no more substance than the claims of snake oil salesmen in the late 19th century. The words *caveat emptor* or 'buyer beware,' have never been more relevant. The problem of ethical concerns about pronunciation instruction is a topic that we encourage language teachers to discuss with their students. We also see a need for more commitment from SLP and TESL training programs to acquaint future professionals with the principles of pronunciation instruction and the difference between accent and intelligibility.

CHAPTER 10

Future directions

When we think of the future, we are tempted to imagine amazing new technologies that will decisively solve the problems of today. Science fiction has often presented us with future scenarios in which technology can be used for enhancing communication. One popular type of device is the 'Universal Translator' – many versions of this exist, including a fish inserted in one's ear (Hitchhiker's Guide to the Galaxy), bacteria that infect the brain of both the speaker and listener (Farscape), a chip embedded in a shirt collar (The Last Starfighter), and communicator pins on a uniform (Star Trek: The Next Generation). If such translators ever become reality, then we presumably won't need to learn new languages, and intelligibility will no longer be an issue. In fact, commercial translation applications now exist, but they remain somewhat restrictive and subject to error. Lucrative careers are still available for human interpreters and translators around the world. Given the current state of translation software, we don't expect any revolutionary changes in the status quo. People will still want to talk directly to each other, communication solutions that are satisfactory for interactions that go beyond basic transactional uses (including pragmatic/cultural adjustments) are not likely to be developed for a very long time. We therefore predict that pronunciation instruction will become more popular long before it fades away.

As we saw in Chapter 2, instruction in L2 pronunciation has existed for centuries; and there is every reason to believe that it will become even more important in the immediate future. Numerous scholars (e.g. Crystal, 2003; Graddol, 2006) have discussed the remarkable impact of English in the 20th and 21st centuries, during which globalization has become a powerful force. The world economy, arts and entertainment, technology, and academia are all dominated by English. While no one knows how long this cultural and technological trend will continue, the need for clear communication skills has become deeply entrenched. In addition, continued large-scale immigration to English-dominant countries such as Australia, Canada, New Zealand, the UK, and the USA is a significant impetus for successful L2 communication. Finally, as baby boomers age, particularly in these immigrant-receiving countries, the number of interactions with L2 speakers will increase exponentially. Researchers (e.g. Duff, Wong, & Early, 2002) have indicated that L2 immigrants are often employed in assisted living and nursing homes, where they encounter difficulties communicating with the residents. This poses important challenges: not only can accented speech sometimes be difficult for younger people to understand, but the difficulties are exacerbated in the elderly by age-related language processing difficulties and hearing loss (Burda, Scherz, Hageman, & Edwards, 2003). Thus it is extremely important that L2 caregivers in these contexts have clear speech.

Of course, if English loses its privileged position in the global context and is replaced by some other language, pronunciation will still matter. Whenever different language groups come into contact (without a universal translator!) the issues related to second language intelligibility and comprehensibility will always arise, just as they do now. In the sections that follow, we discuss the directions in which we hope to see our field progress.

Directions for pronunciation research

Although the last few decades have seen important developments in research on all aspects of L2 pronunciation, we perceive two general themes that are still in need of considerable expansion. First, given the well-established fact that accent is partially independent of comprehensibility and intelligibility, and that the latter two are more important to successful communication, we need more detailed probing of the relationships among these speech dimensions. Such work should focus on the factors that contribute to intelligibility and comprehensibility, including linguistic aspects of L2 speech, processing abilities of the listener, and other situational issues that may affect understanding. Second, there is a clear need for more instructional research on pronunciation to help us identify efficient and effective teaching strategies and techniques.

With respect to methodologies, pronunciation researchers should consider conducting more longitudinal studies, just as investigators in other areas of SLA are being urged to do (Ortega & Iberri-Shea, 2005). One benefit of such studies is that they permit a close examination of the details of phonetic learning to help us understand the acquisition process better. Cross-sectional designs frequently disallow firm conclusions about the process because the participants inevitably differ in ways that are uncontrolled. Another benefit of longitudinal studies of teaching is the possibility of establishing the long-term effects of interventions on learners' pronunciation performance. At present, most studies with before-after designs do not evaluate learners at time points months or even years after the completion of an intervention.

Finally, most of the L2 research that has been conducted thus far has focused on English L2 speakers. Generalizations that can be made for learners of English do not necessarily transfer to learners of other languages. For instance, certain aspects of English prosody, such as lexical stress, may be important for ESL speakers from a wide range of languages, but that same feature may have little or no relevance for learners of other languages in which lexical stress is highly predicable or absent. In addition, prosodic phenomena from other languages such as tone and mora-based timing are highly important in Mandarin and Japanese, respectively. These issues reflect a need for more studies of pronunciation learning in languages other than English, both in instructed and in naturalistic situations.

Directions for teaching

In Chapter 5, we pointed to the limited opportunities for language teachers to obtain L2 pronunciation training. Various surveys have indicated that this is not a localized problem, but one that is found in several immigrant-receiving countries; furthermore, teachers themselves have expressed a desire to learn more about pronunciation issues in order to help their students. The time is right for more resources to be developed and provided to language teachers both pre- and inservice. TESL programs now have an excellent opportunity to enhance their offerings by including a pronunciation-specific course in which teachers learn the practical aspects of teaching as well as the rationale behind them, supported by research. Providing substantive training for teachers would serve as a catalyst for promoting changes in practice that reflect an up-to-date, research-based perspective, founded on the Intelligibility Principle.

A parallel direction for language program directors and materials writers is the development of L2 pronunciation curricula, along with a new approach to materials, including those based on new technologies, that emphasize individual needs over 'one size fits all' packages. Moreover, the development of any new audio and audiovisual materials should be multi-purposed to include a focus on pronunciation learning. For example, videos designed to illustrate pragmatic principles could be accompanied with suggestions for instructors highlighting pronunciation issues. It is unreasonable to expect individual classroom teachers to do this on their own with new resources, but materials developers could easily include awareness-raising activities and other listening practice, along with the primary linguistic focus of the material.

Despite a long tradition in the phonetic sciences that highlights the importance of speech perception in phonological acquisition, much of the current programming and material focuses almost exclusively on production. Yet perceptual learning is clearly tied to accurate speaking. Thus, the available evidence suggests that programming should emphasize perception to a much greater degree.

Directions for assessment

At the program or classroom level, assessment of L2 students' intelligibility and comprehensibility should take place regularly and should guide curriculum structure and learning activities. As noted in several chapters in this volume, learners' pronunciation errors are only partially predictable on the basis of the L1. Rather, what is especially striking about phonetic learning is the large degree of individual variability among speakers. Individualized needs assessments are therefore essential if students are to benefit optimally from the time they spend in the classroom and in self-study. To carry out such assessments, teachers need carefully designed, easy to use assessment tools that incorporate rubrics based on sound principles. The development of such instruments would go a long way to assisting teachers, not only with initial needs assessment, but with formative and summative assessments as well.

Another issue pertaining to assessment concerns International Teaching Assistants (ITAs), who work in post-secondary institutions. In spite of good proficiency in the language in which they are expected to teach, they often face complaints from undergraduate students about their comprehensibility. Although some institutions have developed elaborate programs to assist ITAs, others offer little support. Individualized assessments of these speakers, based on the types of interaction they are required to undertake, would be useful. It would also help to separate out complaints based on accent scapegoating and prejudice from legitimate intelligibility concerns.

Assessment specialists are becoming more cognizant of the role of pronunciation in standardized oral language testing. In particular, the confusion between a strong accent and reduced intelligibility has become an important topic of discussion (Harding, 2011). Although the testing of pronunciation is now on assessors' radar, there is a compelling need for more research on factors influencing rater reliability and construct validity. Large-scale testing and educational measurement organizations (e.g. ETS, IELTS) now have more opportunities to consult with researchers who have the L2 pronunciation expertise to give appropriate guidance. Another aspect of standardized assessment of oral language that requires improvement is the training of individual assessors. For example, as mentioned in Chapter 7, Yates, Zielinski and Pryor (2011) found striking disparities in a study of raters' assessments of students whose proficiency levels had been previously established by IELTS. Their finding suggests that existing assessment procedures and training regimes require re-examination.

Directions for technology

A longstanding problem with technological innovations for pronunciation has been the lack of engagement between pronunciation specialists, whose interests lie mainly in the implementation of well-motivated principles in the pronunciation curriculum, and technical experts, who are concerned with a high quality look and feel for their designs. While we recognize the importance of both contributions, we nonetheless object to an over-emphasis on the 'Wow' factor (Murray & Barnes, 1998) in pronunciation software, especially when it is at the expense of pedagogically sound content and activities.

Implementation issues

As we have argued in Chapter 7, technology has yet to achieve its potential as a complement to classroom based instruction (Levis, 2007; Thomson, 2012a). One route to fulfilling this goal is to utilize user-friendly technology to provide learners with highly individualized practice based on needs established through appropriate assessment. At present, effective automated feedback on precise production difficulties has yet to be realized; this is because of the current state of automatic speech recognition, which for the most part is inadequate as a replacement for human assessors. More research is clearly necessary to advance development in this field.

A closely related problem that could be addressed by technology is the time-consuming nature of individual teacher-based assessment. We can envision the development of a software tool for instructors as follows: first, it would elicit speech samples, and store and organize the audio material automatically. Then it would facilitate systematic audio file presentation to the instructor, along with automated rubrics for online evaluation.

Content issues

Although segmentally-focused software has evolved to the point where it is now useful, at least for perceptual learning, commercial suprasegmental software lags behind. Given the growing awareness of the importance of prosody (at least for ESL), advances in technology to support suprasegmental learning would be useful.

An as yet largely untapped benefit of technology is its potential to expose students to a wide variety of speakers and speaking styles. Some currently available software, developed in light of current research, exploits large databases of speakers to assist learners in establishing a robust new phonemic inventory (e.g. Thomson, 2012b). Individual teachers, on the other hand, have limited options for exposing students to multiple voices. In view of the increasing likelihood of learners' contact with speakers from diverse accent backgrounds, an exclusive focus on a single model, as has tended to be common practice, is no longer sufficient.

Expansion of activity types

Another promising feature of technology is the extent to which it can offer expanded opportunities for interaction and pronunciation learning. Practice with a FOCUS ON FORMS in the classroom can be complemented with awareness-raising activities during virtual L2 interactions in contexts such as Second Life (secondlife.com) and gaming. Like the real world, virtual worlds have their own L2 pronunciation research requirements.

Directions for the larger society

Although this book is geared to researchers and teachers who are interested in the intelligibility and comprehensibility of L2 pronunciation, all human communication is a two-way street; all interlocutors share responsibility for the outcome of any exchange. Communicative success depends on the skills, attitudes, and expectations of all parties in the interaction. Considerable variability exists with respect to these factors. Language teachers, for instance, may be especially skillful in comprehending accented L2 speech, due to their experience, and they are likely, given their job choice, to be open to interacting with language learners and to have realistic expectations about how such interactions play out. For the general public, however, skills, attitudes, and expectations may vary with experience and may be influenced by social factors such as education, geographical location, and economic status. Finally, there are reasons to suppose that people vary in their aptitude for processing speech that differs from their own dialect. As we saw in Chapter 8, it is possible to enhance listeners' ability to understand accented L2 speech; moreover, attitudes and expectations can be changed at least in some cases. As the world becomes smaller, and as societies become increasingly diverse, the need for awareness raising and social change becomes greater than ever. One place to start is the provision of some initial listening training in pre-service programming for teachers, social workers, and others whose future careers will bring them into regular contact with L2 users. Another area of need is in highly diverse workplaces, where employees from a wide range of linguistic backgrounds must communicate with each other. Here we can envision a two-pronged approach to improving communicative success, such that speakers with intelligibility issues can get support at work from a trained ESL instructor, while their co-workers can be helped to become better listeners. In addition, negative attitudes and faulty assumptions should be addressed to promote intercultural understanding, which may lead to increased WTC on the part of all members of the workplace community. We pointed out in Chapter 8 that pragmatic or cultural differences can cause misunderstandings that are blamed on L2 accent, when in fact, accent is not the problem. Programs designed to teach intercultural competence offer promise in eliminating such scapegoating if they are well implemented.

As noted in Chapter 9, the proliferation of accent reduction programs is highly problematic. The scare tactics some use are unethical, the promotion of their services to large businesses and other organizations is questionable, and their promises are often not credible. The available strategies for counteracting their effects are limited, short of government regulation, which is unlikely. However, the growth of legitimate pronunciation courses offered by reputable education institutions with language teachers trained in L2 pronunciation would obviate the demand for expensive and often ineffective accent reduction programs.

In our ten-year longitudinal study, we closely followed the naturalistic (unin-structed) pronunciation development of Mandarin and Slavic language speakers. Many of the participants were relatively intelligible at the beginning, but improved over time, though some, even after such a long time in an English-speaking environment, still struggled to make themselves understood. We strongly suspect that the latter group would have benefited from a pronunciation course, but for whatever reason (e.g. lack of access, lack of time) they were unable to get the help they needed to become more intelligible. One such person is Simon (not his real name, of course), a Mandarin speaker, who after several years is still hard to understand. His language skills have held him back in his career, and even simple exchanges can cause communicative problems because of his pronunciation. Simon's grasp of vocabulary and grammar, although not nativelike, is comparable to that of the other Mandarin speakers in the cohort, but he is trapped by his limited comprehensibility. When asked to identify the most difficult thing about learning English, he named pronunciation. Simon's own contact with English speakers is quite limited, but when asked what advice he would give newcomers, Simon responded: "I think first, always talk. Talk with people if you have any time, any chance." Perhaps Simon would have had more chance to talk with other people if he had been more intelligible. It is our hope that in the near future, people like Simon will have more options, and will succeed in gaining access to effective pronunciation help.

Glossary

accent: Aspects of pronunciation that distinguish members of different speech communities, often the result of regional, ethnic, and class differences. FOREIGN ACCENTS are the result of L1 influence on the L2.

accentedness: The extent of difference perceived by speakers of one linguistic variety when listening to speakers of other varieties.

acoustic measurement: Measurement of the properties of sound, including frequency (pitch), amplitude (volume), and duration (time).

African American Vernacular English (AAVE): A dialect of English spoken primarily in America and most commonly, though not exclusively, by African Americans; other terms used are *Ebonics* and *Black English*.

alveolar: A place of articulation involving the tongue tip and the alveolar ridge as in [t], [d], [s], [z], and [l]. The alveolar ridge is directly behind the top teeth.

aptitude: Second language learning ability or talent.

aspiration: A phonetic feature involving the release of a puff of air. In English, /p/, /t/, and /k/ are always aspirated in initial position in a stressed syllable.

assimilate/assimilation: The process of perceptually matching a sound segment from the L2 to a similar sound in the L1. This can make it difficult for L2 listeners to accurately perceive L2 sounds.

asylum seekers: Refugee claimants who have fled their countries of origin in search of a safe country, usually for political reasons.

Audiolingual Method: A language teaching method, based on behavioural psychology, which emphasizes oral/aural skills, requiring learners to listen to native speaker models and imitate them as closely as possible. With respect to pronunciation the Audiolingual Method adheres to the nativeness principle.

automatic speech recognition (ASR): Technology in which computers determine the content of human speech, often by converting spoken words into textual form.

click: A category of consonants found in some southern African languages such as Xhosa. Click sounds may be used non-linguistically to express dismay by saying *tsk tsk* or to urge a horse to move.

coda: The final component of a syllable. The coda comprises all post-nuclear segments. In /lɛt/ (*let*), /t/ is the coda; however, in /mi/ (*me*), no coda is present.

Communicative Language Teaching (CLT): A language teaching approach that became dominant in the 1980s. Its core principle is to focus on authentic communication rather than mastery of language forms and structure. The move away from focus-on-formS led to a decrease in emphasis on pronunciation in CLT classrooms.

comprehensibility: The degree of effort required by a listener to understand an utterance.

computer-assisted pronunciation training (CAPT): Broadly, the use of computers to teach pronunciation; however CAPT is most often understood as the application of ASR to provide pronunciation feedback to learners. (See AUTOMATIC SPEECH RECOGNITION.)

consonant: A segment in which the articulators impede the flow of air somewhere along the vocal tract, e.g. [p], [d], [s], [dʒ], [k], and [ʔ].

construct validity: The degree to which a test measures what it is supposed measure. For example, a written pronunciation test may lack construct validity because it is likely to provide a poor assessment of oral skills.

contrastive analysis hypothesis (CAH): A proposal that errors in the L2 can be predicted by comparing the structural characteristics of the L1 and the target language.

contrastive stress: A stressed word or phrase that emphasizes a contrast. For instance, a speaker may say, "Could you pass the RED book?" to emphasize that it is not the BLUE book that is needed. See STRESS.

corrective feedback: "An indication to a learner that his or her use of the target language is incorrect. Corrective feedback can be explicit or implicit, and may or may not include metalinguistic information" (Lightbown & Spada, 2006, p. 197).

correlational research: Research that examines the relationship between two variables of interest (e.g. between the extent of contact in an L2 and the degree of comprehensibility). Correlational studies cannot be used to establish causal relationships.

critical period: A hypothesized period of life during which acquisition of a particular skill or behaviour is optimal.

dependent variable: A variable in a research experiment that shows the effects of another variable (independent variable). For example, in a controlled experiment examining the effect of instruction on eliminating epenthesis, frequency of occurrence of epenthesis would be the dependent variable and the presence or absence of pronunciation instruction would be the independent variable.

devoicing: Production of a typically voiced segment without voicing. This can occur as a systematic process in a language, or, in individual speakers, as a result of L1 influence on the L2. For example, a German speaker of English may devoice the final conso-nant in the word 'red' because German does not have voiced consonants in word-final position.

discrimination: The ability to perceive the difference between two sounds or two lon-ger utterances (e.g. recognizing that /l/ and /ɹ/ are different sounds or hearing the dif-ference between *I can go* and *I can't go*).

epenthesis (or insertion): The insertion of a segment not normally present in the tar-get form. For example, Japanese learners of English often insert vowels to break up consonant clusters.

error analysis: "Error Analysis involves a set of procedures for identifying, describing and explaining errors in learner language." (Ellis, 2008, p. 961).

experimental investigation: An empirical study that adheres to all requirements of a true experiment, including random group assignment, manipulation of one or more variables, and a control condition.

flap: A sound produced when one articulator makes contact with another and is quickly withdrawn. In North American English, a flap occurs medially in *butter* (/'bʌɾɹ/). In certain varieties of British English, the same sound is realized as [t].

fluency: The degree to which speech flows easily without pauses and other dysfluency markers such as false starts.

focus on formS: Instruction that is primarily focused on explicit and metalinguistic teaching of grammatical forms and rules.

foreign accent: Patterns of speech resulting from L1 influence on the L2 that are noticeably different from native-speaker productions (see ACCENT).

form-focused instruction: Any language teaching activity that is intended to draw learners' attention to a given linguistic form.

formative assessment: Assessment designed primarily to help teachers determine whether an instructional trajectory should be changed and to provide feedback for students to facilitate improvement.

fossilization: A point during L2 learning when speakers reach a plateau in their L2 language skills, even when exposure to the L2 continues.

fricative: A manner of articulation involving constriction of the vocal tract such that the stream of air moving through the reduced opening produces friction; English examples of fricatives include /θ/, /ð/, /ʃ/, /ʒ/ /s/, /z/, /f/, /v/.

Functional Load: A measure of the "work" done by a speech sound in keeping minimal pairs apart. Brown (1991) and Catford (1987) offer rankings of segmental pairs according to their functional load.

high variability training: Perception training which uses multiple voices to produce variable tokens of a target sound or speech sample rather than a single model.

identification: The specification of which of a particular set of sounds (or longer units) has been uttered, for instance, circling the letter /n/ (as opposed to /l/) when presented with *night*. Identification contrasts with DISCRIMINATION, which requires recognizing whether two utterances are different.

independent variable: A variable in a research experiment that is manipulated to determine its effect on another (dependent) variable; see DEPENDENT VARIABLE.

intelligibility: A measure of the extent to which a listener has understood what a speaker said. Intelligibility is often evaluated through transcriptions, responses to true/false questions, or answers to comprehension questions.

Intelligibility Principle: The notion that that the goal of pronunciation instruction should be to help learners become more understandable by focusing on those aspects of an accent that interfere with listener comprehension; see NATIVENESS PRINCIPLE for a contrasting view.

inter-rater reliability: A statistical measure of the degree of agreement among a group of raters.

interference: In SLA, the ways in which L1 knowledge appear to cause difficulty in the acquisition of aspects of the L2.

International Phonetic Alphabet (IPA): A phonetic transcription system created in 1888 by the International Phonetic Association. IPA is better suited for linguistic analysis than is standard orthography because each distinct sound has its own IPA symbol.

intonation: Variations in the pitch of a speaker's voice in an utterance. Intonation serves some linguistic functions such as indicating a yes/no question; however, it can also convey paralinguistic information about the speaker's attitude toward the listener or toward what is being said.

language identification for the determination of origin (LADO): A type of analysis used by governments to assess the veracity of information given by asylum seekers about their origins.

lexical stress: See WORD STRESS.

light vs. dark /l/: Two allophones of the English phoneme /l/. Typically, light [l] is produced in prevocalic position, and dark [ɫ] is used following vowels.

linking: The interaction between the segment at the end of one word and the segment at the start of the next in fluent speech. For example, in "plant trees" the two /t/ phonemes are often pronounced as one longer sound.

minimal pair: Two words that are identical apart from one phoneme. For example /bæt/ and /bɛt/ constitute a minimal pair.

mirroring: A pronunciation technique in which a learner imitates both speech and body movements of another person.

mora-timed rhythm: A type of rhythm found in Japanese, Hawaiian, Sanskrit and certain other languages. A single syllable can comprise one or more morae, according to its structure.

Nativeness Principle: The notion that the goal of pronunciation instruction is to help learners sound native-like and that all elements of an L2 accent are undesirable; see INTELLIGIBILITY PRINCIPLE for a contrasting view.

palatal: A place of articulation involving the tongue and the palate (the roof of the mouth behind the alveolar ridge).

pause: A break in an utterance comprised of silence (an unfilled pause) or a verbal space filler such "um" or "uh" (a filled pause).

perceptual reorganization: A change in speech perception processes that occurs by the age of 10 to 12 months. This phenomenon, first documented by Janet Werker and colleagues, facilitates L1 learning, but makes it difficult to perceive certain L2 sound distinctions.

performance mistakes: Slips of the tongue, false starts, and other phenomena unrelated to accent.

phoneme: The smallest unit in language that can distinguish meaning.

phonetics: The study of speech, including articulatory phonetics (how speech sounds are produced), acoustic phonetics (the acoustic properties of speech sounds) and auditory phonetics (human processing of speech).

phonics: Rules for determining sound from spelling that make it possible to "sound out a word," taking into account that certain letters and combinations of letters are typically pronounced in a particular way, e.g. 's' is usually pronounced /s/, but when followed by 'h' is usually pronounced /ʃ/.

phonology: An area of linguistics in which the systematic relationships among speech sounds are studied.

phonotactics: The rules that underlie which sound sequences and combinations are possible in a particular language; for example, in English, /ŋ/ cannot occur word-initially.

pitch: The perceptual correlate of sound frequency determined by the rate of vibration of the vocal folds.

pitch track: A visual display of the pitch of speech (e.g. *Praat* displays pitch among many other things).

positive transfer: The beneficial effect of using a structure from the L1 when speaking the L2, when the structure is the same in both languages.

pragmatics: The study of the appropriate use of language in different contexts. There are two subsets of study: (1) pragmalinguistics: knowledge of the linguistic forms necessary to perform speech acts and (2) sociopragmatics: awareness of appropriate social and behavioural norms in a particular culture.

primary stress: The heaviest degree of stress possible within a unit of speech. The term has been used by Hahn (2004) in the sense of 'prominence.' See WORD STRESS, SENTENCE STRESS, PROMINENCE.

prominence: Locations of stress in English that are related to given/new information (new information generally receives more prominence than given information), emphasis (words that the speaker wishes to emphasize are more prominent) and contrastive stress (words are given prominence if they are meant to signal a contrast or contradiction). See STRESS.

pronunciation: The production of the sound system of a language, including segments, prosody, voice quality, and rate.

prosody: The aspects of speech at a higher level than segments (consonants or vowels) e.g. stress, intonation, rhythm, and tone.

recast: The reformulation of an L2 learner's inaccurate production with the error corrected.

Received Pronunciation: A dialect of UK English taught in many countries and considered to be the "standard" accent, but which is spoken by only three percent of the UK population.

register: Differences in language use depending on level of formality, familiarity, and other social conventions. 'How do you do?' and 'Hey' are both greetings but belong to different registers.

reverse linguistic stereotyping: A tendency of listeners to ascribe accent features to spoken language when they are not actually present in the speech, based on a speaker's appearance or other social factors.

rhotic: A type of articulatory configuration that produces an 'r-like' sound. Some dialects of English (e.g. General American English) are considered rhotic because /ɹ/ is pronounced before consonants (as in 'start') and in word-final position (as in 'star'). Many British, Australian, and New Zealand dialects are non-rhotic.

rhythm: The perceived patterns of stress within phrases, clauses, and longer utterances. See STRESS-TIMED RHYTHM, SYLLABLE-TIMED RHYTHM, and MORA-TIMED RHYTHM.

rounding: Positioning the lips in an "O-like" configuration; examples of rounded segments in English include /u/, /o/ and /w/.

schwa: The most common vowel sound in English [ə], often used in unstressed syllables. It is the first sound in _aloud_.

segments/segmentals: Vowels and consonants.

sentence stress: The pattern of strong and weak syllables in a sentence. In English, content words are typically given more stress than function words in a sentence. See PROMINENCE, PRIMARY STRESS, WORD STRESS.

shadowing: A pronunciation technique whereby a learner imitates a speech model, speaking either at the same time or a portion of a second later.

shibboleth: A linguistic marker of a speaker's status as an outsider.

social distance: The extent to which members of a given speaker group share social features with some other speaker group. A large social distance predicts that language learning will be impeded.

stereotype: An oversimplified generalization about a group.

stop: A sound produced by stopping the movement of air in the vocal tract completely; the English stops include /p/, /b/, /t/, /d/, /k/, and /g/.

stress: The prominence that a particular syllable receives within a word or longer utterance typically due, in English, to increased vowel duration, increased volume, and a change in pitch.

stress-timed rhythm: A marked alternation between stressed and weak syllables that characterizes certain languages, including English.

summative assessment: A type of assessment primarily used to judge the performance of learners after instruction. Summative assessment is often employed to evaluate educational program outcomes.

suprasegmental: See PROSODY.

syllable-timed rhythm: A tendency in languages such as French to produce each syllable in an utterance with relatively equal weight.

thought group: A group of words that express a single idea and that are not separated by a noticeable pause.

trill: A rapid repetition of a given articulatory gesture in which an articulator contacts the place of articulation repeatedly and very quickly. Spanish has a phonemic alveolar trill while Arabic and French both have uvular trills.

typological proximity: The degree of similarity between different languages in structural properties.

ultimate attainment: The highest level of proficiency a speaker reaches in a second language.

uvular: A place of articulation involving the tongue and the uvula (the tissue hanging in the throat from the end of the soft palate).

voice quality: The vocal effects of long term settings of the larynx and speech articulators; these settings result in qualities such as nasality, vocal fry, and particular pitch registers.

voiced vs. voiceless: The distinction between sounds that entail vibration of the vocal folds (voiced) during articulation and sounds produced without such vibration (voiceless). In English, /z/ is voiced while /s/ is voiceless.

vowel: Sounds that do not involve obstruction of air in the vocal tract but are determined by the shape of the vocal tract.

Willingness to Communicate (WTC): "the probability of engaging in communication when free to choose to do so" (MacIntyre, Clément, Dörnyei, & Noels, 1998, p. 546).

Window of Maximal Opportunity: The time period during which aspects of L2 pronunciation are most amenable to change.

word stress (lexical stress): The particular pattern of prominence found in an individual word. In English, stressed syllables may be longer, louder, and higher-pitched than unstressed or "weak" syllables (which have a reduced vowel, usually a schwa). Not every stressed syllable has all three characteristics. In other languages, word stress may be signalled differently.

References

Abercrombie, D. (1949). Teaching pronunciation. *ELT Journal, 3*, 113–122.
DOI: 10.1093/elt/iii.5.113

Abrahamsson, N., & Hyltenstam, K. (2008). The robustness of aptitude effects in near-native second language acquisition. *Studies in Second Language Acquisition, 30*(4), 481–509.
DOI: 10.1017/s027226310808073x

Abrahamsson, N., & Hyltenstam, K. (2009). Age of onset and nativelikeness in a second language: Listener perception versus linguistic scrutiny. *Language Learning, 59*(2), 249–306.
DOI: 10.1111/j.1467–9922.2009.00507.x

Albrechtsen, D., Henriksen, B., & Faerch, C. (1980). Native speaker reactions to learners' spoken interlanguage. *Language Learning, 30*(2), 365–396. DOI: 10.1111/j.1467–1770.1980.tb00324.x

American Speech-Language-Hearing Association (ASHA). (2007). *Scope of practice in speech-language pathology* [Scope of Practice]. Retrieved from ⟨http://www.asha.org/policy/SP2007-00283.htm⟩

American Speech-Language-Hearing Association (ASHA). (2010). *Code of ethics* [Ethics]. Retrieved from ⟨http://www.asha.org/policy/ET2010-00309/⟩

Amin, N. (2004). Nativism, the native speaker construct, and minority immigrant women teachers of English as a second language. In L. D. Kamhi-Stein (Ed.), *Learning and teaching from experience: Perspectives on nonnative English-speaking professionals* (pp. 61 80). Ann Arbor, MI: University of Michigan Press. DOI: 10.1017/s0261444808005107

Anderson-Hsieh, J., Johnson, R., & Koehler, K. (1992). The relationship between native speaker judgments of nonnative pronunciation and deviance in segmentals, prosody, and syllable structure. *Language Learning, 42*(4), 529–555. DOI: 10.1111/j.1467–1770.1992.tb01043.x

Archibald, J. (1998). *Second language phonology.* Amsterdam: John Benjamins.
DOI: 10.1017/s0272263110000550

Asher, J.J., & Garcia, R. (1969). The optimal age to learn a foreign language. *Modern Language Journal, 53*(5), 334–341. DOI: 10.1111/j.1540–4781.1969.tb04603.x

Audacity [Computer software] Retrieved from ⟨http://audacity.sourceforge.net/⟩

Bachman, L.F., & Palmer, A. (2010). *Language assessment in practice: Developing language assessments and justifying their use in the real world.* Oxford, UK: Oxford University Press.
DOI: 10.1177/0265532211400870

Baker, W. (2010). Effects of age and experience on the production of English word-final stops by Korean speakers. *Bilingualism: Language and Cognition, 13*(3), 263–278.
DOI: 10.1017/s136672890999006x

Baptista, B.O. (2006). Adult phonetic learning of a second language vowel system. In B. O. Baptista & M. A. Watkins (Eds.), *English with a Latin beat: Studies in Portuguese/Spanish-English interphonology* (pp. 19–40). Amsterdam: John Benjamins. DOI: 10.1075/sibil.31.03bap

Bell, A.M. (1867). *Visible speech.* London: Simpkin, Marshall & Co.

Bent, T., & Bradlow, A.R. (2003). The interlanguage speech intelligibility benefit. *Journal of the Acoustical Society of America, 114*(3), 1600–1610. DOI: 10.1121/1.1603234

Best, C.T., McRoberts, G.W., & Sithole, N.M. (1988). Examination of perceptual reorganization for nonnative speech contrasts: Zulu click discrimination by English speaking adults and infants. *Journal of Experimental Psychology: Human Perception and Performance, 14*(3), 345–360.
DOI: 10.1037//0096–1523.14.3.345

Best, C.T., & Tyler, M.D. (2007). Nonnative and second-language speech perception: Commonalities and complementarities. In O.-S. Bohn & M. J. Munro (Eds.), *Language experience in second language speech learning* (pp. 13–34). Amsterdam: John Benjamins. DOI: 10.1075/lllt.17.07bes

Boersma, P., & Weenink, D. (2014). *Praat: Doing phonetics by computer* [Computer program]. Version 5.3.83. Retrieved from ⟨http://www.praat.org/⟩

Bongaerts, T., Mennen, S., & van der Slik, F. (2000). Authenticity of pronunciation in naturalistic second language acquisition: The case of very advanced late learners of Dutch as a second language. *Studia Linguistica, 54*(2), 298–308. DOI: 10.1111/1467–9582.00069

Bongaerts, T., van Summeren, C., Planken, B., & Schils, E. (1997). Age and ultimate attainment in the pronunciation of a foreign language. *Studies in Second Language Acquisition, 19*(4), 447–465. DOI: 10.1017/s0272263197004026

Bradac, J.J. (1990). Language attitudes and impression formation. In H. Giles & W. P. Robinson (Eds.), *Handbook of language and social psychology* (pp. 387–412). Chichester, UK: John Wiley.

Bradlow, A.R., Akahane-Yamada, R., Pisoni, D.B., & Tohkura, Y. (1999). Training Japanese listeners to identify English /r/ and /l/: Long-term retention of learning in perception and production. *Perception and Psychophysics, 61*(5), 977–985. DOI: 10.3758/bf03206911

Bradlow, A. R., Pisoni, D. B., Akahane-Yamada, R., & Tohkura, Y. (1997). Training Japanese listeners to identify English /r/ and /l/: IV. Some effects of perceptual learning on speech production. *The Journal of the Acoustical Society of America, 101*(4), 2299–2310.

Bragger, J.D., & Rice, D.B. (2000). Foreign language materials: Yesterday, today, and tomorrow. In R. M. Terry (Ed.), *Agents of change in a changing age* (pp. 107–140). Lincolnwood, IL: National Textbook Company.

Breitkreutz, J.A., Derwing, T.M., & Rossiter, M.J. (2001). Pronunciation teaching practices in Canada. *TESL Canada Journal, 19*(1), 51–61.

Brennan, E.M., & Brennan, J.S. (1981a). Accent scaling and language attitudes: Reactions to Mexican American English speech. *Language and Speech, 24*(3), 207–221.

Brennan, E.M., & Brennan, J.S. (1981b). Measurements of accent and attitude toward Mexican-American speech. *Journal of Psycholinguistic Research, 10*(5), 487–501. DOI: 10.1007/bf01076735

Brière, E.J. (1966). An investigation of phonological interference. *Language, 42*(4), 768–796. DOI: 10.2307/411832

Brown, A. (1991). Functional load and the teaching of pronunciation. In A. Brown (Ed.), *Teaching English pronunciation: A book of readings* (pp. 211–224). London, UK: Routledge. DOI: 10.1017/s0272263100011578

Buck, G. (1989). Written tests of pronunciation: Do they work? *ELT Journal, 43*(1), 50–56. DOI: 10.1093/elt/43.1.50

Bueno Alastuey, M.C. (2010). Synchronous-voice computer-mediated communication: Effects on pronunciation. *Calico Journal, 28*(1), 1–20. DOI: 10.11139/cj.28.1.1–20

Burda, A.N., Scherz, J.A., Hageman, C.F., & Edwards, H.T. (2003). Age and understanding speakers with Spanish or Taiwanese accents. *Perceptual and Motor Skills, 97*(1), 11–20. DOI: 10.2466/pms.2003.97.1.11

Burgess, J., & Spencer, S. (2000). Phonology and pronunciation in integrated language teaching and teacher education. *System, 28*(2), 191–215. DOI: 10.1016/s0346-251x(00)00007–5

Burns, A. (2006). Integrating research and professional development on pronunciation teaching in a national adult ESL program. *TESL Reporter, 39*(2), 34–41.

Canadian Association of Speech-Language Pathologists and Audiologists (CASLPA). (2014a). *Code of ethics.* Retrieved from ⟨http://www.caslpa.ca/professional-resources/resource-library/code-ethics⟩

Canadian Association of Speech-Language Pathologists and Audiologists (CASLPA). (2014b). *Scope of practice for speech-language pathology.* Retrieved from ⟨http://www.caslpa.ca/professional-resources/resource-library/scope-practice-speech-language-pathology-canada⟩

Canale, M. (1983). From communicative competence to communicative language pedagogy. In J. C. Richards & R. W. Schmidt (Eds.), *Language and communication* (pp. 2–27). New York, NY: Longman.

Canale, M., & Swain, M. (1980). Theoretical bases of communicative approaches to second language teaching and testing. *Applied Linguistics, 1*(1), 1–47. DOI: 10.1093/applin/i.1.1

Carey, M.D., Mannell, R.H., & Dunn, P.K. (2011). Does a rater's familiarity with a candidate's pronunciation affect the rating in oral proficiency interviews? *Language Testing, 28*(2), 201–219. DOI: 10.1177/0265532210393704

Carroll, J.B., & Sapon, S.M. (1959). *Modern language aptitude test.* San Antonio, TX: Psychological Corporation.

Catford, J.C. (1987). Phonetics and the teaching of pronunciation: A systemic description of the teaching of English phonology. In J. Morley (Ed.), *Current perspectives on pronunciation: Practices anchored in theory* (pp. 83–100). Washington DC: TESOL. DOI: 10.1017/s0272263100008536

Cauldwell, R. (2005). *Streaming speech: Listening and pronunciation for advanced learners of English* [Online]. Birmingham, UK: Speechinaction. DOI: 10.1017/s0025100303221514

Celce-Murcia, M., Brinton, D.M., Goodwin, J.M., with Griner, B. (2010). *Teaching pronunciation: A course book and reference guide* (2nd ed.). New York, NY: Cambridge University Press.

Centre for Canadian Language Benchmarks. (2012). *CLB support kit.* Ottawa, ON: Author.

Champagne-Muzar, C., Schneiderman, E.I., & Bourdages, J.S. (1993). Second language accent: The role of the pedagogical environment. *International Review of Applied Linguistics, 31*(2), 143–160.

Chapelle, C.A. (2009). A hidden curriculum in language textbooks: Are beginning learners of French at U.S. universities taught about Canada? *The Modern Language Journal, 93*(2), 139–152. DOI: 10.1111/j.1540–4781.2009.00852.x

Cho, S., & Reich, G.A. (2008). New immigrants, new challenges: High school social studies teachers and English language learner instruction. *Social Studies, 99*(6), 235–242. DOI: 10.3200/tsss.99.6.235–242

Chun, D.M., Hardison, D.M., & Pennington, M.C. (2008). Technologies for prosody in context: Past and future L2 research and practice. In J. Hansen Edwards & M. Zampini (Eds.), *Phonology and second language acquisition* (pp. 323–346). Amsterdam: John Benjamins. DOI: 10.1075/sibil.36.16chu

Clark, E., & Paran, A. (2007). The employability of non-native-speaker teachers of EFL: A UK survey. *System, 35*(4), 407–430. DOI: 10.1016/j.system.2007.05.002

Collins, B., & Mees, I.M. (1999). *The real Professor Higgins: The life and career of Daniel Jones.* Berlin: Mouton de Gruyter. DOI: 10.1515/9783110812367

Couper, G. (2003). The value of an explicit pronunciation syllabus in ESOL teaching. *Prospect, 18*(3), 53–70.

Couper, G. (2006). The short and long-term effects of pronunciation instruction. *Prospect, 21*(1), 46–66.

Couper, G. (2011). What makes pronunciation teaching work? Testing for the effect of two variables: Socially constructed metalanguage and critical listening. *Language Awareness, 20*(3), 159–182. DOI: 10.1080/09658416.2011.570347

Cruttenden, A. (1994). *Gimson's pronunciation of English* (5th ed.). London, UK: Edward Arnold. DOI: 10.1017/s0025100303231121

Crystal, D. (2003). *English as a global language* (2nd ed.). Cambridge, UK: Cambridge University Press. DOI: 10.1108/09504120410528126

Cucchiarini, C., Neri, A., & Strik, H. (2009). Oral proficiency training in Dutch L2: The contribution of ASR-based corrective feedback. *Speech Communication, 51*(10), 853–863. DOI: 10.1016/j.specom.2009.03.003

Cushing, S. (1995). Pilot-air traffic control communications: It's not (only) what you say, it's how you say it. *Flight Safety Digest, 14*(7), 1–10.

Cutler, C. (2014). Accentedness, "passing" and crossing. In J. M. Levis & A. Moyer (Eds.), *Social dynamics in second language accent* (pp. 145–167). Berlin: DeGruyter. DOI: 10.1515/9781614511762.145

Dahm, M., & Yates, L. (2013). English for the workplace: Doing patient-centred care in medical communication. *TESL Canada Journal, 30, Special Issue 7*, 21–44.

Dalby, J., & Kewley-Port, D. (2008). Design features of three computer-based speech training systems. In M. Holland & F. P. Fisher (Eds.), *The path of speech technologies in computer assisted language learning: From research toward practice* (pp.155–173). New York, NY: Routledge.

Darcy, I., Ewert, D., & Lidster, R. (2012). Bringing pronunciation instruction back into the classroom: An ESL teachers' pronunciation "toolbox". In. J. Levis & K. LeVelle (Eds.), *Proceedings of the 3rd Annual Pronunciation in Second Language Learning and Teaching Conference* (pp. 93–108). Ames, IA: Iowa State University.

Dauer, R. (1983). Stress-timing and syllable-timing reanalyzed. *Journal of Phonetics, 11*(1), 51–62.

Dávila, A., Bohara, A.K., & Saenz, R. (1993). Accent penalties and the earnings of Mexican Americans. *Social Science Quarterly, 74*, 902–916.

de Bot, K. (1983). Visual feedback of intonation I: Effectiveness and induced practice behavior. *Language and Speech, 26*(4), 331–350.

de Bot, K., & Mailfert, K. (1982). The teaching of intonation: Fundamental research and classroom applications. *TESOL Quarterly, 16*(1), 71–77. DOI: 10.2307/3586564

DeKeyser, R.M. (2000). The robustness of critical period effects in second language acquisition. *Studies in Second Language Acquisition, 22*(4), 499–533. DOI: 10.4324/9781410601667

Derwing, T.M. (2003). What do ESL students say about their accents? *Canadian Modern Language Review, 59*(4), 547–566. DOI: 10.3138/cmlr.59.4.547

Derwing, T.M. (2008). Curriculum issues in teaching pronunciation to second language learners. In J. G. Hansen Edwards & M. L. Zampini (Eds.), *Phonology and second language acquisition* (pp. 347–369). Amsterdam: John Benjamins. DOI: 10.1075/sibil.36.17der

Derwing, T.M., Diepenbroek, L.G., & Foote, J.A. (2012). How well do general-skills ESL textbooks address pronunciation? *TESL Canada Journal, 30*(1), 23–44.

Derwing, T.M., Fraser, H., Kang, O., & Thomson, R.I. (2014). L2 accent and ethics: Issues that merit attention. In A. Mahboob & L. Barratt (Eds.), *Englishes in a multilingual world* (pp. 63–80). Berlin: Springer. DOI: 10.1007/978-94-017-8869-4_5

Derwing, T.M., & Munro, M.J. (1997). Accent, intelligibility, and comprehensibility: Evidence from four L1s. *Studies in Second Language Acquisition, 19*(1), 1–16. DOI: 10.1017/s0272263197001010

Derwing, T.M., & Munro, M.J. (2001). What speaking rates do non-native listeners prefer? *Applied Linguistics, 22*(3), 324–337. DOI: 10.1093/applin/22.3.324

Derwing, T.M., & Munro, M.J. (2005a). Second language accent and pronunciation teaching: A research-based approach. *TESOL Quarterly, 39*(3), 379–397. DOI: 10.2307/3588486

Derwing, T.M., & Munro, M.J. (2005b). Pragmatic perspectives on the preparation of teachers of English as a second language. In E. Llurda (Ed.), *Non-native language teachers: Perceptions, challenges, and contributions to the profession* (pp. 179–191). New York, NY: Springer. DOI: 10.1007/0-387-24565-0_10

Derwing, T.M., & Munro, M.J. (2009). Putting accent in its place: Rethinking obstacles to communication. *Language Teaching, 42*(4), 476–490. DOI: 10.1017/s026144480800551x

Derwing, T.M., & Munro, M.J. (2013). The development of L2 oral language skills in two L1 groups: A 7-year study. *Language Learning, 63*(2), 163–185. DOI: 10.1111/lang.12000

Derwing, T.M., Munro, M.J., Abbott, M., & Mulder, M. (2010). *An examination of the Canadian language benchmark data from the citizenship language survey.* Retrieved from ⟨http://www.cic.gc.ca/english/resources/research/language-benchmark/index.asp⟩

Derwing, T.M., Munro, M.J., Carbonaro, M. (2000). Does popular speech recognition software work with ESL speech? *TESOL Quarterly, 34*(3), 592–603. DOI: 10.2307/3587748

Derwing, T.M., Munro, M.J., Foote, J.A., Waugh, E., & Fleming, J. (2014). Opening the window on comprehensible pronunciation after 19 years: A workplace training study. *Language Learning, 64*(3), 526–548. DOI: 10.1111/lang.12053

Derwing, T.M., Munro, M.J., & Thomson, R.I. (2008). A longitudinal study of ESL learners' fluency and comprehensibility development. *Applied Linguistics, 29*(3), 359–380. DOI: 10.1093/applin/amm041

Derwing, T.M., Munro, M.J., Thomson, R.I., & Rossiter, M.J. (2009). The relationship between L1 fluency and L2 fluency development. *Studies in Second Language Acquisition, 31*(4), 533–557. DOI: 10.1017/s0272263109990015

Derwing, T.M., Munro, M.J., & Wiebe, G. (1997). Pronunciation instruction for 'fossilized' learners: Can it help? *Applied Language Learning, 8*(2), 217–235.

Derwing, T.M., Munro, M.J., & Wiebe, G. (1998). Evidence in favor of a broad framework for pronunciation instruction. *Language Learning, 48*(3), 393–410. DOI: 10.1111/0023-8333.00047

Derwing, T.M., & Rossiter, M.J. (2003). The effects of pronunciation instruction on the accuracy, fluency, and complexity of L2 accented speech. *Applied Language Learning, 13*(1), 1–18.

Derwing, T.M., Rossiter, M.J., & Munro, M.J. (2002). Teaching native speakers to listen to foreign-accented speech. *Journal of Multilingual and Multicultural Development, 23*(4), 245–259. DOI: 10.1080/01434630208666468

Derwing, T.M., Rossiter, M.J., Munro, M.J., & Thomson, R.I. (2004). Second language fluency: Judgments on different tasks. *Language Learning, 54*(4), 655–679. DOI: 10.1111/j.1467-9922.2004.00282.x

Derwing, T.M., Thomson, R.I., & Munro, M.J. (2006). English pronunciation and fluency development in Mandarin and Slavic speakers. *System, 34*(2), 183–193. DOI: 10.1016/j.system.2006.01.005

Dlaska, A., & Krekeler, C. (2008). Self-assessment of pronunciation. *System, 36*(4), 506–516. DOI: 10.1016/j.system.2008.03.003

Dlaska, A., & Krekeler, C. (2013). The short-term effects of individual corrective feedback on L2 pronunciation. *System, 41*(1), 25–37. DOI: 10.1016/j.system.2013.01.005

Dörnyei, Z., & Ushioda, E. (2011). *Teaching and researching motivation* (2nd ed.). Harlow, UK: Longman.

Duff, P.A., Wong, P., & Early, M. (2002). Learning language for work and life: The linguistic socialization of immigrant Canadians seeking careers in healthcare. *The Modern Language Journal, 86*(3), 397–422. DOI: 10.1111/1540-4781.t01-1-00157

Eades, D. (2005). Applied linguistics and language analysis in asylum seeker cases. *Applied Linguistics, 26*(4), 503–526. DOI: 10.1093/applin/ami021

Eckman, F.R. (2008). Typological markedness and second language phonology. In J. G. Hansen Edwards & M. L. Zampini (Eds.), *Phonology and second language acquisition* (pp. 95–115). Amsterdam: John Benjamins. DOI: 10.1017/s0272263110000550

Eddy, F.D. (1974). Pierre Delattre, teacher of French. *The French Review, 47*(3), 513–517.

Ellis, R. (2008). *The study of second language acquisition (2nd Edition)*. Oxford: Oxford University Press.

English Language Services Inc. (1966, 1967). *Drills and exercises in English pronunciation* (3 volumes). New York, NY: Collier MacMillan International.

Ensz, K.Y. (1982). French attitudes toward typical speech errors of American speakers of French. *The Modern Language Journal, 66*(2), 133–139. DOI: 10.1111/j.1540–4781.1982.tb06972.x

Esling, J.H. (1994). Some perspectives on accent: Range of voice quality variation, the periphery, and focusing. In J. Morley (Ed.), *Pronunciation pedagogy and theory: New views, new directions* (pp. 49–63). Alexandria, VA: TESOL.

Esling, J.H. (2000). Crosslinguistic aspects of voice quality. In R. D. Kent & M. J. Ball (Eds.), *Voice quality measurement* (pp. 25–35). San Diego, CA: Singular Publishing Group.

Esling, J.H., & Wong, R.F. (1983). Voice quality settings and the teaching of pronunciation. *TESOL Quarterly, 17*(1), 89–96. DOI: 10.2307/3586426

Fayer, J.M., & Krasinski, E. (1987). Native and nonnative judgments of intelligibility and irritation. *Language Learning, 37*(3), 313–326. DOI: 10.1111/j.1467–1770.1987.tb00573.x

Feinstein-Whittaker, M., Wilner, L.K., & Sikorski, L.D. (2012). A growing niche in corporate America. *The ASHA Leader*. Retrieved from ⟨http://www.asha.org/Publications/leader/2012/120313/A-Growing-Niche-in-Corporate-America.htm⟩

Ferguson, C.A. (1975). Toward a characterization of English foreigner talk. *Anthropological Linguistics, 17*(1), 1–14.

Field, J. (2005). Intelligibility and the listener: The role of lexical stress. *TESOL Quarterly, 39*(3), 399–423. DOI: 10.2307/3588487

Fillmore, C.J. (1979). On fluency. In C. J. Fillmore, D. Kempler, & W. S.-Y. Wang (Eds.), *Individual differences in language ability and language behavior* (pp. 85–101). New York, NY: Academic Press. DOI: 10.1016/b978-0-12-255950-1.50012–3

Firth, S. (1992). Pronunciation syllabus design: A question of focus. In P. Avery & S. Ehrlich (Eds.), *Teaching American English pronunciation* (pp. 173–183). Oxford, UK: Oxford University Press.

Flege, J.E. (1987). The production of "new" and "similar" phones in a foreign language: Evidence for the effect of equivalence classification. *Journal of Phonetics, 15*, 47–65.

Flege, J.E. (1988). Factors affecting degree of perceived foreign accent in English sentences. *Journal of the Acoustical Society of America, 84*(1), 70–79. DOI: 10.1121/1.396876

Flege, J.E. (1995). Second-language speech learning: Theory, findings, and problems. In W. Strange (Ed.), *Speech perception and linguistic experience: Theoretical and methodological issues* (pp. 233–277). Timonium, MD: York Press.

Flege, J.E., Bohn, O.-S., & Jang, S. (1997). Effects of experience on non-native speakers' production and perception of English vowels. *Journal of Phonetics, 25*(4), 437–470. DOI: 10.1006/jpho.1997.0052

Flege, J.E., & Davidian, R.D. (1984). Transfer and developmental processes in adult foreign language speech production. *Applied Psycholinguistics, 5*(4), 323–347. DOI: 10.1017/s014271640000521x

Flege, J.E., & Fletcher, K.L. (1992). Talker and listener effects on degree of perceived foreign accent. *Journal of the Acoustical Society of America, 91*(1), 370–389. DOI: 10.1121/1.402780

Flege, J.E., & Liu, S. (2001). The effect of experience on adults' acquisition of a second language. *Studies in Second Language Acquisition, 23*(4), 527–552.

Flege, J.E., & MacKay, I.R.A. (2011). What accounts for 'age' effects on overall degree of foreign accent? In M. Wrembel, M. Kul, & K. Dziubalska-Kołaczyk (Eds.), *Achievements and perspectives in the acquisition of second language speech: New Sounds 2010*, Volume 2 (pp. 65–82). Bern: Peter Lang.

Flege, J.E., Munro, M.J., & MacKay, I.R.A. (1995). Factors affecting strength of perceived foreign accent in a second language. *Journal of the Acoustical Society of America, 97*(5), 3125–3134. DOI: 10.1121/1.413041

Flege, J.E., Munro, M.J., & Skelton, L. (1992). Production of the word-final English /t/ – /d/ contrast by native speakers of English, Mandarin, and Spanish. *Journal of the Acoustical Society of America, 92*(1), 128–143. DOI: 10.1121/1.404278

Flege, J.E., Takagi, N., & Mann, V. (1995). Japanese adults can learn to produce English /ɹ/ and /l/ accurately. *Language and Speech, 38*(1), 25–55.

Flege, J.E., Yeni-Komshian, G.H., & Liu, S. (1999). Age constraints on second-language acquisition. *Journal of Memory and Language, 41*(1), 78–104. DOI: 10.1006/jmla.1999.2638

Foote, J.A., Holtby, A.K., & Derwing, T.M. (2011). Survey of the teaching of pronunciation in adult ESL programs in Canada, 2010. *TESL Canada Journal, 29*(1), 1–22.

Foote, J., & Smith, G. (2013, September). *Is there an app for that?* Paper presented at the 5th Pronunciation in Second Language Learning and Teaching Conference, Ames, Iowa.

Foote, J.A., Trofimovich, P., Collins, L., & Urzúa, F.S. (2013). Pronunciation teaching practices in communicative second language classes. *The Language Learning Journal*. Advance online publication. DOI:10.1080/09571736.2013.784345

Foster, Paul. (2005). Racism from home shocks Britons working at a call centre in India. *The Telegraph*. Retrieved from ⟨http://www.telegraph.co.uk/news/uknews/4194939/Racism-from-home-shocks-Britons-working-at-call-centre-in-India.html⟩

Foster, Pauline, & Skehan, P. (1996). The influence of planning and task type on second language performance. *Studies in Second Language Acquisition, 18*(3), 299–323. DOI: 10.1017/s0272263100015047

Fraser, H. (2001). *Teaching pronunciation: A handbook for teachers and trainers. Three frameworks for an integrated approach*. Sydney, Australia: Department of Education Training and Youth Affairs (DETYA)

Fraser, H. (2006). Helping teachers help students with pronunciation: A cognitive approach. *Prospect, 21*(1), 80–96.

Fraser, H. (2009). The role of 'educated native speakers' in providing language analysis for the determination of the origin of asylum seekers. *The International Journal of Speech, Language and the Law, 16*(1), 113–138. DOI: 10.1558/ijsll.v16i1.113

Fraser, H. (2013). Language analysis for the determination of origin (LADO). In C. A. Chapelle (Ed.), *The encyclopedia of applied linguistics* (pp. 2920–2922). Hoboken, NJ: Blackwell Publishing.

French, L., Collins, L., Gagné, N., & Guay, J.-D. (2014, March). *A look at long-term effects of intensive instruction on L2 skills*. Paper presented at the American Association for Applied Linguistics Conference, Portland, Oregon.

Gatbonton, E., & Segalowitz, N. (2005). Rethinking communicative language teaching: A focus on access to fluency. *The Canadian Modern Language Review, 61*(3), 325–353. DOI: 10.3138/cmlr.61.3.325

Gatbonton, E., Trofimovich, P., & Segalowitz, N. (2011). Ethnic group affiliation and patterns of development of a phonological variable. *The Modern Language Journal, 95*(2), 188–204. DOI: 10.1111/j.1540–4781.2011.01177.x

Gibson, M. (1997). Nonnative perception and production of English attitudinal intonation. *The 23rd LACUS Forum*. Retrieved from ⟨http://www.lacus.org/volumes/23/40.gibson.pdf⟩

Gilbert, J. (1984). *Clear speech: Pronunciation and listening comprehension in North American English.* New York, NY: Cambridge University Press. DOI: 10.1017/cbo9781139523172

Gilbert, J. (2010). Pronunciation as orphan: What can be done? *Speak Out, 43*, 3–7.

Gilbert, J. (2011). *Clear speech* [Application for mobile devices]. New York, NY: Cambridge University Press.

Gilbert, J. (2012). *Clear speech: Pronunciation and listening comprehension in North American English; Teacher's resource and assessment book* (4th ed.). New York, NY: Cambridge University Press. DOI: 10.1017/cbo9781139523172

Giles, H. (1970). Accent mobility: A model and some data. *Anthropological Linguistics, 15*(2), 87–105.

Gimson, A.C. (1970). *An introduction to the pronunciation of English* (2nd ed.). London, UK: Edward Arnold. DOI: 10.1017/s0022226700003078

Gluszek, A., & Dovidio, J.F. (2010). The way they speak: A social psychological perspective on the stigma of nonnative accents in communication. *Personality and Social Psychology Review, 14*(2), 214–237. DOI: 10.1177/1088868309359288

Golombek, P., & Rehn Jordan, S. (2005). Becoming "black lambs" not "parrots": A poststructuralist orientation to intelligibility and identity. *TESOL Quarterly, 39*(3), 513–533. DOI: 10.2307/3588492

Goodwin, J. (2008, September 23). A conversation with Janet Goodwin, Applied Linguistics, UCLA [Video file]. Retrieved from ⟨https://www.youtube.com/watch?v=6c6k54axw24⟩

Goodwin, J. (2013). Pronunciation teaching methods and techniques. In C. A. Chapelle (Ed.), *The encyclopedia of applied linguistics* (pp. 4725–4734). Hoboken, NJ: Blackwell Publishing.

Graddol, D. (2006). *English next*. London, UK: British Council. Retrieved from ⟨http://www.british-council.org/learning-research-english-next.pdf⟩

Granena, G., & Long, M.H. (2013). Age of onset, length of residence, language aptitude, and ultimate L2 attainment in three linguistic domains. *Second Language Research, 29*, 311–343. DOI: 10.1177/0267658312461497

Grant, L. (2010). *Well said: Pronunciation for clear communication* (3rd ed.). Boston, MA: Heinle & Heinle.

Greene, J., & Wells, E. (1927). *The cause and cure of speech disorders: A textbook for students and teachers on stuttering, stammering and voice conditions.* New York, NY: The Macmillan Company. DOI: 10.1001/archpedi.1927.04130240179022

Griffen, T.D. (1980). A nonsegmental approach to the teaching of pronunciation. *Revue de Phonétique Appliquée, 54*, 81–94.

Guion, S.G., & Pederson, E. (2007). Investigating the role of attention in phonetic learning. In O.-S. Bohn & M. J. Munro (Eds.), *Language experience in second language speech earning: In honor of James Emil Flege* (pp. 57–76). Amsterdam: John Benjamins. DOI: 10.1075/lllt.17.09gui

Guiora, A.Z., Acton, W.R., Erard, R., & Strickland, F.W. (1980). The effects of benzodiazapene (valium) on permeability of language ego boundaries. *Language Learning, 30*(2), 351–361. DOI: 10.1111/j.1467–1770.1980.tb00323.x

Guiora, A.Z., Beir-Hallahmi, B., Brannon, R.C. L., Dull, C.Y., & Scovel, T. (1972). The effects of experimentally induced changes in ego states on pronunciation ability in a second language: An exploratory study. *Comprehensive Psychiatry, 13*(5), 421–428. DOI: 10.1016/0010-440x(72)90083-1

Gynan, S.N. (1985). Comprehension, irritation and error hierarchies. *Hispania, 68*(1), 160–165. DOI: 10.2307/341633

Hahn, L.D. (2004). Primary stress and intelligibility: Research to motivate the teaching of suprasegmentals. *TESOL Quarterly, 38*(2), 201–223. DOI: 10.2307/3588378

Hahn, M.K. (2002). *The persistence of learned primary phrase stress patterns among learners of English* (Unpublished doctoral dissertation). University of Illinois at Urbana-Champagne, IL, USA.

Hakuta, K., Bialystok, E., & Wiley, T. (2003). A test of the critical period hypothesis for second language acquisition. *Psychological Science, 14*(1), 31–38. DOI: 10.1111/1467-9280.01415

Harding, L. (2011). *Accent and listening assessment: A validation study of the use of speakers with L2 accents on an academic English listening test.* Frankfurt, Germany: Peter Lang.

Hardison, D.M. (2004). Generalization of computer-assisted prosody training: Quantitative and qualitative findings. *Language Learning and Technology, 8*(1), 34–52.

Henderson, A., Frost, D., Tergujeff, E., Kautzsch, A., Murphy, D., Kirkova-Naskova, A., Waniek-Klimczak, E., Levey, D., Cunningham, U., & Curnick, L. (2012). The English Pronunciation Teaching in Europe Survey: Selected results. *Research in Language, 10*(1), 5–27. DOI: 10.2478/v10015-011-0047-4

Hewings, M. (2004). *Pronunciation practice activities: A resource book for teaching English pronunciation.* Cambridge, UK: Cambridge University Press.

Hincks, R., & Edlund, J. (2009). Promoting increased pitch variation in oral presentations with transient visual feedback. *Language Learning and Technology, 13*(3), 32–50.

Honey, J. (1989). *Does accent matter?* London, UK: Faber and Faber.

Hu, X., Ackermann, H., Martin, J.A., Erb, M., Winkler, S., & Reiterer, S.M. (2013). Language aptitude for pronunciation in advanced second language (L2) learners: Behavioural predictors and neural substrates. *Brain and Language, 127*(3), 366–376. DOI: 10.1016/j.bandl.2012.11.006

Hyltenstam, K., & Abrahamsson, N. (2001). Age and L2 learning: The hazards of matching practical "implications" with theoretical "facts". *TESOL Quarterly, 35*(1), 151–170. DOI: 10.2307/3587863

Hymes, D. (1966). *Language in culture and society.* New York, NY: Harper and Row. DOI: 10.1017/s0022226700001547

Ioup, G., Boustagui, E., El Tigi, M., & Moselle, M. (1994). Reexamining the critical period hypothesis: A case study of successful adult SLA in a naturalistic environment. *Studies in Second Language Acquisition, 16*(1), 73–98. DOI: 10.1017/s0272263100012596

Isaacs, T. (2014). Assessing pronunciation. In A. J. Kunnan (Ed.), *The companion to language assessment* (pp. 140–155). Hoboken, NJ: Wiley-Blackwell.

Isaacs, T., & Thomson, R.I. (2013). Rater experience, rater scale length, and judgments of L2 pronunciation: Revisiting research conventions. *Language Assessment Quarterly, 10*(2), 135–159. DOI: 10.1080/15434303.2013.769545

Iverson, P., Hazan, V., & Bannister, K. (2005). Phonetic training with acoustic cue manipulations: A comparison of methods for teaching English /r/-/l/ to Japanese adults. *Journal of the Acoustical Society of America, 118*(5), 3267–3278. DOI: 10.1121/1.2062307

Jamieson, D., & Morosan, D. (1986). Training non-native speech contrasts in adults: Acquisition of the English /θ/ and /ð/ contrast by francophones. *Perception and Psychophysics, 40*(4), 205–215. DOI: 10.3758/bf03211500

Jenkins, J. (2002). A sociolinguistically based, empirically researched pronunciation syllabus for English as an international language. *Applied Linguistics, 23*(1), 83–103.
DOI: 10.1093/applin/23.1.83

Jenkins, J. (2006). Current perspectives on teaching world Englishes and English as a lingua franca. *TESOL Quarterly, 40*(1), 157–181. DOI: 10.2307/40264515

Jesperson, O. (1904). *How to teach a foreign language*. London: S. Sonnenschein & Co.

Johansson, S. (1978). Studies of error gravity: Native reactions to errors produced by Swedish learners of English. *Gothenburg Studies in English, 44*. Gothenburg, Sweden: Acta Universitatis Gothoburgensis. DOI: 10.2307/3586814

Jordan, M. (2010). Arizona grades teachers on fluency. *The Wall Street Journal*. Retrieved from ⟨http://online.wsj.com/news/articles/SB10001424052748703572504575213883276427528⟩

Kachru, B.B. (1985). Standards, codification and sociolinguistic realism: The English language in the outer circle. In R. Quirk & H. G. Widdowson (Eds.), *English in the world: Teaching and learning the language and literatures* (pp. 11–30). Cambridge, UK: Cambridge University Press.

Kachru, B.B. (1991). Models of English for the third world: White man's linguistic burden or language pragmatics. In A. Brown (Ed.), *Teaching English pronunciation: A book of readings* (pp. 31–52). London, UK: Routledge.

Kalin, R. and Rayko, D.S. (1978) Discrimination in evaluative judgments against foreign-accented job candidates. *Psychological Reports, 43*, 1203–1209.

Kang, O., & Rubin, D. (2009). Reverse linguistic stereotyping: Measuring the effect of listener expectations on speech evaluation. *Journal of Language and Social Psychology, 28*(4), 441–456.
DOI: 10.1177/0261927x09341950

Kang, O., & Rubin, D. (2012). Inter-group contact exercises as a tool for mitigating undergraduates' attitudes toward nonnative English-speaking teaching assistants. *Journal on Excellence in College Teaching, 23*(3), 159–166.

Kang, O. & Rubin, D. (2014). Reverse linguistic stereotyping. In J. Levis & A. Moyer (Eds.), *Social dynamics in second language accent* (pp. 239–253). Berlin: DeGruyter Mouton.

Kelly, L.G. (1969). *25 centuries of language teaching*. Rowley, MA: Newbury House Publishers.

Kennedy, S., & Trofimovich, P. (2010). Language awareness and second language pronunciation: A classroom study. *Language Awareness, 19*(3), 171–185.
DOI: 10.1080/09658416.2010.486439

Kibishi, H., Hirabayashi, K., & Nakagawa, S. (2015). A statistical method of evaluating the pronunciation proficiency/intelligibility of English presentations by Japanese speakers. *ReCall, 27*(1), 58–83. DOI: 10.1017/S0958344014000251

Kossan, P. (2011). Arizona teacher accent scrutiny halted. *The Arizona Republic*. Retrieved from ⟨http://www.azcentral.com/arizonarepublic/news/articles/2011/09/12/20110912arizona-teacher-accent-scrutiny-halted.html⟩

Koster, C.J., & Koet, T. (1993). The evaluation of accent in the English of Dutchmen. *Language Learning, 43*(1), 69–92. DOI: 10.1111/j.1467–1770.1993.tb00173.x

Krashen, S.D. (1981). *Second language acquisition and second language learning*. Oxford, UK: Pergamon. DOI: 10.1017/s0272263100004733

Krashen, S.D. (1985). *The input hypothesis: Issues and implications*. London, UK: Longman.
DOI: 10.2307/3586393

Lacey, M. (2011). In Arizona, complaints that an accent can hinder a teacher's career. *New York Times*. Retrieved from ⟨http://www.nytimes.com/2011/09/25/us/in-arizona-complaints-that-an-accent-can-hinder-a-teachers-career.html?_r=3&ref=todayspaper⟩

Lado, R. (1957). *Linguistics across cultures.* Ann Arbor, MI: University of Michigan Press.

Lado, R. (1961). *Language testing: The construction and use of foreign language tests.* London, UK: Longman. DOI: 10.2307/323564

Lado, R., & Fries, C.C. (1958). *English pronunciation: Exercises in sound segments, intonation, and rhythm* (Vol. 3). Ann Arbor, MI: University of Michigan Press.

Larson-Hall, J. (2006). What does more time buy you? Another look at the effects of long-term residence on production accuracy of English /ɹ/ and /l/ by Japanese speakers. *Language and Speech, 49*(4), 521–548. DOI: 10.1177/00238309060490040401

Laver, J. (1980). *The phonetic description of voice quality.* Cambridge, UK: Cambridge University Press. DOI: 10.1017/s0025100300002292

Lee, J., Jang, J., & Plonsky, L. (2014). The effectiveness of second language pronunciation instruction: A meta-analysis. *Applied Linguistics.* DOI: 10.1093/applin/amu040

Lenneberg, E.H. (1967). *Biological foundations of language.* New York, NY: Wiley. DOI: 10.1002/bs.3830130610

LeVelle, K., & Levis, J. (2014). Understanding the impact of social factors on L2 pronunciation: Insights from learners. In J. M. Levis & A. Moyer (Eds.), *Social dynamics in second language accent* (pp. 97–118). Berlin: DeGruyter Mouton. DOI: 10.1515/9781614511762.97

Levis, J.M. (1999). Intonation in theory and practice: Revisited. *TESOL Quarterly, 33*(1), 37–63. DOI: 10.2307/3588190

Levis, J.M. (2005). Changing contexts and shifting paradigms in pronunciation teaching. *TESOL Quarterly, 39*(3), 369–377. DOI: 10.2307/3588485

Levis, J. (2007). Computer technology in teaching and researching pronunciation. *Annual Review of Applied Linguistics, 27*, 184–202. DOI: 10.1017/s0267190508070098

Levis, J., & Barriuso, T.A. (2012). Nonnative speakers' pronunciation errors in spoken and read English. In J. Levis & K. LeVelle (Eds.), *Proceedings of the 3rd Annual Pronunciation in Second Language Learning and Teaching Conference* (pp. 187–194). Ames, IA: Iowa State University.

Levis, J., & Cortes, V. (2008). Minimal pairs in spoken corpora: Implications for pronunciation assessment and teaching. In C. A. Chapelle, Y.-R. Chung, & J. Xu (Eds.), *Towards adaptive CALL: Natural language processing for diagnostic language assessment* (pp. 197–208). Ames, IA: Iowa State University.

Levis, J.M., & Grant, L. (2003). Integrating pronunciation into ESL/EFL classrooms. *TESOL Journal, 12*(2), 13–19.

Levis, J., Link, S., Sonsaat, S., & Barriuso, T.A. (2013, September). *Native and nonnative teachers of pronunciation. Does language background make a difference in learner performance?* Paper presented at the Pronunciation in Second Language Learning and Teaching Conference, Ames, Iowa.

Liberman, I.Y., Shankweiler, D., Fischer, F.W., & Carter, B. (1974). Explicit syllable and phoneme segmentation in the young child. *Journal of Experimental Child Psychology, 18*(2), 201–212. DOI: 10.1016/0022–0965(74)90101–5

Lightbown, P. & Spada, N. (2006). *How languages are learned* (3rd ed.). New York: Oxford University Press.

Linguistic Society of America (LSA). (2010). *Resolution on the Arizona teachers' English fluency initiative.* Retrieved from ⟨http://www.linguisticsociety.org/about/what-we-do/resolutions-statements-guides/arizona-teachers-initiative⟩

Lippi-Green, R. (2012). *English with an accent: Language, ideology, and discrimination in the United States* (2nd ed.). London, UK: Routledge. DOI: 10.1017/s1360674300240276

Lloyd James, A. (1940). *Speech signals in telephony.* London, UK: Sir I. Pitman & Sons.

Lord, G. (2010). The combined effects of immersion and instruction on second language pronunciation. *Foreign Language Annals, 43*(3), 488–503. DOI: 10.1111/j.1944–9720.2010.01094.x

MacDonald, D., Yule, G., & Powers, M. (1994). Attempts to improve English L2 pronunciation: The variable effects of different types of instruction. *Language Learning, 44*(1), 75–100. DOI: 10.1111/j.1467–1770.1994.tb01449.x

MacDonald, S. (2002). Pronunciation: Views and practices of reluctant teachers. *Prospect, 17*(3), 3–18.

MacIntyre, P.D. (2007). Willingness to communicate in the second language: Understanding the decision to speak as a volitional process. *The Modern Language Journal, 91*(4), 564–576. DOI: 10.1111/j.1540–4781.2007.00623.x

MacIntyre, P.D., Clément, R., Dörnyei, Z., & Noels, K.A. (1998). Conceptualizing willingness to communicate in a L2: A situational model of L2 confidence and affiliation. *The Modern Language Journal, 82*(4), 545–562. DOI: 10.1111/j.1540–4781.1998.tb05543.x

MacKay, I.R. A., & Flege, J.E. (2004). Effects of the age of second language learning on the duration of first and second language sentences: The role of suppression. *Applied Psycholinguistics, 25*(3), 373–396. DOI: 10.1017/s0142716404001171

Mahboob, A., Uhrig, K., Newman, K., & Hartford, B.S. (2004). Children of a lesser English: Status of non-native English speakers as college-level English as a Second Language teachers in the United States. In L. Kamhi-Stein (Ed.), *Learning and teaching from experience: Perspectives on nonnative English-speaking professionals* (pp. 100–120). Ann Arbor, MI: University of Michigan Press.

Mai, R., & Hoffman S. (2014). Accents in business communication: An integrative model and propositions for future research. *Journal of Consumer Psychology, 24*(1), 137–158. DOI: 10.1016/j.jcps.2013.09.004

Major, R.C. (1987). Phonological similarity, markedness, and rate of L2 acquisition. *Studies in Second Language Acquisition, 9*(1), 63–82. DOI: 10.1017/s0272263100006513

Marx, N. (2002). Never quite a 'native speaker': Accent and identity in the L2 and the L1. *Canadian Modern Language Review, 59*(2), 264–281. DOI: 10.3138/cmlr.59.2.264

Massaro, D.W. (2003). A computer animated tutor for spoken and written language learning. In S. L. Oviatt, T. Darrell, M.T. Maybury, & W. Wahlster (Eds.), *Proceedings of the 5th International Conference on Multimodal Interfaces* (pp. 172–175). New York, NY: ACM Press. DOI: 10.1145/958462.958466

McArthur, T. (2001). World English and world Englishes: Trends, tensions, varieties, and standards. *Language Teaching, 34*(1), 1–20. DOI: 10.1017/s0261444800016062

McCroskey, J.C., & Richmond, V.P. (1991). Willingness to communicate: A cognitive view. In M. Booth-Butterfield (Ed.), *Communication, cognition and anxiety* (pp. 19–37). Newbury Park, CA: Sage.

McGregor, A., & Sardegna, V. (2014, March). *Pronunciation improvement through an awareness-raising approach.* Paper presented at the American Association for Applied Linguistics Conference, Portland, Oregon.

Meyers, C.M. (2013). Mirroring project update: Intelligible accented speakers as pronunciation models. *TESOL Video News: The Newsletter of the Video and Digital Media Interest Section.* Retrieved from ⟨http://newsmanager.commpartners.com/tesolvdmis/issues/2013-07-27/6.html⟩

Miller, J. (2003). *Audible difference: ESL and social identity in schools.* Bristol, UK: Multilingual Matters.

Milovanov, R., Pietilä, P., Tervaniemi, M., & Esquef, P.A.A. (2010). Foreign language pronunciation skills and musical aptitude: A study of Finnish adults with higher education. *Learning and Individual Differences, 20*(1), 56–60. DOI: 10.1016/j.lindif.2009.11.003

Miyawaki, K., Jenkins, J.J., Strange, W., Liberman, A.M., Verbrugge, R., & Fujimura, O. (1975). An effect of linguistic experience: The discrimination of [r] and [l] by native speakers of Japanese and English. *Perception & Psychophysics, 18*(5), 331–340. DOI: 10.3758/bf03211209

Morgan, B. (2009). Fostering transformative practitioners for critical EAP: Possibilities and challenges. *Journal of English for Academic Purposes, 8*(2), 86–99. DOI: 10.1016/j.jeap.2008.09.001

Morgan, B. (2010). Fostering conceptual roles for change: Identity and agency in ESEA teacher preparation. *Kritica Kultura, 15*, 34–55.

Morley, J. (1991). The pronunciation component in teaching English to speakers of other languages. *TESOL Quarterly, 25*(3), 481–520. DOI: 10.2307/3586981

Moulton, W.G. (1962). Toward a classification of pronunciation errors. *The Modern Language Journal, 46*(3), 101–109. DOI: 10.1111/j.1540–4781.1962.tb01773.x

Moussu, L., & Llurda, E. (2008). Non-native English-speaking English language teachers: History and research. *Language Teaching, 41*(3), 315–348. DOI: 10.1017/s0261444808005028

Moyer, A. (2007). Do language attitudes determine accent? A study of bilinguals in the USA. *Journal of Multilingual and Multicultural Development, 28*(6), 502–518. DOI: 10.2167/jmmd514.0

Moyer, A. (2014). The social nature of L2 pronunciation. In A. Moyer & J. M. Levis (Eds.), *Social dynamics in second language accent* (pp. 11–29). Berlin: De Gruyter. DOI: 10.1515/9781614511762.11

Munro, M., & Mann, V. (2005). Age of immersion as a predictor of foreign accent. *Applied Psycholinguistics, 26*(3), 311–341. DOI: 10.1017/s0142716405050198

Munro, M.J. (2003). A primer on accent discrimination in the Canadian context. *TESL Canada Journal, 20*(2), 38–51.

Munro, M.J., & Derwing, T.M. (1994). Evaluations of foreign accent in extemporaneous and read material. *Language Testing, 11*(3), 254–266. DOI: 10.1177/026553229401100302

Munro, M.J., & Derwing, T.M. (1995a). Foreign accent, comprehensibility, and intelligibility in the speech of second language learners. *Language Learning, 45*(1), 73–97. DOI: 10.1111/j.1467–1770.1995.tb00963.x

Munro, M.J., & Derwing, T.M. (1995b). Processing time, accent, and comprehensibility in the perception of native and foreign-accented speech. *Language and Speech, 38*(3), 289–306.

Munro, M.J., & Derwing, T.M. (1998). The effects of speaking rate on listener evaluations of native and foreign-accented speech. *Language Learning, 48*(2), 159–182. DOI: 10.1111/1467–9922.00038

Munro, M.J., & Derwing, T.M. (2001). Modeling perceptions of the accentedness and comprehensibility of L2 speech: The role of speaking rate. *Studies in Second Language Acquisition, 23*(4), 451–468.

Munro, M.J., & Derwing, T.M. (2006). The functional load principle in ESL pronunciation instruction: An exploratory study. *System, 34*(4), 520–531. DOI: 10.1016/j.system.2006.09.004

Munro, M.J., & Derwing, T.M. (2008). Segmental acquisition in adult ESL learners: A longitudinal study of vowel production. *Language Learning, 58*(3), 479–502. DOI: 10.1111/j.1467–9922.2008.00448.x

Munro, M.J., & Derwing, T.M. (2015a). A prospectus for pronunciation research methods in the 21st century. *Journal of Second Language Pronunciation, 1*(1), 11–42. DOI: 10.2307/3588486

Munro, M.J., & Derwing, T.M. (2015b). Intelligibility in research and practice: Teaching priorities. In M. Reed & J. M. Levis (Eds.), *The handbook of English pronunciation* (pp. 377–396). Hoboken, NJ: Wiley Blackwell.

Munro, M.J., Derwing, T.M., & Morton, S.L. (2006). The mutual intelligibility of L2 speech. *Studies in Second Language Acquisition, 28*(1), 111–131. DOI: 10.1017/s0272263106060049

Munro, M.J., Derwing, T.M., & Saito, K. (2013, June). *Aspiring to aspirate: A longitudinal study of English voiceless stop acquisition.* Paper presented at the Canadian Association of Applied Linguistics Conference, Victoria, BC.

Murphy, J.M., & Baker, A.A. (2015). History of ESL pronunciation teaching. In M. Reed & J. M. Levis (Eds.), *The handbook of English pronunciation* (pp. 36–65). Hoboken, NJ: Wiley Blackwell.

Murray, L., & Barnes, A. (1998). Beyond the "wow" factor: Evaluating multimedia language learning software from a pedagogical viewpoint. *System, 26*(2), 249–259.
DOI: 10.1016/s0346-251x(98)00008-6

Nation, I.S.P. (1989). Improving speaking fluency. *System, 17*(3), 377–384.
DOI: 10.1016/0346-251x(89)90010-9

Nguyen, B. (1993). Accent discrimination and the Test of Spoken English: A call for an objective assessment of the comprehensibility of non-native speakers. *California Law Review, 81*(5), 1325–1361. DOI: 10.2307/3480920

Nilsen, D.L. F., & Nilsen, A.P. (1971). *Pronunciation contrasts in English.* New York, NY: Simon and Schuster.

Nilsen, D.L. F., & Nilsen, A.P. (2010). *Pronunciation contrasts in English* (2nd ed.). Long Grove, IL: Waveland Press.

Norton Peirce, B. (1995). Social identity, investment, and language learning. *TESOL Quarterly, 29*(1), 9–31. DOI: 10.2307/3587803

Ohala, J.J. (2006). Phonetics: Overview. In K. Brown (Ed.), *Encyclopedia of language and linguistics* (2nd ed., pp. 468–470). Boston, MA: Elsevier.

Olive, J.P. (1998). "The talking computer": Text to speech synthesis. In D. G. Stork (Ed.), *HAL's legacy: 2001's computer as dream and reality* (pp. 101–129). Cambridge, MA: The MIT Press.

Ortega, L., & Iberri-Shea, G. (2005). Longitudinal research in second language acquisition: Recent trends and future directions. *Annual Review of Applied Linguistics, 25*, 26–45.
DOI: 10.1017/s0267190505000024

Oyama, S. (1976). A sensitive period for the acquisition of a nonnative phonological system. *Journal of Psycholinguistic Research, 5*(3), 261–283. DOI: 10.1007/bf01067377

Oyama, S. (1982). A sensitive period for the acquisition of a nonnative phonological system. In S. Krashen, R. Scarcella, & M. Long (Eds.), *Child-adult differences in second language acquisition* (pp. 20–38). Rowley, MA: Newbury House.

Palmer, J. (1976). Linguistic accuracy and intelligibility. In G. Nickel (Ed.), *Proceedings of the 4th International Congress of Applied Linguistics* (pp. 505–513). Stuttgart, Germany: Hochschul Verlag.

Patkowski, M.S. (1990). Age and accent in a second language: A reply to James Emil Flege. *Applied Linguistics, 11*(1), 73–89. DOI: 10.1093/applin/11.1.73

Penfield, W., & Roberts, L. (1959). *Speech and brain mechanisms.* Princeton, NJ: Princeton University Press. DOI: 10.1002/bjs.18004720433

Pennington, M.C. (1998). The teachability of phonology in adulthood: A re-examination. *International Review of Applied Linguistics in Language Teaching, 36*(4), 323–341.
DOI: 10.1515/iral.1998.36.4.323

Pennington, M.C., & Richards, J.C. (1986). Pronunciation revisited. *TESOL Quarterly, 20*(2), 207–225. DOI: 10.2307/3586541

Perlmutter, M. (1989). Intelligibility rating of L2 speech pre- and post-intervention. *Perceptual and Motor Skills, 68*, 515–521. DOI: 10.2466/pms.1989.68.2.515

Pica, T. (1994). Questions from the language classroom: Research perspectives. *TESOL Quarterly, 28*(1), 49–79. DOI: 10.2307/3587198

Pickering, L., Menjo, S., & Bouchard, J. (2012, June). *'Are you telling me or asking me?' International intelligibility in call center interaction and implications for EFL.* Paper presented at the Australian Council of TESOL Associations International TESOL Conference, Cairns, Australia.

Pike, K.L. (1945). *The intonation of American English.* Ann Arbor, MI: The University of Michigan Press.

Piller, I. (2002). Passing for a native speaker: Identity and success in second language learning. *Journal of Sociolinguistics, 6*(2), 179–208. DOI: 10.1111/1467–9481.00184

Pinget, A.-F., Bosker, H.R., Quené, H., & de Jong, N.H. (2014). Native speakers' perception of fluency and accent in L2 speech. *Language Testing, 31*(3), 349–365.
DOI: 10.1177/0265532214526177

Piske, T., MacKay, I.R. A., & Flege, J.E. (2001). Factors affecting degree of foreign accent in an L2: A review. *Journal of Phonetics, 29*(2), 191–215. DOI: 10.1006/jpho.2001.0134

Politzer, R.L. (1978). Errors of English speakers of German as perceived and evaluated by German natives. *The Modern Language Journal, 62*(5–6), 253–261.
DOI: 10.1111/j.1540–4781.1978.tb02395.x

Porter, D., & Garvin, S. (1989). Attitudes to pronunciation in EFL. *Speak Out, 5,* 8–15.

Prator, C.H. (1951). *Manual of American English pronunciation for adult foreign students.* New York, NY: Rinehart.

Prator, C.H., & Robinett, B.W. (1984). *Manual of American English pronunciation.* New York, NY: Harcourt College Publishers.

Preston, D.R. (1999). A language attitude approach to the perception of regional variety. In D. R. Preston (Ed.), *Handbook of perceptual dialectology* (pp. 359–373). Amsterdam: John Benjamins. DOI: 10.1075/z.hpd1.30pre

Price, O. (1665). *The vocal organ.* Menston, Yorkshire: Scholar Press, A Scholar Press Facsimile.

Prodromou, L. (2007). A reader responds to J. Jenkins's "Current perspectives on teaching world Englishes and English as a lingua franca". *TESOL Quarterly, 41*(2), 409–413.
DOI: 10.2307/40264515

Purcell, E.T., & Suter, R.W. (1980). Predictors of pronunciation accuracy: A re-examination. *Language Learning, 30*(2), 271–287. DOI: 10.1111/j.1467–1770.1980.tb00319.x

Purnell, T., Idsardi, W., & Baugh, J. (1999). Perceptual and phonetic experiments on American English dialect identification. *Journal of Language and Social Psychology, 18*(1), 10–30.
DOI: 10.1177/0261927x99018001002

Rajagopalan, K. (2010). The soft, ideological underbelly of the notion of intelligibility in discussions of 'World Englishes.' *Applied Linguistics, 31*(3), 465–470. DOI: 10.1093/applin/amq014

Ramus, F., Nespor, M., & Mehler, J. (1999). Correlates of linguistic rhythm in the speech signal. *Cognition, 73*(3), 265–292. DOI: 10.1016/s0010-0277(99)00058-x

Ranta, L., & Meckelborg, A. (2013). How much exposure to English do international graduate students really get? Measuring language use in a naturalistic setting. *Canadian Modern Language Review, 69*(1), 1–33. DOI: 10.3138/cmlr.987

Reed, M., & Michaud, C. (2005). *Sound concepts: An integrated pronunciation course.* New York, NY: McGraw-Hill.

Richards, J.C., & Rodgers, T.S. (2014). *Approaches and methods in language teaching* (3rd ed.). Cambridge, UK: Cambridge University Press. DOI: 10.1177/003368820203300208

Riney, T.J., & Flege, J.E. (1998). Changes over time in global foreign accent and liquid identifiability and accuracy. *Studies in Second Language Acquisition, 20*(2), 213–243.
DOI: 10.1017/s0272263198002058

Robinson, R. (1617). *The art of pronunciation.* London: Nicholas Oakes.

Rogers, H. (2005). *Writing systems: A linguistic approach.* Malden, MA: Blackwell Publishing.

Rossiter, M.J. (2009). Perceptions of L2 fluency by native and non-native speakers of English. *The Canadian Modern Language Review, 65*(3), 395–412. DOI: 10.3138/cmlr.65.3.395

Rossiter, M.J., Derwing, T.M., & Jones, V.M.L.O. (2008). Is a picture worth a thousand words? *TESOL Quarterly, 42*(2), 325–329.

Rubin, D.L. (1992). Nonlanguage factors affecting undergraduates' judgments of nonnative English-speaking teaching assistants. *Research in Higher Education, 33*(4), 511–531. DOI: 10.1007/bf00973770

Rubin, D. (2012). The power of prejudice in accent perception: Reverse linguistic stereotyping and its impact on listener judgments and decisions. In J. Levis & K. LeVelle (Eds.), *Proceedings of the 3rd Annual Pronunciation in Second Language Learning and Teaching Conference* (pp. 11–17). Ames, IA: Iowa State University.

Ryan, E.B., & Carranza, M. (1975). Evaluative reactions of adolescents toward speakers of standard English and Mexican-American accented English. *Journal of Personality and Social Psychology, 31*(5), 855–863. DOI: 10.1037/h0076704

Ryan, E.B., Carranza, M., & Moffie, R.W. (1977). Reactions towards varying degrees of accentedness in the speech of Spanish-English bilinguals. *Language and Speech, 20*(3), 267–273.

Rymer, R. (1993). *Genie: A scientific tragedy.* New York, NY: Harper Perennial.

Saalfeld, A.K. (2012). Teaching L2 Spanish stress. *Foreign Language Annals, 45*(2), 283–303. DOI: 10.1111/j.1944–9720.2012.01191.x

Saito, K., & Lyster, R. (2012). Effects of form-focused instruction and corrective feedback on L2 pronunciation development of /ɹ/ by Japanese learners of English. *Language Learning, 62*(2), 595–633. DOI: 10.1111/j.1467–9922.2011.00639.x

Sardegna, V.G. (2011). Pronunciation learning strategies that improve ESL learners' linking. In J. Levis & K. LeVelle (Eds.), *Proceedings of the 2nd Annual Pronunciation in Second Language Learning and Teaching Conference* (pp. 105–121). Ames, IA: Iowa State University.

Schachter, J. (1974). An error in error analysis. *Language Learning, 24*(2), 205–214. DOI: 10.1111/j.1467–1770.1974.tb00502.x

Schairer, K.E. (1992). Native speaker reaction to non-native speech. *The Modern Language Journal, 76*(3), 309–319. DOI: 10.1111/j.1540–4781.1992.tb07001.x

Schmidt, A.M., & Sullivan, S. (2003). Clinical training in foreign accent modification: A national survey. *Contemporary Issues in Communication Science and Disorders, 30*, 127–135.

Schumann, J. (1976). Social distance as a factor in second language acquisition. *Language Learning, 26*(1), 135–143. DOI: 10.1111/j.1467–1770.1976.tb00265.x

Schumann, J. (2013). Societal responses to adult difficulties in L2 acquisition: Toward an evolutionary perspective on language acquisition. *Language Learning, 63, Issue Supplement s1*, 190–209. DOI: 10.1111/j.1467–9922.2012.00744.x

Schumann, J., Holroyd, G., Campbell, R.N., & Ward, F.A. (1978). Improvement of foreign language pronunciation under hypnosis: A preliminary study. *Language Learning, 28*(1), 143–148. DOI: 10.1111/j.1467–1770.1978.tb00310.x

Scovel, T. (1988). *A time to speak: A psycholinguistic investigation into the critical period for human speech.* New York, NY: Harper and Row.

Segalowitz, N. (2007). Access fluidity, attention control, and the acquisition of fluency in a second language. *TESOL Quarterly, 41*(1), 181–186.

Segalowitz, N., & Hulstijn, J.H. (2005). Automaticity and second language learning. In J. F. Kroll & A. M. B. De Groot (Eds.), *Handbook of bilingualism: Psycholinguistic approaches* (pp. 371–378). Oxford, UK: Oxford University Press.

Seidlhofer, B. (2010). Giving VOICE to English as a lingua franca. In R. Facchinetti, D. Crystal, & B. Seidlhofer (Eds.), *From international to local English – and back again* (pp. 147–163). Frankfurt, Germany: Peter Lang. DOI: 10.1075/eww.33.2.06wer

Shaw, G.B. (1912). *Pygmalion* [Play]. DOI: 10.5325/shaw.31.1.0009

Sheldon, A., & Strange, W. (1982). The acquisition of /r/ and /l/ by Japanese learners of English: Evidence that speech production can precede perception. *Applied Psycholinguistics, 3*(3), 243–261. DOI: 10.1017/s0142716400001417

Singleton, D. (2001). Age and second language acquisition. *Annual Review of Applied Linguistics, 21,* 77–89. DOI: 10.1017/s0267190501000058

Sisson, C.R. (1970). The effect of delayed comparison in the language laboratory on phoneme discrimination and pronunciation accuracy. *Language Learning, 20*(1), 69–88. DOI: 10.1111/j.1467–1770.1970.tb00046.x

Sobkowiak, W. (2012). This is Tom = /zyzys'tom/: Pronunciation in beginners' EFL textbooks then and now. *Research in Language, 10*(1), 111–122. DOI: 10.2478/v10015-011-0028-7

Spada, N. (1997). Form-focused instruction and second language acquisition: A review of classroom and laboratory research. [State of the Art Article] *Language Teaching, 30*(2), 73–87. DOI: 10.1017/s0261444800012799

Spada, N. (2011). Beyond form-focused instruction: Reflections on past, present and future research. *Language Teaching, 44*(2), 225–236. DOI: 10.1017/s0261444810000224

Strain, J.E. (1963). Difficulties in measuring pronunciation improvement. *Language Learning, 13*(3–4), 217–224. DOI: 10.1111/j.1467–1770.1963.tb01432.x

Strange, W., & Dittmann, S. (1984). Effects of discrimination training on the perception of /r-l/ by Japanese adults learning English. *Perception and Psychophysics, 36*(2), 131–145. DOI: 10.3758/bf03202673

Stuparyk, M. (1996, July 14). New Canadians eager to master English: Course helps Canadianize accents. *The Edmonton Journal,* G6.

Sustarsic, R. (2003). Application of acoustic analysis in English phonetics teaching. In M.-J. Solé, D. Recasens, & J. Romero (Eds.), *Proceedings of the 15th International Congress of Phonetic Sciences* (pp. 2841–2844). Barcelona, Spain: Universitat Autònoma de Barcelona.

Surtees, V. (2013). Mobile tracking of L2 interactions: Identifying speech act contexts for inclusion in pragmatic assessment tools. Paper presented at the Canadian Association of Applied Linguistics Conference, Victoria, Canada.

Suter, R.W. (1976). Predictors of pronunciation accuracy in second language learning. *Language Learning, 26*(2), 233–253. DOI: 10.1111/j.1467–1770.1976.tb00275.x

Swan, M., & Smith, B. (Eds.). (2001). *Learner English: A teacher's guide to interference and other problems.* Cambridge, UK: Cambridge University Press. DOI: 10.1017/cbo9780511667121

Sweet, H. (1900). *The practical study of languages: A guide for teachers and learners.* New York, NY: Henry Holt & Co.

Szpyra-Kozłowska, J. (2015). *Pronunciation in EFL instruction: A research-based approach.* Bristol, UK: Multilingual Matters.

Tajima, K., Port, R., & Dalby, J. (1997). Effects of temporal correction on intelligibility of foreign-accented English. *Journal of Phonetics, 25*(1), 1–24. DOI: 10.1006/jpho.1996.0031

Tam, J. (2012). *Reduction study.* Retrieved from ⟨http://www.joannatam.net/reductionStudy.html⟩

Tergujeff, E. (2010). Pronunciation teaching materials in Finnish EFL textbooks. In A. Henderson (Ed.), *English pronunciation: Issues and practices (EPIP): Proceedings of the First International Conference* (pp. 189–205). Chambéry, France: Université de Savoie.

Tergujeff, E. (2012). English pronunciation teaching: Four case studies from Finland. *Journal of Language Teaching and Research, 3*(4), 599–607. DOI: 10.4304/jltr.3.4.599–607

Tergujeff, E. (2013). *English pronunciation teaching in Finland* (Doctoral dissertation). University of Jyväskylä, Finland. DOI: 10.4304/jltr.3.4.599–607

The Leadership Conference Education Fund. (2008, March 3). Accents [Video file]. Retrieved from ⟨http://www.youtube.com/watch?v=84k2iM30vbY⟩

Thomas, E.R. (2014). L2 accent choices and language contact. In A. Moyer & J. M. Levis (Eds.), *Social dynamics in second language accent* (pp. 119–144). Berlin: De Gruyter. DOI: 10.1515/9781614511762.119

Thompson, I. (1991). Foreign accents revisited: The English pronunciation of Russian immigrants. *Language Learning, 41*(2), 177–204. DOI: 10.1111/j.1467–1770.1991.tb00683.x

Thompson, J. (2011). *English is stupid.* Caledon, ON: Thompson Language Center.

Thomson, R.I. (2004). Buyer beware: Professional preparation and TESL certificate programs in Canada. *TESL Canada Journal, Special Issue 4*, 41–57.

Thomson, R.I. (2011). Computer assisted pronunciation training: Targeting second language vowel perception improves pronunciation. *Calico Journal, 28*(3), 744–765. DOI: 10.11139/cj.28.3.744–765

Thomson, R.I. (2012a). Improving L2 listeners' perception of English vowels: A computer-mediated approach. *Language Learning, 62*(4), 1231–1258. DOI: 10.1111/j.1467–9922.2012.00724.x

Thomson, R.I. (2012b). *English accent coach* [Online game]. Retrieved from ⟨www.englishaccent-coach.com⟩

Thomson, R.I. (2013a). Accent reduction. In C. A. Chapelle (Ed.), *The encyclopedia of applied linguistics* (pp. 8–11). Hoboken, NJ: Wiley-Blackwell.

Thomson, R.I. (2013b). ESL teachers' beliefs and practices in pronunciation teaching: Confidently right or confidently wrong? In J. Levis & K. LeVelle (Eds.), *Proceedings of the 4th Annual Pronunciation in Second Language Learning and Teaching Conference* (pp. 224–233). Ames, IA: Iowa State University.

Thomson, R.I. (2014). Myth 1: Accent reduction and pronunciation instruction are the same thing. In L. Grant (Ed.), *Pronunciation myths* (pp. 160–187). Ann Arbor, MI: The University of Michigan Press.

Thomson, R.I., & Derwing, T.M. (2014). *The effectiveness of L2 pronunciation instruction: A narrative review. Applied Linguistics.* DOI: 10.1093/applin/amu076

Thomson, R.I., Nearey, T.M., & Derwing, T.M. (2009). A modified statistical pattern recognition approach to measuring the crosslinguistic similarity of Mandarin and English vowels. *Journal of the Acoustical Society of America, 126*(3), 1447–1460. DOI: 10.1121/1.3177260

Timmis, I. (2002). Native speaker norms and International English: A classroom view. *ELT Journal, 56*(3), 240–249. DOI: 10.1093/elt/56.3.240

Trofimovich, P., & Baker, W. (2006). Learning second language suprasegmentals: Effect of L2 experience on prosody and fluency characteristics of L2 speech. *Studies in Second Language Acquisition, 28*(1), 1–30. DOI: 10.1017/s0272263106060013

Trofimovich, P., Lightbown, P.M., Halter, R.H., & Song, H. (2009). Comprehension-based practice: The development of L2 pronunciation in a listening and reading program. *Studies in Second Language Acquisition, 31*(4), 609–639. DOI: 10.1017/s0272263109990040

Truscott, J. (1996). The case against grammar correction in L2 writing classes. *Language Learning, 46*(2), 327–369. DOI: 10.1111/j.1467–1770.1996.tb01238.x

Tsukada, K., Birdsong, D., Bialystok, E., Mack, M., Sung, H., & Flege, J. (2005). A developmental study of English vowel production and perception by native Korean adults and children. *Journal of Phonetics, 33*(3), 263–290. DOI: 10.1016/j.wocn.2004.10.002

University of Iowa. (2001). Phonetics: The Sounds of American English [Software]. Iowa City, IA: Author. Retrieved from ⟨http://www.uiowa.edu/~acadtech/phonetics/english/english_main.html⟩

Usher, J. (1995). Teaching pronunciation: Inhalation/exhalation helps students distinguish sounds. *Contact, 21*, 14–15.

Vandergrift, L., & Goh, C. (2012). *Teaching and learning second language listening: Metacognition in action.* New York, NY: Routledge. DOI: 10.1017/s0272263112000812

van Loon, J. (2002). Improving pronunciation of adult ESL students. *TESL Canada Journal, 20*(1), 83–88.

Varonis, E., & Gass, S. (1982). The comprehensibility of nonnative speech. *Studies in Second Language Acquisition, 4*(2), 114–136. DOI: 10.1017/s0272263112000812

Walker, R. (2011). *Teaching the pronunciation of English as a Lingua Franca.* Oxford: Oxford University Press. DOI: 10.1093/applin/ams035

Wang, Z., Arndt, A.D., Singh, S.N., Biernat, M., & Liu, F. (2013). "You lost me at hello": How and when accent-based biases are expressed and suppressed. *International Journal of Research in Marketing, 30*(2), 185–196. DOI: 10.1016/j.ijresmar.2013.10.001

Wang, X., & Munro, M.J. (2004). Computer-based training for learning English vowel contrasts. *System, 32*(4), 539–552. DOI: 10.1016/j.system.2004.09.011

Wardhaugh, R. (1970). The contrastive analysis hypothesis. *TESOL Quarterly, 4*(2), 123–130. DOI: 10.2307/3586182

Watt, D., & Taplin, J. (1997). The least one should expect of TESL/TEFL programs. *TESL Canada Journal, 14*(2), 72–74.

Webster, N. (1828). *An American dictionary of the English language.* New York, NY: S. Converse.

Webster, N. (1836). *The American spelling book; Containing, the rudiments of the English language, for the use of schools in the United States.* Philadelphia, PA: Johnson & Warnka.

Weinberger, S.H. (2015). *The speech accent archive.* Fairfax, VA: George Mason University. Retrieved from ⟨http://accent.gmu.edu⟩

Weinreich, U. (1953). *Languages in contact: Findings and problems.* New York, NY: Publications of the Linguistic Circle of New York.

Wennerstrom, A. (2000). The role of intonation in second language fluency. In H. Riggenbach (Ed.), *Perspectives on fluency* (pp. 102–127). Ann Arbor, MI: University of Michigan Press.

Werker, J.F., & Tees, R.C. (2002). Cross-language speech perception: Evidence for perceptual reorganization during the first year of life. *Infant Behavior and Development, 25*(1), 121–133. DOI: 10.1016/s0163-6383(02)00093-0

Weyant, J. M. (2007). Perspective taking as a means of reducing negative stereotyping of individuals who speak English as a second language. *Journal of Applied Social Psychology, 37*, 703–716.

Winke, P., Gass, S., & Myford, C. (2013). Raters' L2 background as a potential source of bias in rating oral performance. *Language Testing, 30*(2), 231–252. DOI: 10.1177/0265532212456968

Yates, L. (2007). *The not-so-generic skills: Teaching employability communication skills to adult migrants.* North Ryde, NSW: NCELTR.

Yates, L., & Zielinski, B. (2009). *Give it a go: Teaching pronunciation to adults.* Sydney, NSW: AMEP Research Centre, Department of Immigration and Citizenship. Retrieved from ⟨http://www.ameprc.mq.edu.au/__data/assets/pdf_file/0011/157664/interactive_sm.pdf⟩

Yates, L., Zielinski, B., & Pryor, E. (2011). The assessment of pronunciation and the new IELTS Pronunciation scale. In J. Osborne (Ed.), *IELTS research reports* (Vol. 12, pp. 1–46). Melbourne, VIC: IDP: IELTS Australia and British Council.Zielinski, B.W. (2008). The listener: No longer the silent partner in reduced intelligibility. *System, 36*(1), 69–84. DOI: 10.1016/j.system.2007.11.004

Zielinski, B. (2012). The social impact of pronunciation difficulties: Confidence and willingness to speak. In J. Levis & K. LeVelle (Eds.), *Proceedings of the 3rd Annual Pronunciation in Second Language Learning and Teaching Conference* (pp. 18–26). Ames, IA: Iowa State University.

Zielinski, B., & Yates, L. (2014). Myth: Pronunciation instruction is not appropriate for beginner-level learners. In L. Grant (Ed.), *Pronunciation myths* (pp. 56–79). Ann Arbor, MI: University of Michigan Press.

Subject Index

Author Index